Cannibal Culture

Cannibal Culture

Art, Appropriation, and the Commodification of Difference

Deborah Root

Westview Press
A Member of the Perseus Books Group

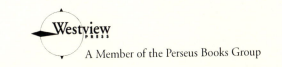

Published in 1996 in the United States of America by Westview Press, 5500 Central Avenue, Boulder, Colorado 80301-2877, and in the United Kingdom by Westview Press, 12 Hid's Copse Road, Cumnor Hill, Oxford OX2 9JJ

Library of Congress Cataloging-in-Publication Data
Root, Deborah.
Cannibal culture: art, appropriation, and the commodification of difference / Deborah Root.
p. cm.
Includes bibliographical references and index.
ISBN 0-8133-2088-7 (hc) — ISBN 0-8133-2089-5 (pb)
1. Art and society. I. Title.
N72.S6R66 1996
701'.03—dc20
95-20261
CIP

Printed and bound in the United States of America.

The paper used in this publication meets the requirements of the American National Standard for Permanence of Paper for Printed Library Materials Z39.48-1984.

PERSEUS POD ON DEMAND

10 9 8 7 6

Contents

Preface viii
Acknowledgments xv

1 Fat-Eaters and Aesthetes: The Politics of Display 1

The White Cannibal, 8
Aristocratic Dreams, 12
From Spectacle to Display, 16
Alibis of Appreciation, 18
Entitlement, 21
A New World Order, 24

2 The Luxurious Ambivalence of Exoticism 27

Alluring Foreigners, 29
Exotic Histories, 32
Tropes of Difference, 34
Fragments of Culture, 41
Connoisseurs of Ambivalence, 43
Colonial Desires, 47
Exotic Sites: Blood and Flowers, 49
Exotic Imaginaries, 51
Surrealist Dreams, 53
Bataille, 55
Eisenstein: Mexico as Redemption, 60
Artaud: Redemptive Madness, 63

3 Conquest, Appropriation, and Cultural Difference 67

Salvaging Culture, 73
Authenticity and Cultural Integrity, 78
Deterritorialization and Recoding: National Agendas, 82
The New Age: Appropriating the Spirit, 87
Desperate People: Honky Shamans and Wannabe Indians, 97
Grey Owl and the Problem of Identity, 102

4 Art and Taxidermy: The Warehouse of Treasures 107

Resacralization of the Authentic Object, 110
Temporality and Writing, 112
Necrophilia, 116
Authentic Details, 118
Commodity Fetishism, 120
The Commodification of the Proper Name, 127
Class and Gender Anxieties, 130
Dead Art, 136
Critical Styles and Death, 142
The Marketing of Marginality, 145
Art and Commerce, 147

5 Dreams and Landscapes: The Delineation of Wild Spaces 151

Western Culture and How It Got That Way, 153
How Ideas About Land Structure Ideas About People, 159
Orientalist Dreams, 161
Colonial Representation and Landscape, 165
Colonial Nightmares, 171
Travel and Delirium, 173
Aristocratic Dreams, 176
Sexual Ambivalences, 177
Land and Madness, 179
Escape and Authority, 183

6 The Smoking Mirror 187

The State, Again, 195
Signs and Omens, 197
Refusing the Cannibal, 202

Notes 207
Bibliography 219
About the Book and Author 225
Index 227

Preface

It is November 1994 in Toronto, and performance artist Guillermo Gómez-Peña sits in a bamboo cage in the Dufferin Mall. He wears studded driving gloves and a feathered hat beaded with a Native eagle design. He devours a human heart made of rubber. He repeatedly raises a clenched fist. Sometimes he speaks to the audience in a language meant to sound unfamiliar, then turns and clutches a package of Ancient Grains breakfast cereal, the front of which displays a photograph of a carved head unearthed at Teotihuacán. Sometimes he slumps drunkenly against the bars of the cage. As we stare at the man in the cage, Coco Fusco works the crowd. Dressed in feathers and face paint, she offers free interviews to shoppers, inquiring if we would prefer to holiday in an indigenous village in Chiapas or scuba dive off Port-au-Prince. She wants to know if we imagine grass skirts to be inconvenient. She assigns interviewees a number, and they move obediently to stand in front of Gómez-Peña's cage, awaiting the performance of what the artists call "ethnic talent" that he has created, seemingly just for them.

In Fusco and Gómez-Peña's performance the museum collapses into the shopping mall, where cultural difference becomes another commodity to be bought and sold. The mall has become the true axis of Western culture as most of us experience it in North America. Here, as elsewhere, commodification works by repetition and the recognition this fosters: Most of the shops are franchises, and the products on exhibition are identical to those on display in other cities. This particular mall lies at the center of "multicultural" Toronto, and on a typical afternoon you can see people wearing West African *lappas,* Indian saris, or rock-and-roll clothes, shoppers who are likely to know a thing or two about colonial history. Despite the appearance of plurality, Toronto remains a colonial city in which many prefer to forget the past or, rather, to assume that colonial history is something that is finished, over and done with, as archaic as the British North America Act and the fur traders of the Hudson Bay Company. Multiple histories exist here, those of what the newspapers call "new Canadians" watching the performance at the Dufferin Mall, those of the Mohawks and Anishnabe, those of the Scots and Irish who settled here, those of ex-Americans like myself. Some histories are more visible than others, and it is perhaps too easy to ignore those stories that challenge the illusion that culture is fixed and unitary.

In the *zócalo* in Mexico City hundreds of dancers honor Cuauhtémoc, the last Aztec king who was tortured to death by Hernán Cortés. On the site of the great ceremonial center of imperial Tenochtitlán, they dance in precise movements, each dancer performing the gesture of a particular star, all together becoming a constellation, a community that remembers history and culture. The drum pounds out the heartbeat of the nation, while the smoking copal mingles with the automobile exhaust and factory effluvia that blanket the largest metropolis in the world. Banners adorn the square, announcing to passersby, QUETZALCOÁTL: YOU ARE NOT WHITE. YOU HAVE NO BEARD. As I lingered in the *zócalo,* I was reminded of other dancers I had witnessed a few years earlier. Near Montreal, after the barricades have been dismantled in one of the Mohawk territories besieged by the Canadian Army in the Oka summer of 1990, bundles of sage burn as drummers in Kahnawake beat out the American Indian Movement song, and people—both Native and non-Native—press around the circle, singing and raising clenched fists. (Later we hear that a white entrepreneur in Quebec is seeking to market a Mohawk warriors board game.)

It was in Mexico City and Kahnawake that I began to grasp the elision of multiple histories that had been at the base of my intellectual training, and I understood that the universalist discourses of high theory were unable to account for or at times even recognize the subtleties of cultural difference and colonial representation. These questions are being worked out elsewhere, on the ground, in a multitude of sites where power advances and retreats, mutates and coalesces, and is displaced. The writing of *Cannibal Culture* came out of an attempt to find a different way to talk about cultural difference and the corresponding ambiguities of perception and understanding. This not only meant that it was time to lay the big books aside, but that it also had become necessary to recognize the limits of understanding: There are things about other cultures I will never quite grasp, histories I will never quite know, even if I have friends in these communities who are willing to explain nuances to me. The fiction that it is possible to stand back and make judgments about difference or authenticity, that it is possible to know in advance what this difference will look like, was revealed to me as no more than intellectual arrogance.

Sometimes—and perhaps especially from the rather narrow vistas of academic institutions—there is a tendency to imagine that the cultural world dreamed up by people working for corporations is seamless, that the commodification of culture has in some profound way succeeded. Cynicism can be seductive and can itself presuppose a universalist stance. But the drummers in Mexico City and Kahnawake, the ongoing struggles over land rights and NAFTA, the sometimes bitter debates over representation and power, make it clear that colonialism is not something over and done with, even if efforts to address questions of power quickly become commodities in their own right. If colonial histories continue to play out, then culture continues to be a battleground.

If culture remains a site of contestation, then the colonial histories that have informed the way cultural difference was taken up in the West will continue to be an issue. People sometimes speak of "postcolonialism" as if something has been decided, as if the mixing and fragmentation of culture and history such as occur in the Dufferin Mall are neutral and not themselves a function of imperial agendas put into play long ago. The mall remains a place where colonial histories continue to be reenacted, as do the museum and the university, even if these sites can become points of disruption and performance art. The man in the cage forces us to consider the differences and similarities between museums and shopping malls and between the art world and mass media. Colonial representation works much as it has always done. Gómez-Peña's display of his own body as a living museum specimen underlines the extent to which a vast range of sites of Western cultural practice are underpinned by an imperial project that continually seeks to exercise and display power over foreign bodies.

In one sense the link between mall and museum is obvious. The real problem is finding a way to think through the concept of Western culture, that vast construct that seems able to encompass an infinite number of sites, histories, and forgettings. On the one hand, I believe it is important to hold onto a set of generalities about what Western culture is or, rather, what kinds of mentalities and practices make up this approach to the world. It then becomes possible to recognize the sites where this mentality is manifested, from malls to museums, high art to television, and to look at the differences and similarities of each site. On the other hand, it is important to keep seeing where the pretensions to universality have broken down, both inside and outside Western centers and both in the past and present. How can we learn to remember, and to think through issues of colonialism and power, without taking the position of the conquerors and without reproducing the mentalities that made conquest thinkable again and again?

There exists a set of practices and ideas that can be recognized as Western culture, but that culture is not now nor has it ever been one thing, one historical moment or site from which power is seamlessly transmitted across the globe. It looks this way sometimes because of how certain modalities of hierarchy and abstraction are able to migrate across time and space.

Part of the problem is the persistence of a historical legacy of appropriation. As the West sought to affirm colonial domination over territory, the world increasingly came to be imagined as a vast warehouse of images: Other cultures became signs and fragments of a world destroyed in advance and of a difference and authenticity that could be aestheticized and consumed in the West. Although the West was always able to incorporate difference into its agendas, it nevertheless sought to maintain a rigid line of demarcation between "them" and "us," between Europe and its "others." This is the true ruse of colonialist thinking and one that continues to underlie much contemporary thinking about culture. The apparent availability in the marketplace of a vast range of cultural and historical impedimenta can elide the persistence of the system of values that has always fueled the colonial machine.

Because cultural difference has long been conceived as a redemptive solution to the ambivalence of a Western culture established in the destruction of its own traditions, the appropriation of other aesthetic and spiritual modes is ultimately self-referential. This means that any attempt to perceive another culture based on the commodification and consumption of difference will fail. Understanding never really was the point. This self-referentiality has permeated intellectual practices as well, even some streams of thought that seek to address questions of difference. In the stretch-limo world of the 1980s the power brokers of this city embarked on a campaign to attach the adjective *world-class* to Toronto's cultural products. (The immigrant community of the Dufferin Mall was never imagined as world-class.) Large segments of the intellectual community scurried to keep up, taking their orders from Paris, New Haven, or other centers of discursive authority. But in the end the self-referentiality of the project went nowhere, and the city was left with the New World Order and the illusion of seamlessness that goes along with it. What underlies this desire to be world-class, to speak to and of the world, to possess a master discourse that will explain and account for vast multiplicities of experience and history?

We all have our blind spots, and those of us schooled in the Western tradition have often been too quick to assume a universality that does not exist. Our conceptual maps tend to lack a way to conceive the immanence of violence and power in the ideals and practices that have become dominant in the Western tradition. Mass death has tended to be conceived as something accidental, something outside the ordinary run of events. I think the difficulty in coming to terms with the peculiarities of the Western will to power has to do with the absence of a central metaphor capable of describing the link between consumption and death. The consumptive mentality has in many respects been normalized, as has the violence that underpins and is the effect of systems of universal judgment. Certainly the aestheticization of difference is coextensive with the romance with violence that has become so characteristic of contemporary Western society.

There have been many writers and artists in the West who have addressed these problems, but these have tended to be idiosyncratic thinkers. I have learned a great deal about the nature of power from writers such as

Friedrich Nietzsche, Gilles Deleuze and Felix Guattari, and Michel Foucault, but I have also come to understand the importance of a somewhat different range of issues from thinkers who locate their practice on the rather more distant margins of the Western tradition. This is not to suggest that theory is less valuable than practice, or vice versa; my concern is to open up these questions to other kinds of knowledge and other ways of theorizing hierarchy and violence and their relation to the control of nature. After reading the works of First Nations writers Jack Forbes and Leslie Marmon Silko, after talking to cultural activists in the Native communities in Canada, and after attempting to think through questions of Aztec historiography, I felt I could begin to address issues of power and culture from a rather more detached perspective and do so in a way that does not assume the centrality of Western concerns.

One way to conceive of the issues at stake in this text is to turn to the metaphors of other cultures. This can be tricky, as it can easily veer into appropriation and into thinking of ideas as existing in a kind of shopping mall, where we can select bright, shiny objects of thought off the shelves if we possess the right currency. I came to think that the problem lies, not in talking about or deriving lessons from other cultural paradigms—many of us tend to do this anyway, regardless of whether we write about it—but in doing so within a rhetoric of radical difference. This means imagining another culture as wholly other, exaggerating and aestheticizing the differences that do exist, and placing all firmly in the past. The task becomes how to recognize and respect differences without reproducing the us-them couplet of colonialist thinking or a master code that treats difference as if it were one thing. All cultures face the problems of how to live on the earth and how to organize power and address questions of consumption. Many cultures possess a conceptual map that grasps the nature of violence and power and explains it through a metaphor of consumption. Often this is conceived as a cannibal that visits the community in hard times and that must be faced up to and addressed ceremonially so that it will not devour its own. Looking the monster in the face is a technique for controlling it, and the lesson of the cannibal stories is that violence and paranoia are most likely to become problems in societies that refuse to acknowledge the cannibal at the heart of all culture and all community.

In this way the failure of Western culture to come to terms with the centrality of its consumptive impulse is both a failure of reflexivity and a function of the aestheticization and consumption of difference. Violence ultimately turns against itself, and sick societies produce sick people who no longer go elsewhere to live out their fantasies of control. As I write these lines, a serial killer is hunting women in my Toronto neighborhood. We have all begun to watch one another, to search for the visible marks of the cannibal on passersby. Such people are imagined to be wholly other, somehow separate from the society in which they live. The killer is perhaps the most obvious and extreme incarnation of the will to consume, but the cannibal has many other guises. The displacement and projection of ferocity and rage onto the outsider are a fiction that links up to the notion that the Aztecs or the Arabs were the bearers of a violence that Europe had gone beyond. But these qualities have always been inside, always part of us.

Cannibal Culture is an attempt to construct a topography of the West's will to aestheticize and consume cultural difference. The various sites in which this occurs are organized around the central image of the legendary cannibal monster who consumes and consumes, only to become hungrier and more destructive. This monster takes many forms and has been called by many different names. I imagine the cannibal as a map that at times may be called "Tezcatlipoca," sometimes "*wétiko,*" sometimes "deterritorialization and recoding," and sometimes "empire." I have located several sites where this cannibalization of difference is manifested, including ethnographic and art museums, various kinds of tourist attractions, French surrealist thinking, the New Age industry, nineteenth-century painting and opera, contemporary film, and advertisements for cosmetics and perfume. Some of these are sites of projection, which reveal more about Western obsessions than about the places that are the objects of interest. Araby and Mexico are examples of this. Other sites are institutions in which versions of cultural difference are displayed to the public at large, as in ethnographic exhibitions or, somewhat differently, in operas such as *Madama Butterfly.* The text is structured around a series of problematics, including exoticism, appropriation, and land, to underline how such abstractions can inform myriad seemingly disparate practices.

Although *Cannibal Culture* is critical of many Western institutions, I am not suggesting that museums or oil paintings are by definition corrupt or purely propagandistic or are somehow part of a colonialist conspiracy to pervert the truth about other cultures. Nor am I attempting to juxtapose an inauthentic mode of representation against an authentic one. I do not think it useful to seek a pure or originary space from which to judge representations of culture, and it would be extremely difficult to locate uncommodified forms of culture, even assuming we wanted to do so. Cultures have always been mixed and in flux, and to assume a pure space of resistance or authenticity is to refuse to recognize the extent to which we are all complicit with systems of power and authority, as we are all complicit with the cannibal.

I was able to think through many of these issues through the historical encounter between the Spaniards and the Aztecs, and for this reason the Aztecs are present throughout this text, at times implicitly. I begin *Cannibal Culture* with an Aztec story for two reasons. First, the Méxica have been treated as the nightmare of Western culture in a way that has always made me suspicious. The main reason for this treatment is human sacrifice; never mind that various kinds of human sacrifice saturate Western institutions from the time of the Greeks and Romans to the present. Reading account after account of the pious horror (and sometimes delight) experienced by Europeans in the face of Aztec Mexico, I felt that there has been an unwillingness to recognize the extent to which the Aztec state did what all states do, regardless of the fact that it organized the displays of death rather more explicitly than in the West. It was precisely this explicitness that illuminated questions that had been suppressed in the West. I realized that if I wanted to understand the nature of imperial power in general, I would have to look at the lessons offered by the Méxica rather than treat them as something incomprehensible. Second, as I sought to piece together the Aztecs' stories of their transformation from nomadic wanderers into an imperial power, I came to understand that, despite their will to conquer, the Méxica possessed a metaphoric map able to account for the ruses and seduction of imperial violence.

The Aztec stories are a smoking mirror that reveals the true nature of the state without the pretensions of the benign polis and the redemptive god. They are able to articulate the link between violence and representation. Thus, the stories that circulate in this book also circulate around a mirror and what can happen when we look into it.

Deborah Root

Acknowledgments

The writing of a book is truly a collective process and grows out of many discussions and chance encounters with people and ideas. I have benefited from the willingness of friends and colleagues to contribute their ideas and expertise and to argue with many of my conclusions.

Writers Lang Baker and Dot Tuer graciously read drafts of the manuscript (despite their own deadlines) and provided intellectual stimulation and moral support during the often onerous process of writing this book. Their willingness to engage in debate was extremely valuable in helping me clarify the ideas in this book.

Visual artist Christine Davis engaged in ongoing and illuminating discussions about art theory and practice and was generous with books and articles. Her work was always very thought provoking.

Special thanks to Larry Lyons for many of the photographs that appear in this book.

I also wish to thank those who helped make this book possible: Shonagh Adelman, Donna Baker, Kass Banning, Jody Berland, Jake Boots, Sharon Brooks, Rosemary Coombe, Barbara Freedman, Jamelie Hassan, Tariq Hassan-Gordon, Amy Irwin, Peter Kulchyski, Dvora Levinson, Susan Lord, Janine Marchessault (who consistently offered special encouragement and support), Kellie Masterson, Jen Metcalf, Mahmut Mutman, Amanda Pask, Andy Payne, Beverly Pierro, Allison Roberts, Amresh Sinha, Wedlidi Speck, Meyda Yegenoglu, and Dilip Yogasundram.

The editors at Westview Press were supportive throughout the writing of this text, and I wish to thank Gordon Massman, production editor Jane Raese, and copyeditor Jess Lionheart. The Royal Ontario Museum courteously provided photographs. I am also indebted to the Province of Ontario Arts Council, which provided generous support.

This book is for Lang, whose love and care have sustained me far beyond a project such as this. The memory of sweet Maia suffused the writing of the text because she well understood the problems of power and difference.

D. R.

1

Fat-Eaters and Aesthetes: The Politics of Display

A few years before Cortés landed on the coast of Mexico, evil omens began to appear in the capital city of Tenochtitlán that warned of the imminent arrival of the Spaniards and the destruction of the Aztec empire. One omen was a strange, ashen-colored bird fished out of the lake surrounding the city. This bird wore a mirror in its forehead in which could be seen the night sky and certain constellations. As Motecuzoma gazed into the mirror, the black starry night dissolved to show strange warriors coming toward him, riding deer and fighting among themselves. When the king asked his magicians to look into the mirror, both the image and the bird suddenly disappeared.

What made this omen so particularly disturbing to Emperor Motecuzoma and so clearly a portent of the destruction of the city? The appearance of the bird meant it was a message from Tezcatlipoca (see Figure 1.1) to his subject and surrogate, Motecuzoma. Tezcatlipoca is the Smoking Mirror, the black god of the north, of night, and of magicians and robbers. He sometimes appears as a handsome, flute-playing youth and sometimes as a jaguar. Smoking Mirror controls the forces of death and destruction and was referred to in Tenochtitlán as "the enemy on both sides" and "the tyrannical one," yet he also creates and bestows wealth and dignity. The presence of Tezcatlipoca saturates the institutions of kingship and human sacrifice in Aztec Mexico.

The story of a doomed king gazing into a mirror recalls the demise of another ruler, the god-king Quetzalcoátl-Topilzín of Tula, the Toltec kingdom on which the Méxica people, or Aztecs,[1] based their legitimacy and whose history and mythology they appropriated. Here, Quetzalcoátl's brother fomented a revolution in order to impose human sacrifice and militarist ideals on the Toltec city. The evil brother was, of course, Tezcatlipoca the Smoking Mirror, and he bested his brother by a ruse: through trickery and malice, Tezcatlipoca made his brother look into a mirror, and the sight of his face so shocked and horrified Quetzalcoátl that he became drunk and

FIGURE 1.1 Tezcatlipoca (after Codex Borgia, *D. Root)*

committed incest with his sister. In shame Quetzalcoátl was forced to flee the city, leaving it to Tezcatlipoca and the forces of human sacrifice and militarism. Bad omens began to announce Tula's impending collapse. In the cyclical histories of Méxica cosmology the fall of Tula mirrored the imminent fall of Tenochtitlán, with Tezcatlipoca appearing as the mocking destroyer.

Tezcatlipoca plays a double game. His ambivalent relation to his subjects exemplifies how despotic authority operates and seduces again and again. No matter how power is represented, no matter how often it appears as something kindly, benevolent, or beautiful, Tezcatlipoca waits to hand us the mirror, revealing the connections between wealth and death, power and disaster. In the contemporary imperial systems of the Western tradition violence and beauty continue to go hand in hand, fragments endlessly reflecting each other but all pointing to the scornful hunger of Tezcatlipoca. If the despot is imagined as the sign that all other signs refer to, we can see that the various manifestations of despotic authority are able to devour images as much as human bodies.

The Aztecs recognized that human flesh was necessary to the functioning of the state, and they knew the extent to which violence and the consumption of bodies were immanent to empire. At some point a deal was cut: The Aztecs were allowed to consume the wealth of the people they conquered, but it cost them blood. The Smoking Mirror was very explicit in his demand for blood, and the Aztecs were rigorous in upholding the ceremonies that honored this demand. The sacrificial victim climbed the pyramid to meet the obsidian knife, and after the heart had been cut out of the body and the blood offered to the gods, the arms and legs were distributed to the priests who administered the sacrificial cult. The eating of human flesh was strictly ritualized in Tenochtitlán, and complex cosmological questions regarding the transmutation of matter circumscribed the cannibal ceremonies. At the same time, however, the Aztecs made a point of eating foreign enemies rather than Méxica. It is always someone else's flesh that is the meal of choice.

Does Tezcatlipoca walk in the West? Does Tezcatlipoca still demand blood in exchange for power? Is it possible that, despite the European claim to rationality and the ideal of the democratic polis, violence and cannibalism have a ceremonial function here similar to that of the Aztec state? Elaborate systems of representation distract attention from the extent to which our system also depends on the ritualized killing of human beings. The Western powers launched a war in the Persian Gulf and bodies were consumed amid a ceremonial display and repetition of images of the Western family, of individual heroism, and of cultural self-congratulation. "Baghdad lit up like a Christmas tree," one pilot said, thus articulating a display of power that was more exhilarating than negotiations or sanctions could ever be because it aestheticized the idea of dead bodies. Violence became something beautiful. The Christmas tree image elides what was occurring on the streets of Baghdad as the bombs fell, and all we are left with is the pilot's pleasure of mastery. The words of the U.S. pilot offer no more than a glimpse of how cannibal power works, but they promise so much more. The smoking mirror offers a dream of plentitude and perfection, but as Tezcatlipoca and Louis Althusser have shown in their different ways, the image of the face of power can operate only as another ruse.

Different societies approach questions of power and representation differently, and some are much more suspicious of authority than the Western tradition is and have developed techniques to contain the representation of power. Some societies see power as quite dangerous and unattractive (although always interesting).[2] Others bring the problem right out into the open and give power a name, which can be another version of the same thing. In recognizing that power can be named as such, we can see how the Méxica stories illuminate the nature of power, which remains behind the mirror in the Western tradition because we are unwilling to gaze into its face. The Aztec metaphor suggests another way to approach Western ambivalence about representation and imperial authority. It is worth paying attention to Tezcatlipoca because he demonstrates that the state is and always has been a cannibal monster continually seeking flesh to consume. Let us return to the story of the two brothers.

That the fall of the Toltec state appeared in the Aztec writings as the result of a conflict between enemy brothers was indicative of how destructive the antagonism between these two figures was. Each brother represented a rival view of militarism and human sacrifice—in short, how violence should be organized and represented by the state. I sometimes wonder if these stories suggest that the outcome of the struggle could have been different and that, barring Tezcatlipoca's treachery, the Méxica could have created a different kind of state, where bodies were not consumed by wars and the sacrificial block. It is important to remember that the expansionist ideals of imperial Tenochtitlán, the economy based on tribute, and the mass human sacrifice of prisoners of war were all instituted and maintained by the military-religious-merchant elites of the city. As in Europe, it was not the hunters, farmers, or ordinary people living in small villages who established the cannibal regimes.

Certainly it was at least in part through the honoring of Quetzalcoátl that people were able to maintain nonmilitaristic ideals within a militaristic economy. Quetzalcoátl was presented as a dupe and victim of sorcery and tricks, yet was always more benevolent and helpful to people than Tezcatlipoca. But the veneration of Quetzalcoátl as the Toltec god par excellence—and as the god of learning, science, and the priesthood—did not change the fact that it was the sorcerer Tezcatlipoca, the Smoking Mirror, who ultimately won. In imperial Tenochtitlán, Tezcatlipoca was elevated to the supreme god and worshiped as Tloque Nahuaque—Master of the Near and the Close—the god who was always there.

Quetzalcoátl, in contrast, was taken up by the priesthood. High priests were given the title of "Quetzalcoátl," which at first glance seems fitting given the view of the Toltecs as the source of all knowledge and culture and of the figure of Quetzalcoátl as the exemplary Toltec sovereign. Quetzalcoátl's peaceful reign in Tula (until all the trouble at the end, of course), his identification with the priesthood and with the virtues of harmony, wisdom, and learning, were evoked again and again in the Méxica priestly texts, which seems somewhat contradictory given Quetzalcoátl's well-known opposition to human sacrifice and the priests' rather intense dedication to it. The ideals extolled in the Quetzalcoátl literature were nevertheless presented as antithetical to the sorcery and discord wrought by Tezcatlipoca, and the Méxica writings were careful to distinguish between the two figures and the qualities and values with which each was associated.

Because of the constant emphasis on the differences between the two brothers, it is easy to forget that Quetzalcoátl was a ruler as well as a priest, which meant that he maintained political sovereignty in Tula, with all the hierarchy and violence implied by an institution of royal authority. The priestly ideal personified by Quetzalcoátl occluded his despotic function or, rather, purified and rendered benign the idea of the despot or supreme lord. Quetzalcoátl became the ruse of imperial power, appearing as what the state was at its best and what kings at their best were capable of offering the people. But we know better. The despotic face of the wise king was revealed by Tezcatlipoca, who brought about the fall of Tula by displaying to Quetzalcoátl his face: "Then he gave him the mirror and said: 'Look and know thyself my son, for thou shalt appear in the mirror.' Then Quetzalcoátl saw himself; he was very frightened and said: 'If my vassals were to see me, they might run away.'"[3]

Tezcatlipoca's sorcery is stronger than Quetzalcoátl's arts and sciences because it is capable of revealing the despot to be not the benign face of Quetzalcoátl but the fearsome face of the enemy on both sides. Illusions fall down, all is revealed, and the face in the mirror is that of the sign all other signs refer to: power. Tezcatlipoca teaches that the state operates and maintains its authority through violence and terror. The sovereign of Tenochtitlán himself recognizes this and indeed becomes king by revealing Tezcatlipoca's absolutist demands and by enacting a performance in which this is displayed for all to see. The human sovereign's relationship to the deity is one of abjection and self-abasement before a greater power, here the despotic authority of the god. In the formal speech made by the Méxica king to Tezcatlipoca on the occasion of his ascension to the throne, the king says, "O master, O our lord, O lord of the near, of the nigh, O night, O wind, thou hast inclined thy heart. Perhaps thou hast mistaken me for another, I who am a commoner, I who am a labourer. In excrement, in filth hath my lifetime been—I who am unreliable, I who am of filth, of vice. And I am an imbecile."[4]

The device of making the sovereign say such things publicly was instituted, not only I think, to underline his humility before the god but also to absolutize the idea of despotic authority *in itself*. The king's willingness to express his subordination becomes a way to represent the broader concept of formal authority, and the point emphasized in the speech is that the symbolic system must be ordered hierarchically, with a chain of command in which everyone is implicated. Even a sovereign has a master. This is what is important, not any particular god or ruler.

The story of the two brothers explains despotic violence and militarism while seeming to maintain an ideal of the benign state, but the triumph of Tezcatlipoca functions as a recognition that political authority is always underlain by chaos and death.

The other principal gods, and their functions and activities, turn out to be different guises or aspects of the Smoking Mirror. The god of war, Huitzilopochtli, is revealed as the blue Tezcatlipoca of the south; the flayed god, Xipe Totec, is the red Tezcatlipoca of the east, and even the brother-enemy Quetzalcoátl becomes the white Tezcatlipoca of the west. Lamenting the fate of the unfortunate Quetzalcoátl distracts us from the extent to which the ideals associated with Tezcatlipoca's triumph—that is, the ideals of the state, of militarism, and of human sacrifice—were affirmed in the Méxica cities.

One of the attributes of Tezcatlipoca is invisibility—in some paintings he is represented only by footprints—and this ability to become invisible at will increases his power and fearsomeness. Indeed, even though the name Tezcatlipoca is generally translated as "Smoking Mirror," a more accurate rendition would be "The Smoke That Mirrors." Obsidian mirrors were used for divination by the Méxica (and the Aztec mirrors that reached Europe after 1521 were used for the same purpose by magicians such as John Dee and Nostradamus). Magicians gazed into the mirror and waited for images to form. The sense of a smoke that mirrors is suggestive of a double quality of veiling and revealing through reflection; the smoke both obscures and reflects the image of the inquirer. The face of power is never fully revealed but always veils itself. And here it is the god himself, the despotic deity Tezcatlipoca, who reflects the image of the people and of the priests who seek knowledge of the future and of the affairs of state.

Tezcatlipoca's mirror has a name; it is called "The Place from Which He Watches." The invisible god sees all and knows all. The shock and horror provoked in both Quetzalcoátl and Motecuzoma by the presence in the mirror are not difficult to understand—both figures were reminded that the watching eye of power was on them, that the despotic gaze was everywhere, even on the supreme leaders of the state. They were also reminded that they, too, reflected the face of the despot, a truth that Quetzalcoátl found impossible to bear. And this despotic gaze implies a destructive quality that both observes and reflects the power of kings.

I chose (or perhaps appropriated) the example of the two Mexican brothers to illustrate something that can be overlooked in Western culture: Power is never benign. When the mask of the good king is stripped away, the face underneath is always that of Tezcatlipoca, whether he is called Good Queen Bess or John F. Kennedy. Tezcatlipoca—or at least his manifestations in the human world—is a cannibal, an entity that needs neverending streams of blood and human bodies to consume and whose desires are organized around death. In societies with hierarchies that control bodies and determine which ones will live and which ones will die, there is always some spectacle of violence (even if it sometimes takes place behind closed doors, with only a few witnessing or partaking). Most sacrificial spectacles, which take explicit and implicit forms, display and symbolize the link between power and representation for all to see. All are implicated, and people are kept in line. Power swallows life.

The story of the two brothers shows us that the Méxica recognized the nature of a hierarchical political system, but once social and religious power was concentrated in the hands of an elite, the system became extremely difficult for ordinary people to change, even assuming they wanted to do so. The Méxica sacrificial system is not, I think, an anomaly among hierarchical social systems, which is why it can illuminate the blind spots and failures in the Western tradition. The specific form this system took—the pyramids, the lines of prisoners awaiting the sacrificial block—was more explicit than many others about its need to consume human bodies and to display this ability to consume for all to see. I am not describing the Méxica state as a cannibal system in order to separate Aztec Mexico from the equally cannibalistic European social orders and derisively mark it as "barbarian" (or some such epithet). Much like the system that has come to dominate the West, the Méxica symbolic and political economy had to feed off violence in order to reproduce and survive. The Aztecs understood the ambivalence of power, its ability to simultaneously seduce and demand, and its facility in taking on a life of its own. The particular manifestations of imperial authority (as demanded by Tezcatlipoca) became extremely difficult to divert from the cannibal path once it had reached a certain point. And, again, some people benefited from such a system. The story of the two brothers also shows that Tezcatlipoca is perhaps easier to recognize, if not control, if he is understood within a sacred order.

Because most Spaniards who invaded Mexico in the sixteenth century refused to look squarely at the implications of power, they could not tolerate the explicitness of the Méxica state's organization of violence and mass death. For example, in Tenochtitlán prisoners of war were sent to the sacrificial pyramids, while in Paris in the same years thousands were slaughtered in the streets in the Saint Bartholomew's Day massacre. The European state was—and is—as much a cannibal as the Aztec, but mass death in Europe tends to be classified as an accidental phenomenon rather than as something intrinsic to the functioning of the system. Despite example after example of Western atrocities, it is always someone else who is the cruel and pitiless barbarian.

These harsh words are not intended to negate the many critical streams in European thinking that have addressed questions of violence and power and, in particular, the ambivalence these are able to generate. But I think we must face the possibility that something is dreadfully wrong with society and that this is somehow connected to the bloody history of Western culture, a bloodiness that surpasses all others, including the Aztecs and their human sacrifice. But is it even possible to look at our cannibal nature? We remember the consequences of looking in Tezcatlipoca's mirror—Quetzalcoátl lost his power and had to leave the city.

The Aztec state rendered absolutely and unmistakably explicit the nature and consequence of a hierarchical and imperial social order, something that is prettied up in the Western tradition with notions of "civilization," the aesthetics of high culture, and the Greek polis as the source of democratic political organization. This disavowal continues to obtain today. The Méxica are presented as a horrific, incomprehensible society where violence was totally out of control—unlike us. European writing about Aztec society focuses almost exclusively on human sacrifice, which is described in such a way as to obscure the links among the different versions of violence from above. (A great deal of perplexed head-shaking goes on as Western academics attempt to account for Aztec state institutions; Claude Lévi-Strauss refers to the Aztecs as "that open wound on the flank of Americanism."[5]) This refusal has its consequences in the classificatory schemes of both Western art and science, particularly those of ethnologists and museologists: The Aztec court art that was not immediately destroyed or melted down is housed in European museums with the egalitarian societies defined as "primitive" and "savage" rather than with the real savages, the court cultures of Europe and the ancient Near East.

The White Cannibal

Power dazzles and blinds, and those closest to its heart are often unable to see anything beyond its reflections. Those who affirm a more marginal relation to the dominant culture sometimes more easily see the nature of that system and notice what those closer to the center may overlook. In the 1991 novel by Native American writer Leslie Marmon Silko (*Almanac of the Dead*), the old woman Yoeme recognizes the profound bond between Méxica and Spaniard, particularly the resemblances between the way the Aztec and European states organized violence:

> Yoeme alleged the Aztecs ignored the prophecies and warnings about the approach of the Europeans because Montezuma and his allies had been sorcerers who had called or even invented the European invaders with their sorcery. Those who worshipped destruction and blood secretly knew each other. Hundreds of years earlier, the people who hated sorcery and bloodshed had fled north to escape the cataclysm prophesied when the "blood worshippers" of Europe met the "blood worshippers" of the Americas. Montezuma and Cortes had been meant for each other.[6]

Silko is suggesting that the Spanish and Aztecs acknowledged and understood each other in the beginning because both societies were organized around violence or, more accurately, around a conceptual system that generated individual and collective excitement from blood and suffering. I think that she is right and that this moment was so shocking to the invading Christians that they had to immediately deny that Aztecs and Europeans had anything in common. The Aztecs were not "civilized," the Spanish said, although they manifested the same traits as other civilized societies, even if they were not Christian. Looking into that particular mirror was a bit too unsettling. To admit the Aztecs into the ranks of civilized societies was to put the notion of civilization itself into question.

What are the implications of this mutual recognition? And what may be learned from the refusal of this moment in Western thinking? Let us begin by looking at how violence has become aestheticized in Western culture. We have seen that the Méxica stories articulate a complex chain of religious and political concepts whereby the origin of violence and the state is explained through Tezcatlipoca's trickery. By looking at how Tezcatlipoca is situated within the Aztec symbolic economy, which is to say how it is represented in various sites in the culture, we can see how questions of authority permeate areas of culture that at first glance seem entirely unrelated to issues of political power. The conceptual diagram I call "Tezcatlipoca" links Aztecs and Europeans and reveals otherwise overlooked affinities between different sites and different representational forms. When looking at different sites in the Western symbolic economy, we will keep watch for the traces of Tezcatlipoca's presence, for those moments when despotic authority is articulated and when human (and other) bodies are consumed.

Within Western culture there has been a tendency to project the categories of violence and of bloodthirsty, barbaric religious practices onto colonized people. This is nothing new; we can trace it as far back as Herodotus's conceptions of Persian and Scythian cultures.[7] What is less immediately obvious is the extent to which a European cannibal spirit (or Tezcatlipoca-type figure) animates our own relation to culture and violence in a way that continues to be elided and disavowed in our tradition. This is less extreme than it first appears: The cannibal seeks human bodies to eat, and the desire for flesh generates escalating desire. This hunger for flesh is generalized into society as a whole when consumption is treated as a virtue and seen as a source of pleasure and excitement in itself. Consumption is power, and the ability to consume excessively and willfully becomes the most desirable aspect of power. At the same time, both Aztec and European are constructs that elide the internal conflicts and dissension within each society and that therefore function as generalizations imposed from the outside. (Comanche writer Paul Chaat Smith remarks, "We never imagine sullen teenagers in Tenochtitlán, that fabled Aztec metropolis, in some pre-Columbian Zona Rosa dive, badmouthing the wretched war economy and the ridiculous human sacrifices that drove their empire."[8]) There are syncretic elements in both cultures. But generalizing about how violence is organized and represented may tell us something about the links between consumption and blood sacrifice. By reading this problem through the figure of the cannibal, as an image that continues to evoke fear and horror, we can argue that what is really at stake here is consumption.

Wasi'chu, the Lakota term used for white people, delineates a particular mentality, a bizarre obsession that is organized almost entirely around consumption and excess. *Wasi'chu* means "fat-eater," or "greedy one who takes the fat," and describes someone whose desires are out of control, entirely without limit or thought for the future.[9] The cravings of the fat-eater have an atemporal quality and must be satisfied regardless of the eventual consequences for future generations or the community as a whole. The term describes a real phenomenon, an endless hunger that results in the literal consumption of land and bodies, a hunger that can only be temporarily satisfied and then breaks out anew. The hunger grows and grows, and the provisions required to feed it can only increase as the desire to control and organize people and cultures intensifies. Lust for "the fat" continues to careen unchecked across the earth. *Wasi'chu* does not simply describe a racial category or set of characteristics; *wasi'chus* have been noticed among those non-Europeans who subscribe to Western values. Rather, *wasi'chu* is a state of mind that Lakota people observed in European invaders, initially during the Black Hills gold rush of the 1880s, when white desire was wholly organized around an obsession with gold. As in Mexico, where Native writers also spoke with some astonishment about Spanish greed as exemplified by a fetishization of gold, the cost of that gold to people and land was not a consideration for colonizers obsessed with dreams of wealth.[10]

Native American writer Jack Forbes has explored this idea and in *Columbus and Other Cannibals* situates the essential failure of the Western or European model of society in the unchecked will to consume that is at the heart of the Western mentality.[11] Again, this is not a racial matter but a particular state of mind. We need to be very clear that this mentality, which has been dominant in the West for the past several centuries, had to be imposed by force on European populations (as it later was on Native populations), a process that involved the violent suppression of heretics and others defined as heterodox and culturally deviant. Regardless of whether we speak of Europe or of colonized territories, the imposition of the *wasi'chu* values was, and is, always linked to violence.

Forbes attributes the desire for unfettered consumption to the phenomenon of cannibal psychosis, or what in the Cree language is termed *wétiko,* which is possession by evil cannibal monster spirits. Forbes suggests that many of us—and "us" means all those who in some way live off and in relation to Western culture, which is nearly everyone—have literally been transformed into cannibals, consuming human bodies for profit. The *wétiko* psychosis, like *wasi'chu,* is characterized by a need or desire that grows and grows until it is completely out of control and in effect possesses the person who succumbs to it. People are consumed, their bodies devoured by other, more rapacious people in many different ways, some of the most immediately obvious being in systems of slave labor, in pointless and destructive wars undertaken for profit, and in the killing of people to "free" their land for development projects. Forbes describes the Western ethos as a highly contagious disease with hideous effects whose sufferers are nevertheless highly rewarded in this culture.

I was initially uneasy with Forbes's use of a disease metaphor to characterize Western consumption. Such metaphors must be approached with extreme caution, particularly when generated by people wielding coercive authority who are juxtaposing a "healthy" population (always themselves) against a deviant and troublesome population whose land or wealth is coveted. In some cases these metaphors have been used to justify genocide. Yet it seems evident that Forbes does not speak as someone positioned to buttress institutional power but as someone seeking to account for the levels of violence in mainstream society. Moreover, Forbes does not really use the concept of *wétiko* as a metaphor but as a technical medico-spiritual term for a particular approach to the world. This disease is able to cross populations to produce certain kinds of recognizable effects in the people who have contracted it. Both *wasi'chu* and *wétiko* emphasize consumption, which exists at the heart of Western culture, and both traditions characterize consumption in very literal and concrete terms. By consumption I am not necessarily talking about visits to the mall (although this may well be a site of consumption) but rather more generally about an ontological condition involving an approach to reality and state of mind that have as their central obsession "the fat."

In the old stories the *wétiko* monsters always come from the far north and possess hearts of ice. This association of consumption with coldness initially seemed curious to me, as I imagined gluttony to be driven by heat—in other words, by a kind of lust. But Nietzsche reminds us that "the coldest of cold monsters" is the state, which endlessly feeds off lies and death: "It is the destroyers who set snares for many and call it the state: they hang a sword and a hundred desires over them."[12]

Nietzsche paid a very high price for his insights (and one that may have been too dear), and he is right to link the production of infinite, destructive desire to a fixed hierarchical system. When authority is organized around a rigidly predetermined scale of values, people cease to believe that they belong to the world in which they live. The state engenders profound passivity in its citizens (which is, after all, the point), and kindness has no place in the balance books of the palace functionaries. If we understand *wétiko* psychosis as a description of the state, and vice versa, it is no longer surprising that every act of consumption seeks to break through this paralysis, this system that seems frozen in place and hence itself exudes a glacial quality.

The state can be a tricky adversary, in part because of its ability to present itself as a neutral manifestation of the will of the people. In this way the state conceals its presence. Michael Taussig eloquently shows how state terror operates through silence and produces that frigid isolation in which the cannibal monster thrives. Speaking of how Colombian death squads distribute fear and silencing throughout the populace, Taussig writes, "The point about silencing and the fear behind silencing is not to erase memory. Far from it. The point is to drive the memory deep within the fastness of the individual so as to create more fear and uncertainty in which dream and reality comingle."[13]

Ultimately, the state both produces and consumes fear. The individual becomes her own police force, her own imaginary torturer. And thus the social order reproduces itself: If anything can happen, then it is better to toe the line. This is another example of the way power pacifies by intermittently allowing a glimpse of its face, a sight that invariably stuns people into fearful silence and submission. Taussig explains how the different sites of terror operate by concealing the extent of their terror-producing activities (in other words, their cannibal natures), which reminds us of Nietzsche's insistence that the state exists through lies. The topography of terror always turns out to be a map of the face of the state, behind which the countenance of the blood-loving Tezcatlipoca is visible.

Aristocratic Dreams

It is all too obvious that in contemporary society people are taught to define themselves by the goods they possess and to follow orders so they can acquire more goods. It is not so much that wealth equals power but that wealth equals consumption equals power. We can imagine our own seduction: "Let's go to Paris! Why not? Hire somebody to clean the house; hire somebody to provide a range of pleasures (and to smile while doing so), to walk the dog, to mine gold." There are many versions of the dream. (A few years ago I was transfixed by a provincial lottery ad in which a folksinger sang in a soft, insinuating voice; "Have the freedom to do what you want to do; it's a good life, oh yeah," while the camera panned people sleeping in the morning sun. Wealth was never more seductive.) Some streams of the Western tradition have recognized that excessive consumption leads to moral and spiritual death, but many of these critiques appear in puritan versions of Christian discourses that rhetorically frame the solution to the problem around renunciation. More interesting are those critiques that originally came out of so-called folk cultures, most obviously the vampire stories.

In the European tradition the figure of the vampire can be thought of as a variant of the *wétiko* cannibal monster (and possibly as a less articulated and complex version of Tezcatlipoca). I am not suggesting any historical links between *wétikos* and vampires and am in fact focusing on the differences between the two figures. I think that the different ways that the will to consume has been made flesh are each indicative of a larger attitude toward violence and cannibalism and, by extension, of the relation of the individual to the community as a whole.

Vampire stories seem to be of enduring interest—witness the enormous success of the Anne Rice novels—perhaps because for the European vampire the consumption of flesh is eroticized. The desire that grows out of balance is represented as being ultimately sexual in nature. The European vampire usually has an attractive, seductive side deriving from his (less often, her) air of aristocratic dissipation, itself fascinating to many and a sign of the ambivalence and danger he embodies. We see this again and again. The aristocratic glamor of Gary Oldman's Dracula in the recent *Bram Stoker's Dracula* (1992; see Figure 1.2) exemplifies this dangerous male allure—Dracula is as irresistible to the audience as he is to his victims. We are reminded of other aristocrats, such as the marquis de Sade and Gilles de Rais, and how their apparently pure individualism and lack of conscience were manifested in extreme, yet affectless violence toward others, especially those considered weak—in other words, women, peasants, and children (always the preferred sacrificial victims). These aristocrats also seem to be of enduring interest, and their will to violence has been aestheticized in ways very similar to vampire stories. Because of the vampire's allure, we experience ambivalence toward his power over life and death. The vampire's ability to seduce, and his power over human bodies, appears to us as a kind of absolute freedom and manifestation of personal will.

We are taught to want to "eat the fat" because to do so is to possess and experience an illusion of total power and freedom. Thus, freedom appears as the ability to do as we please with other bodies and, by extension, with other species and with the land itself. Respect—and community—becomes no more than an irritating limit on desire, something best left to peasants and drones.

The continuing ability of the vampire to fascinate, erotically or otherwise, is only one indication of the extent to which contemporary society has aestheticized *wétiko* sickness and we ourselves have become cannibal. We can see this aestheticization in films, commodities, and various other cultural products in which the ability to take or control life is glamorized. As I understand the cannibal stories, in traditional societies the cannibal spirits are recognized as beings to be avoided except in very specific ceremonial contexts, whereas in the commodified version of the European tradition those who would be recognized as cannibals elsewhere are seen as sexy and fun. Again, this eroticization of the vampire refers to the aristocratic ideal of excess circulating around a languorous figure who has no affect, the despotic sign all the other signs refer to. But there are different kinds of vampires. Power is glamorous, and we learn to feed off evil. We

FIGURE 1.2 *Mina (Winona Ryder) is seduced by Dracula's (Gary Oldman) eternal charms in* Bram Stoker's Dracula. *(Copyright © 1992 Columbia Pictures Industries, Inc. All rights reserved. Used by permission.)*

see it again and again: Powerful people are always surrounded by lackeys who are eager to please, even if this means abasing themselves. If we think about the matter carefully, bearing in mind all the cautionary tales in the Western folk tradition, a wiser course of action would be to back away slowly from, rather than to associate with, those who seek to manifest raw power. Indeed, this is the response of people who understand power as a form of cannibalism.

Because power is a desirable aspiration in Western culture, it is difficult to maintain a conceptual framework that recognizes sites of dominance and authority and that is able to call these into question. A process of naturalization renders authority shifting, even invisible, and at times we can see only the glamor.

However, the ambivalence and unease that the notion of abstract power over life and death generates are often displaced onto those who have been directly subject to this power. Historically, Europeans' tendency to attribute cannibalism to people they sought to colonize (as well as to internal "deviants," such as Jews and witches, both of whom were subjected to blood libels) seems to have been a way of displacing and drawing attention away from the extent to which European elites were prepared to consume bodies. The fascination remains, provided it does not come too close to home. European and North American tourists travel to see "cannibals" in New Guinea and others whom they believe to celebrate frightful, bloodthirsty, yet fascinating rites.[14] This fascination with other people's customs, of course, also displaces cannibalism to somewhere far away. In the movies cannibalism continues to be displaced onto foreigners old and new as well as onto contemporary serial killer–type psycho criminals, who are presented as cultural outsiders by virtue of their madness. (Interestingly, neither the audience nor the victim characters ever recognize the insane murderers in advance, as they are initially indistinguishable from "normal" people.) People visiting museums in Western capitals can see the signs of unspeakable rituals formerly practiced elsewhere and breathe sighs of relief that "we" have gone beyond such horrors.

The urge and the willingness to consume human bodies, entire cultures, and species of plants and animals have continued, in part, because there are immediate rewards for doing so. There are profits to be made from such exploitation. But there are other reasons people willfully turn themselves into cannibals and vampires. *Wétiko* psychosis isolates us from other people—and indeed makes the idea of profound attachments with others appear as impossible, naive foolishness—from the land, and from other forms of life. It is, I think, this separation from the world in which we live that makes us susceptible to the disease. The cannibal monster is able to invade our bodies at this weak point and transform isolation into a roaring, painful emptiness before presenting us with what seems the only certain cure for that isolation: more consumption, more accumulation, and, for some, more ironic distance about the process. People attempt to connect with one another through objects and through the shared excitement those objects generate. Those who are unable to do so sometimes resort to more explicitly violent means: The person who unloads a semiautomatic into a crowded shopping mall is simultaneously denying and expressing intense isolation.

What feeds the cannibal and makes it grow? To comprehend and account for the cannibal, we have to be willing to use a different kind of language, one that can describe certain kinds of phenomena as evil. As I understand it, the cannibal is able to live and grow where there is a void—which is to say, an absence of a particular element (or cluster of elements) that is necessary to the cohesion and balance of the whole. This is true of individuals as well as societies.

Most traditional societies recognize the existence of evil. If evil is denied or repudiated in a culture, there will be no ceremonies to deal with it. There will be only an empty space where evil would, in another system, be recognized and ceremonially confronted.[15] I think that because we have displaced cannibalism onto deviants and foreigners, the desire to consume, and the temporary excitement produced by the act of consumption, is able to expand and metastasize, colonizing and destroying Western culture from within. The chickens do come home to roost, as we can see from the rising and apparently uncontrollable levels of violence that permeate contemporary culture. Because we have refused to recognize the extent to which the cannibal lives inside us and at the heart of our culture, the cannibal monster becomes larger and larger. I said previously that we of Western culture are unwilling to stare the monster in the face: A traditional person would explain that this is why the monster's appetite increases. I think societies that refuse to glamorize power understand that the only way to keep *wétiko* value systems from taking root is to recognize the seductiveness of consumption and to collectively devise ways of minimizing it. This is what most anthropologists and other "experts" from the *wétiko*-dominated outside fail to understand: The ceremonies that various societies employ to address destructive cannibal spirits confront a real, concrete social issue in a practical manner. We in the West can see the results of cannibal psychosis everywhere but seem paralyzed, unable to recognize and name it for what it is, unable to do anything about it.

From Spectacle to Display

The Aztec state had to display its ability to consume bodies, and the public nature of many of the sacrifices and the exhibition of human skulls on skull racks seem to have been as important as the killing itself. We are dazzled and seduced by the display of consumption, and there seems to be a direct link between accumulation of wealth and the ability to display for all to see the power of life and death. Many of the displayed things are beautiful, which produces an identification of power and beauty and thereby further entrenches and normalizes consumption as the defining quality of the culture. The way beauty and art have been used to justify a very wide range of cannibal behaviors is central to the notions of exoticism and appropriation that are the subject of this book. Certainly, *wétiko* psychosis appears and is manifested in aesthetics—and in both the high and low versions—and aesthetics continue to be the site where the disease is manifested in some of its most complex and ambivalent ways.

Consumption can be displayed in many ways. Both objects and people can serve to exhibit cannibalistic qualities, and specific individuals can be presented in such a way that they embody consumption itself: Lifestyles of the Rich and Famous. There is a relation between the relatively harmless experience of pleasure when buying, for instance, a new pair of earrings and the pleasure and excitement supposedly felt in the presence of famous, wealthy people. Celebrities are often cannibals, but their glamor gives cachet to their cannibalistic practices or, rather, celebrity is in many respects dependent upon *wétiko* behavior. (There are also historical reasons for this, and Forbes notes that the heroes of Western history have almost always been major *wétikos*.[16])

In contemporary capitalist culture celebrities are marketable. Thus, they exercise a great deal of power because of their wealth and fame, and this power—which comes down to power over other bodies—is presented again and again in various media as fascinating, and erotic, in itself. In part this eroticization of power has to do with how celebrity is generated in our society, but it is also because these people are able to satisfy cannibalistic desires, if and when they so please, much as the aristocratic vampires of another era did. Not everyone responds to the same precise manifestation of abstract power, of course: One person may become aroused by contact with a wealthy industrialist, whereas another may find musicians or actors more exciting. Famous celebrity artists are continually surrounded by sycophants, if Andy Warhol's diaries are anything to go by. The important point is that in our culture cannibal types continue to be glamorized and represented as romantic objects of desire and their ways of life held out as something to strive for.

This glamorization of *wétiko* and this linking of it to notions of celebrity can in some instances become an extremely contradictory and ambivalent mode of desire. We read newspaper and magazine stories from time to time about mass murderers who, although they are on death row, have devoted followings of women who wish to marry them. But are such extreme examples really any different from the generalized fetishization of consumption and celebrity? The cannibal faces constantly change, and who among us can really remember what Donald Trump looks like? All we remember is the excess.

Following Jack Forbes, I have stressed that *wétiko* is not a metaphor but a real phenomenon with real effects. Cannibal psychosis involves the consumption of real bodies. But it is also useful to extend the definition of cannibalism to forms of consumption that occur beyond the physical body of the individual or even the community. It is possible to consume somebody's spirit, somebody's past or history, or somebody's arts and to do so in such a way that the act of consumption appears beautiful and heroic. The sites where this consumption takes place can be some of the most cherished institutions in Western culture: art galleries, libraries, museums, universities.

Alibis of Appreciation

Art can operate as an alibi for cannibal power because of its ability to gild ugly social and historical facts with the patina of taste and beauty. Certain forms of aesthetic practice are believed to be able to elicit lofty sentiments (particularly, but not exclusively, those that fall into the category of high culture) and hence can obscure the conditions under which these same lofty sentiments are made possible. The presence of art can draw attention away from the extent to which its practice continues to be dependent on a rhetoric of exclusion and mastery. This is not simply to say that, for instance, oppressed serfs toiled so that the lords could appreciate oil painting. Rather, the issue is the way in which ideas of beauty (especially in the highly aestheticized incarnations of old master painting, symphonic music, ballet, opera, and the like) have been abstracted from their social and cultural matrix, imagined as something separate and transcendent that makes all the violence and repressions of history thinkable. The old idea that beauty is somehow good in itself has excused many unattractive moments. Art is often utilized to explain and naturalize the display of authority (and of dead bodies), and the effects of this display can be extremely subtle and complex, profoundly influencing how we understand cultural, sexual, and other differences.

Every now and then the smoke dissolves, and we recognize the mysterious affinity between consumption—of images as much as bodies—and the representation and aestheticization of violence and authority. There are many permutations of this link; power is never seamless, nor is it absolutely confident at all times, which is one reason aesthetics can appear to construct a space outside of power, the space ostensibly necessary to liberate the imagination. But the existence of conceptual zones supposedly untouched by banal authority is so often possible only because this authority hovers nearby and in such a way that the artist or connoisseur is able to benefit from it. Power is merely one step removed from the art object, which in the end means only that art is not banking or law. Now I am not saying that because aesthetic production in late or any other kind of capitalism is linked to the economic and political context in which it occurs, all artistic endeavors are completely pointless and corrupt. None of us is uncontaminated by the market, and part of the problem is the insistence that a pure space can indeed be located and occupied if only we are virtuous enough. It is a more difficult and painful task to look into the complicities, both historical and contemporary, of mainstream and "alternative" aesthetics with power, colonialism, racism, and a host of other oppressions and to do so in such a way that goes beyond self-congratulatory condemnation of the artists and writers we do not like.

Because of the high ideals associated with Western art, many people have been unwilling to recognize that aesthetics are dependent on very explicit sets of power relations. This unwillingness seems disingenuous at best. This dependency is obvious in the way particular kinds of images of colonized cultures are carefully and habitually maintained as sources of what gets called "inspiration." Within Western aesthetics other cultural traditions have been assigned the role of artistic resource, to be harvested pretty much at the pleasure of the colonizers (this is similar to the way images of women of all colors have continually functioned within the same aesthetic), although the specifics of this appropriation have shifted over time. Gold and images, images and gold: both were carried off to Europe. Treating another culture as an aesthetic resource can work in many different ways. For instance, in 1845 Parisian critic Théophile Gautier wrote:

> It is strange, we believe we have conquered Algeria, but Algeria has conquered us. Our women already wear scarves interwoven with threads of gold, streaked with a thousand colours, which have served the harem slaves, our young men are adopting the camel hair burnous. ... Hashish is taking the place of champagne; our Spahi officers look so Arab one would think they had captured themselves in a *smala;* they have adopted all the Oriental habits, so superior is primitive life to our so-called civilization. If this goes on, France will soon be Mahometan and we shall see the white domes of mosques rounding themselves on our horizons. ... We should indeed like to live to see the day.[17]

A number of issues are raised in this quotation. By 1845 France had finally subdued most of Algeria in one of the bloodiest colonial wars of the nineteenth century. Conquest of territory meant control over the people inhabiting the territory, and the new power relationship between the two countries meant that the external trappings of Algerian aesthetics and culture—Gautier mentions costume, hashish, and architecture—were now available for French aesthetes to investigate and consume. Gautier was an extremely influential critic in France; indeed, he coined the notorious term *art for art's sake* (he was interested in a certain kind of excess, and as part of his project to épater les bourgeois he used to walk a live lobster down the Champs Elysees). It is perhaps too easy to overlook the extent to which Gautier's comments reflect the colonial relationship between France and Algeria because he rhetorically frames his remarks as admiration. He loves Algeria! He adores the clothes and the way of life of the people, all the way from hashish to Islam. He happily, which is to say, ironically, insists that the "primitive" life of Algeria is superior to the "civilized" life of Paris (and assumes his readers are Frenchmen who know what he means by these terms). Yet Gautier continues to wholeheartedly support brutal French policies in Algeria. How can this be?

Gautier is not unusual in his willingness to take up the paraphernalia of a culture while calling for or remaining indifferent to the suppression of the people whose objects he acquires and esteems. Nor is he unusual in his tendency to frame his desire for this exotic culture in an ironic mode. In many ways Gautier epitomizes the double man, the man of modernity who plays the double game, on the one hand presenting himself as an antiestablishment bohemian aesthete and on the other supporting the governments that funnel money into his pocket. Gautier is one of the first to occupy the new role of culture broker, based on a new kind of elitism, ostensibly more democratic than the elitism of the ancien régime but much more cynical. His use of irony exemplifies this cynicism; it implies a community of similarly inclined people who are in on the joke, as it were, because they are able to recognize what the speaker is doing and know how to interpret ambiguous statements. This use of irony further implies a symbolic order in which every statement could be made to mean something else but in which a despotic entity at the center decides the "true" meaning of the statement and uses it as a way to adjudicate who is in and who is out.[18] Because a remark can mean anything, the interest in cultural difference can appear as pure consumption, without affect or respect and finally without connection. Again, we are reminded that some cannibals have as their primary interest human bodies; some, precious, beautiful, or grotesque objects; and others, aesthetic sensibilities.

I want to be very careful here. People are curious about one another, which is not necessarily something horrible. We must not assume too much in advance about people's motives, even if these people happen to be male or white or seem to share traits with the oppressor. Nor is this a question of enforcing the one true way or a notion of cultural purity that, however tempting, puts us back in the same conceptual box from which we started. But, this said, it seems obvious that Gautier's brand of appreciation has something quite nasty behind it and that this way of thinking has in many respects been normalized in the dominant stream of Western culture. A fascination with other cultures has been a way for a certain type of aesthete to imagine an outside to the exhaustion and disasters of European culture. Fantasizing a space of pure difference can be the result of battle fatigue or of battle fatigue as a sophisticated pose. Susan Sontag, in her introduction to Antonin Artaud's writings, describes the modernist interest in Asian societies, Western magic, and earth-based cultures: "What unites the East, the ancient antinomian and occult traditions in the West, and the exotic communitarianism of pre-literate tribes is that they are elsewhere, not only in space but in time."[19] In effect, an aestheticized taste for societies far removed from where we actually are can become a way of never having to put the assumptions of our own culture into question or recognize what constitutes the line of demarcation between inside and outside, here and there. The Westerner remains in charge, and the outside remains inside, the aesthetic property of the avant-garde.

Admiration of a foreign culture or a foreign aesthetic system can connote broad-mindedness and at the same time flatter the aesthetic or political pretensions of the connoisseur. The regard for difference can also become another way to control what has been determined to fall into the category marked "foreign"; certainly this can be its effect on the ground, especially when people are stripped of their art and ceremonial objects so that Western admirers can look at them in conveniently located museums. In this way appreciation à la Gautier becomes no more than another manifestation of the colonial mentality. It can operate as an alibi for various forms of colonial encroachment and can serve as an attempt to domesticate and bring under control difference not only with respect to bodies but also in terms of aesthetic codes and conventions. More important, it can presuppose the right to decide what is valuable and interesting. What this comes down to is the assumption that the colonist possesses the master code within which all data, all people and customs, all art objects, can be assimilated and judged.

In this way of thinking it is the colonist—or the museum expert, the anthropologist, the judge at the land claims court—who will decide what is authentic and, by extension, what is worth paying attention to, saving, or stealing. The world exists as a warehouse of treasure, with the plunder of choice this time more aesthetic than explicitly material. The aestheticized appreciation of difference can elide the extent to which the possibility of this appreciation continues to be based on ugly and unequal power relations. It still comes down to a question of who takes and who gives.

Entitlement

That Gautier's love of Algeria veils a colonialist agenda seems evident. The link between aesthetic appreciation and imperial expansion is mirrored in other, more explicit forms of cultural consumption in which sacred objects are seized (and often renamed art in the process) and removed to the capitals of Europe and North America. Gautier's elegant discursive style draws attention away from his certainty that he has a right to anything that catches his eye in the new colony of Algeria. Bombastic enthusiasm can perform a similar function and elide the fact that questions of possession have already been decided by the new masters. It also seems to be a way of demonstrating this right to appropriate for all to see. At a certain point in history the old smash-and-grab colonial mentality merged with notions of scientific expertise, which was to have profound implications for how the world was imagined in the West. Nineteenth-century colonialists believed that the art and artifacts of people across the globe were by definition for the taking, precisely because the Westerners' supposedly greater, scientific perspective entitled them to bring the arts of all other cultures under their purview.

American explorer John Lloyd Stephens, who wrote the influential *Incidents of Travel in Central America, Chiapas, and Yucatan* in 1841, exemplified the confidence of the period when he enthused to his partner in 1841 about a project he had initiated to purchase Copán, a classic-period Mayan ceremonial center located in Honduras: "An operation! (Hide your heads, ye speculators in up-town lots!) To buy Copan! remove the monuments of a by-gone people from the desolate region in which they were buried, set them up in the 'great commercial emporium' [New York City], and found an institution to be the nucleus of a great national museum of American antiquities!"[20] Stephens's hyperbolic, exclamatory style was typical of his time (I am strangely reminded of Walt Whitman), and his rather stunning confidence led him to try buying not only Copán but also other Mayan cities. His remark that these monuments are situated in "desolate regions"—when in fact these areas are populated—is symptomatic of the belief that if these arts and monuments are not recognized by white people or located in a place to which Westerners have easy access, they do not really exist. If a tree falls in the forest, does a listener have to be white to hear it? Does he have to be a scientist? The idea that there must be a central geographical locus in which the people who matter will have access to the fragments of world culture that they have decided are worth preserving continues to persist in some circles in the West. Here the proper nucleus is imagined as New York (Stephens was an American); other times it is London or Paris. The dogma that North American or European cities are the appropriate depots of world culture is shifting, but not without a fight.

Stephens wrote in the mid-nineteenth century, but his insistence on Western entitlement has not been entirely laid to rest in the West. A universalized notion of art, which has always sought to encompass the arts of other cultures, has been taken even further as museums and other art institutions come under fire for retaining cultural property that was confiscated during the colonial period or through other doubtful means.

A Shiva figure was removed from a temple in South India in the 1970s and sold a few years later to a private collector for $405,000. The Indian government wanted the figure (called the Nataraja) back, and the case went to court in London, where the sale had taken place. There were a number of interesting legal arguments, some of which turned on the question of whether the deity (or the deity's lingam) in fact owned the work. The court decided in favor of India and ordered the Nataraja returned to the temple. This profoundly irritated American arts writer Stephen Weil, who wrote, "Our great Western collections have themselves become cultural artifacts. Arching above once-individual cultures, there is today a collective cultural patrimony that has been formed by the flow, mingle and merge of history. ... What's at stake has become *our* heritage, too."[21]

Weil takes the British court's decision as an opportunity to argue against the return of cultural treasures in general, an argument I suspect is not entirely atypical of Western curators and collectors. His agenda is obvious in the way he constantly constructs his audience as Western by reiterating the pronoun *our,* from which India is clearly excluded. Like Gautier, Weil manipulates notions of inclusion and exclusion to justify possession of foreign cultural material. Weil evidently imagines that the connoisseur of such a piece would be a Westerner and has no time for the idea that the Nataraja might be an object of religious veneration; his argument about Western collections assumes that a religious image can be classified according to Western criteria as art, which is to say, as something dead and without spirit. He seems to be saying that because certain art treasures have been removed to the West, the cultures from which they were removed no longer have any specificity or indeed any say in the matter; they can only be "once-individual." It is a peculiar logic: Weil is suggesting that because India (and elsewhere) in some respects has become Westernized, Indian art should remain in the West because these are more or less the same place.

It is what Weil leaves out that is interesting and the way he deploys seemingly neutral but universalized terms, such as "history," as a way of explaining and justifying the presence of religious objects in Western collections. These collections have been formed by historical forces, he asserts, which appear as both an impartial entity and a fait accompli. Weil seems to find the idea unthinkable that the connoisseur of fine art would have to travel to Delhi instead of London or New York to see art objects, a view that echoes Stephens's characterization of Honduras as a "desolate region."

Western collectors and museums are obviously under pressure both from foreign governments demanding the return of cultural material and from the current economic climate, which demands that public institutions generate income. Museums need important art pieces to attract paying customers. Today museums have to construct fairly extreme arguments to justify their ownership of certain pieces, yet both the great Western museums and the non-Western governments that seek the return of art treasures are complicit in defending the primacy of the museum itself. Both seek to prevent ceremonial items from going back to the people who made them and to the communities that might use such objects in a nonmuseum context. Both agree that the national museum is the only proper house for such objects, and the quibbling really concerns which national institution will administer which version of heritage. This is not to say that the Nataraja should not return to India. But this does not solve the problems of judgment and expertise that led to the seizing of such objects in the first place. It also does not address the abstraction of aesthetic and ceremonial objects from the cultural contexts in which they were made and used. As long as museums validate ceremonial objects as fine art, the illegal trade in these objects will continue to flourish.

A New World Order

Gautier wrote at a time when most Europeans took for granted their "right" to decide the good and to control and determine the fate of the rest of the world. Yet his remarks seem curiously contemporary, even "postcolonial,"[22] in the way he juxtaposes a superior primitive against an inferior civilization as part of an apparently admiring embracing of a foreign aesthetic. The evidence lies in his ironic remarks about Islam. Irony can function as a smoking mirror that veils and displaces power, and although we know where Gautier stands, his breathless remarks produce a sense of ambivalence that, again, can mean anything. Ambivalence really is the point here because it means that power will never quite reveal its face and that, as René Descartes would have it, we are fully in charge of what we are experiencing. Gautier articulates his appreciation of Algerian aesthetics wholly within the context of colonial conquest and does not begin to question his evident belief that Arab culture exists only for French aesthetes. Gautier supports a physical conquest of territory as the basis of a European conquest of Algerian aesthetics, a view that at first glance looks like an antiquated, typically nineteenth-century colonialist position, one that has been tossed onto the ash-heap of history everyone has heard so much about.

But think, How many non-Native collectors who adore, say, traditional Native American beadwork also work to support Native sovereignty and land rights? What are the links between past and present when institutions such as the Royal Ontario Museum mount a show on classical Mayan art from Mexico at a time when Mayan-speaking people in Chiapas are under extreme pressure from a pro–free trade Mexican government? How many North Americans who wear clothing from "exotic" countries or select "exotic" designs for their bedsheets question European and North American economic and political policies in the countries in which the beautiful objects originated? Perhaps more to the point, do these consumers know anything at all about the people who create these designs? For most, these questions do not exist, or, more correctly, they briefly emerge before being suppressed and displaced onto the knick-knack being purchased. This is possible because so many people in the West have been subject to a conceptual system that separates people from the art and culture they create. Nineteenth century–style colonial enterprises have for the most part become too expensive for the Western powers to engage in, but the conquest and commodification of traditional aesthetic forms and traditional spirituality remain possible. The question of the extent to which cultures will be able to exist outside of world capital or, rather, on whose terms hybridity will occur hardly ever comes up when images of differences are being "appreciated" and consumed.

Colonists have sought gold in various forms, scientific and art institutions have sought objects, and aesthetes have sought images. Although in recent years some attention has been paid to the conditions of acquisition, collection, and display of museum objects, the manifold ways in which complexes of images have been taken up and aestheticized need more critical attention. Capital moves very quickly, and multinational corporations operate unchecked by borders. A mere one hundred years ago the configurations of world power apparent today would have been unimaginable to most living in the heart of the West. As Iain Chambers points out, Lagos and Mexico City have in many respects become more typical centers of world culture than Paris or New York.[23] Despite the fact that the old distinction between center and periphery has altered, many people in the West cling to fantasies of power, and the West's former colonies continue to be utilized as a source of images. Many of these images have a long history in the Western imaginary and are both explicitly and implicitly associated with colonial sensibilities—for instance, supposedly free approaches to sexuality, great luxury, absolute power, and adventure. My task is to consider the ways in which these imaginary meanings can attach to particular objects and the ways specific meanings are able to migrate over time and space. In this sense I am describing what can be no more than a trace, the shade of a Western colonial ideal that is dead but, like the vampire count, continues to live on and on.

2

The Luxurious Ambivalence of Exoticism

> What would you say if a blonde homecoming queen fell in love with a short Japanese businessman? He treats her cruelly, then goes home for three years, during which time she prays to his picture and turns down marriage from a young Kennedy. Then, when she learns he has remarried, she kills herself. Now, I believe you would consider this girl to be a deranged idiot, correct? But because it's an Oriental who kills herself for a Westerner—ah!—you find it beautiful.[1]

Song Liling's retelling of the Madame Butterfly story in David Henry Hwang's 1988 play *M. Butterfly* reminds the spectator that the death of the foreign woman has been transformed into a sacrificial moment in a Western dream. Butterfly is a phantom, she is insane, she is an aestheticised object whose self-immolation offers a tableau of submission to the worldly consumer of images. Butterfly's death becomes another swirling form in Tezcatlipoca's mirror, one that veils and reveals Western preoccupations while promising an answer to the mystery of difference and ambivalence. Tezcatlipoca promises to tell the truth, but his promise, as always, is a trick.

The Madame Butterfly story, most famously rendered in Giacomo Puccini's 1904 opera (see Figure 2.1), continues to absorb and enchant Western audiences. We can trace this enduring fascination in a wide range of venues; for instance, in pop culture in Malcolm McLaren's 1980s dance tune that featured Puccini's famous death aria, a perennial favorite of opera companies large and small; in David Henry Hwang's play *M. Butterfly*, which turns the story on its head by revealing the Butterfly character to be a Chinese man; and in David Cronenberg's 1993 movie version of the play, which transforms Hwang's script into a relatively straightforward narrative of romantic betrayal. Recently Madame Butterfly has been relocated to Vietnam in the blockbuster musical *Miss Saigon* (see Figure 2.2). In Puccini's opera the stereotypically exquisite Japanese woman kills herself for the love of an arrogant American man. In Hwang's *M. Butterfly* the

FIGURE 2.1 Madama Butterfly *(courtesy of the Canadian Opera Company, Toronto)*

FIGURE 2.2 Miss Saigon *(courtesy of the Princess of Wales Theatre, Toronto)*

French functionary Rene Gallimard allows himself to be seduced by his expectations of Asia and of exotic sexuality; thinking he is seducing a Chinese woman with his European charm and expertise, he is in turn deceived by a Maoist male agent who understands how to manipulate Gallimard's cultural blindness and obsession with his own authority.

The functionary longs to be seduced and enchanted by difference, and everything he sees and experiences in Beijing can be subsumed under this desire. Indeed, Gallimard never questions his fantasy construction of the Asian woman but instead maintains and affirms his make-believe opus for years, believing himself to be in love with the properly submissive woman of his colonialist dreams. Hwang's retelling of the Butterfly story reminds us that today we cannot be quite so sanguine about such quaint conceits as the price of fixed gender and ethnic identities becomes more evident. The "truth" of these identities is increasingly called into question.[2] The consequences of essentialist notions of ethnicity and culture were always brutally obvious to the woman who was directed by the operatic narrative to sacrifice herself, and the rest of us are increasingly coming to understand racism as a system that fixes everyone in her or his place in a way that damages all.

There are many spectacles of death and of sacrifice in Western culture, and there are many ways to render these displays intensely beautiful and moving. Sometimes sacrificial events are made to seem more splendid or more sublime if they use a foreign vocabulary, or, rather, the strangeness of the images draws the spectator's attention away from the didactic function of the story and from the question of precisely what is being displayed. The foreign woman dies. This is how one version of the story is supposed to go, as we can see from the repetition of Butterfly's suicide. But the autosacrificial event does not float in time and space but is given meaning through its fictional context, its essential foreignness: This death makes sense to the Western spectator precisely because the woman is coded as Japanese. The death of the woman occurs within a structure of recognition in which surrounding objects explain and bracket the event—the scarlet brocade, the incense, the paper lanterns, and the dagger direct the spectator to find the death enthralling. The foreign woman dies in an apparent act of self-sacrifice, but, as usual, it is only ventriloquism.

Alluring Foreigners

Why do certain manifestations of foreignness continually reappear as a source of fascination in so many streams of Western culture? Why have certain cultures, objects, and people been coded as exotic in Western aesthetics and others not? Exoticism in its commodified form appears as a sophisticated appreciation of other cultures or as an aestheticized nostalgia for a different place or time, but the content of exotic images links it closely to colonialism and to contemporary systems of economic and cultural domination. The process of exotification is another kind of cultural cannibalism: That which is deemed different is consumed, its aesthetic forms taken up and used to construct a dream of the outside and sometimes of escape from the Western nightmare. Exotic images feed particular cultural, social, and political needs of the appropriating culture. This is why colonial adventures continue to be romanticized and why the consumption of the spectacle of difference is able to make the alienated Westerner feel alive.

The word *exotic* technically means "foreign," and biologists speak of an exotic plant or species without the word immediately suggesting the fascination and ambivalence it evokes in a cultural context. Different places have come to stand for different sensibilities in Western thinking, and images and commodities from those places have been able to summon, point to, and substitute for these sensibilities. It is these complexes of ideas, and the acquisitions and appropriations that underpin them, that can most properly be called exoticism. As with Rene Gallimard's fantasy of the perfect Asian woman, the content of exotic images is generally extremely conventional and hackneyed but continues to reappear, and to work, again and again.

People everywhere do seem to be interested in and curious about cultural differences, and I am not suggesting that the problem of exoticism lies in this interest. Some people find cultural and social differences interesting and stimulating, and although somewhat questionable in certain contexts, this is not necessarily an issue in itself. Differences clearly do exist between cultures, and the issue is not that these are noticed but how these come to be aestheticized and by whom. The problem seems to occur when cultural difference is construed through particular systems of authority and is charged or energized for its own sake or, to put the issue somewhat differently, when this interest goes out of balance in such a way that the fact of difference itself is able to produce intense excitement and pleasure at the cost of negating the people or culture that is the source of interest. This imbalance seems most likely to occur when a notion of abstract difference is maintained, as opposed to a recognition of many everyday differences. The key issue is how a culture comes to be aestheticized by people who have no stake in that community and in particular by those who exercise authority over the culture or people being rendered exotic. This aestheticization is dependent on a mechanism whereby differences are abstracted from their cultural context and rendered strange or curious (a process that seems to relate to the fascination with cultural difference as display of grotesquerie in early museums).

Exotic images and cultural fragments do not drop from the sky but rather are selected and named as exotic within specific cultural contexts; certain fragments of a cultural aesthetic are selected and rendered exotic, whereas others are rejected. The reason for this has to do with power, that is, with who is in a position to decide which fragments are interesting and to whom. This is not to suggest that faceless authority decides in advance what the rest of us are to see, reproducing repressive culture seamlessly and effortlessly (although this may sometimes seem the case). Cultural authority is not a question of a conspiracy but of the existence of a context in which decisions about cultural value can be articulated and put into practice: *Madame Butterfly* can usually find the funding to be staged because the music is loved, because it supports the status quo, because it replenishes prejudices about women, about Asia, about the United States. At the same time, an abstract category of phenomena determined to be exotic or interesting implies the existence of a fictional individual at the center who adjudicates what will be of interest and to whom. This process of abstraction means that the encounter between different cultures is rarely framed as a series of events in which exchange or dialogue takes place; rather, the world appears as something from which a universalized, European "one" selects traits. And because this selection is always ambivalent, a single, decontextualized attribute can be utilized to evoke nearly anything the would-be colonist fancies. The aestheticization of colonized peoples can always be differentially valorized, at times seen as fascinating and at other times seen as a sign of decadence or insubordination.

When difference itself is all that is necessary to create excitement, or to resuscitate a tired narrative, what has been determined to be different is positioned so that it is unable to move out of the conceptual box in which it has been placed. Questions of power, representation, and veracity of the images are displaced. This positioning constructs fixed identity on both sides, for both the creator or consumer of the exotic image and the person standing in for the source. This, of course, was Gallimard's trouble in *M. Butterfly:* The fixed racial and sexual identities he assigned to Song Liling shackled him equally to a particular identity, although he could not see this. In the streams of exoticism that locate authenticity in other cultures, the image of authenticity and the potential for liberation attributed to cultural difference are based on the assumption that European culture is dead; because cultural transformation is no longer possible, Westerners must look elsewhere for meaning. Does this belief serve to close off the margins that do exist within Western culture? This extremely complicated problem is the subject of Chapter 6, but if we keep in mind that racism is a system that controls everyone under its purview, we can begin to see how notions of fixed identity and cultural purity have limited understandings of Western culture, as much as they have of societies subject to Western colonialism.

Exotic Histories

In the early eighteenth century the balance of power between Europe and the traditional centers of wealth and military power, specifically the Islamic world and the prosperous Asian countries, began to shift. It was at this point that "foreign" traits that had formerly been anathematized in the West came to be valorized and seen as a source of excitement and inspiration for writers and artists. At first this process involved the European aristocracy taking up stylistic elements, such as dressing à la turque or buying carpets and other luxury goods.

As colonial adventures became more common, and as bourgeois standards of sexual conduct began to be universalized in Europe after the eighteenth century, notions of individualized, erotic "freedom" and adventure began to be located elsewhere, sometimes in the past but more frequently and conveniently in the colonies. Many Europeans looked to other societies to provide aesthetic titillation but at the same time required sites where various kinds of adventures could be undertaken and put into practice. The European countries had colonies not only to extract profits but also to have access to territory where dreams of absolute power could be imagined and lived out. Fantasies could be played out in colonial situations in a way that was impossible at home and with much less anxiety about the process, an obvious example being all the petty bureaucrats in British India who were able to live as if they were lords. Because the ancien régime functioned as the primary model of unfettered desire, the specific power fantasies played out in the colonies tended to refer to aristocratic values and protocols, but now all the peasants were brown.

What came to be called "the other" became a pretext for talking about European concerns, as in Montesquieu's *Lettres persanes,* which utilized an image of Asian despotism to criticize absolutist rule before the 1789 revolution in France. At the same time, notions of "progress" (which has always had its critics) came to be coupled with a nostalgia for so-called primitive life, which was believed to exist in a state of nature, without rules or constraints. *Sans loi, sans roi, sans foi,* the saying went, evoking a society without lawyers, kings, and priests, a state of affairs that many felt was all to the good. Social practices such as plural marriage or warrior societies came to be seen as exemplary of this pristine state of nature, and half-understood versions of land-based peoples, and of their social or religious institutions, circulated in European intellectual communities (a relatively recent example being the interest, originating with Marcel Mauss, in the Kwagiutl potlatch).

During the nineteenth century the colonial process was undertaken in an increasingly wide and brutal manner and accompanied by endless rhetoric about Europe's "civilizing mission" and the enormous favor the West was doing the world. Traditional, land-based people were, by definition and indeed by their very essence, seen as threats to this mission, and if they refused to be subdued were subject to extermination attempts. Colonial terminology from this period is instructive: In the U.S. West aboriginal people who followed the old ways were termed "renegades," as opposed to the so-called progressives who supported U.S. assimilation policies. Yet one result of the policies of assimilation, put into place all over the world by missionaries and colonial functionaries, was the emergence—at the heart of Europe and articulated in a variety of European aesthetic forms—of an ever-increasing nostalgia for what people imagined the old ways to be. Europe appeared not only as the site of progress but also as a dead, industrialized place where everything had already been decided.

I want to be very clear here: Most Europeans (including critical thinkers such as Karl Marx and Friedrich Engels) did not want traditional societies to actually exist as such but rather to operate as a set of signs that, like Madame Butterfly, ultimately referred to and reinforced the hegemony of the West. Westerners with rarefied tastes wanted the fascinating art forms, the foods, and the amusingly costumed people to remain available for various forms of consumption. The nostalgia for the old ways was, and in many respects continues to be, no more than regret for the loss of aesthetic *styles,* not for the loss of the social, political, economic, and ceremonial institutions on which the aesthetic traditions were dependent and through which meaning was achieved. Because many Europeans believed in some version of the end of history and asserted the world-historical destiny of Western culture, they consequently assumed the inevitable disappearance of other cultures, which meant that cultural difference could be imagined only as something existing in relation to and at the pleasure of the West. This kind of thinking remains a problem.

By the twentieth century in most parts of the world aesthetic traditions were even further disarticulated from the societies in which they occurred, although new, syncretic styles were generated in colonial contexts, often as a way of resisting the assimilation process.[3] The older styles had for some time been inserted into a system of commodification, with Western galleries, museums, and private collectors influencing the production of aesthetic objects. Film became a new medium for the old colonial tale, and many people's ideas of what cultures other than their own were like came from the movies. Imperial messages were promulgated in film after film. Edward Said talks about the shift in Western perceptions of the Islamic world in his seminal work *Orientalism,* focusing on the links between the European military domination of the Muslim world and the way the latter also came to be represented in aesthetic and scholarly works. It is a mistake to separate these areas as they reinforce and give credence to each other. For instance, the Western fascination with cultural difference can be organized to promote the appropriation and construction of an exotic aesthetic and to enforce notions of science and "knowledge." This construction of exoticism further promotes a notion of expertise and of the professionals who are believed to be qualified to elucidate different cultures.[4]

So-called primitive societies continued to be looked to as a source of authenticity as Western intellectuals became increasingly pessimistic about the direction European culture was taking. Many post–World War I writers and artists in Europe believed that non-Western, traditional societies were able to clarify the nature of community and collective action, which in their view had been debased by modern systems of production and individualism. These societies were accessible to Europeans primarily through ethnological texts, and through the insights of writers such as Mauss, whose highly influential "Essai sur le don" (1923) attempted to account for the processes underlying social phenomena, in particular the binding of the community through ritualized gift exchange. The juxtaposition of a supposedly authentic tribal society with a corrupt urban one persists today, although less in scientific discourses such as ethnology than in obviously aestheticized venues that range from movies to clothing to New Age religions.

Tropes of Difference

The specific forms or tropes of exoticism that function in the West have particular histories and employ particular narrative structures; for instance, the sacrificial death of the Asian woman in the opera *Madame Butterfly* and, more recently, in the musical *Miss Saigon*. According to literary theory, a trope is a conceptual mechanism that organizes images. So whereas a narrative strings together events, a trope binds together or organizes many diverse concepts, symbols, and associations into one idea, like a rope binding together many strands. Thus, notions of sublimity, violence, or eroticism, all of which can fall under the general rubric of exoticism, function as tropes that continue to structure our perceptions of cultural difference. The precise ways in which tropes of difference are able to function can be extremely complex and often involve ambivalent valorizations of specific traits or qualities. Because exoticism works by generating excitement and delirium precisely from the viewer's ambivalent relation to difference, qualities that in one context are classified as negative—such as violence—can with the proper distance produce delight, desire, and, of course, the edge of danger and ambiguity that supplies an added frisson. A particular image can be used to suggest almost anything. Tropes differ from stereotypes precisely because of this ability to do so many things at once; consequently tropes are harder to challenge than stereotypes because they are multifarious and draw from a range of sources, some of which precede European

colonialism. The tropic images continue to work even after the stereotypes are challenged. For example, William McGregor Paxton's *The New Necklace* (1910) utilizes exotic paraphernalia to bind together long-standing notions of class and gender (see Figure 2.3). Although the wealthy white woman is the bearer of exotic images, the painting reinforces the trope of Asia as the source of luxury and opulence as well as a range of ideas about women as consumers. The messages conveyed by this work are layered and complex.

A quick glance across the exotic conventions apparent in both popular and high culture can provide a schematic sketch of some of these tropes. There are, of course, many other possible examples, but for the moment I am interested in the tropes of violence, the primitive and the savage, the sublime, passivity and timelessness, and the erotic and the people and cultures with whom these are associated.

Violence appears most commonly and ubiquitously in representations of Mexico, the Muslim world, and Iroquois people, among many others. The trope of violence includes specific stereotypes: The oldest example, Islam, has been represented as combining the glittering, barbaric splendor of the sultans with hideous executions and religious fanaticism. Notions of violence and fanaticism constantly appear in contemporary characterizations of the Islamic world, and the Western filmgoer or newspaper reader has learned to recognize these characterizations as accurate. The American-in-a-foreign-prison drama *Midnight Express* (1978) made a point of punctuating each instance of gratuitous violence with the Islamic call to prayer, just in case the viewer failed to grasp the point of the narrative. Aztec Mexico is incessantly described in terms of human sacrifice, whereas the contemporary country seems pervaded with evil *bandidos* and dangerous, hostile *federales*. Iroquois people continue to be presented in history books and recent films such as *Last of the Mohicans* (1992) and *Black Robe* (1991) as extremely frightening and opaque, always eager to torture innocent Christian colonists.

The key point is that violence has become a floating category that can be retrieved and used to characterize nearly any culture or people in a range of colonial histories and in representations old and new. The Western trope of the inherent violence of non-Western peoples is always available to explain acts of resistance or anti-Western sentiment or to add a jolt to a story line in need of one.

The trope of *the primitive and the savage* has underpinned Western descriptions of Africa, North and South America, and Melanesia, among others. This trope often reflects an apparently irreconcilable discursive tension between the notion of the good and gentle primitive and that of the bad and violent savage. This division continues to be apparent in contemporary discussions of "human nature," with much ink spilled over the question of whether human beings are inherently aggressive. In Western texts that range from popular films to canonical "literature," Africa appears again and again as the home of cannibalism and fear, exemplifying in the European tradition what Sally Price calls "the night side of man."[5] (A somewhat different version of this is apparent in some accounts of Africa as the source of the AIDS virus.)

North and South America are the site where the conflict between good and bad images of the primitive plays out most exhaustively and has done so since the earliest European invasions of these lands. As early as 1550 the famous debate between Juan Ginés de Sepúlveda and Bartolomé de Las Casas on the essential nature of the people of the Americas turned on a distinction between a view that aboriginal people were inherently slavish and wicked and a belief that they were innocent children of nature who manifested an inherent godliness. Europeans have consistently been fascinated with the cannibalism and sacrifices they saw or thought they saw in the Americas, but indigenous people have also been presented as gentle children of nature. We can see this tension in film after film, and the representation of Native people as gentle and pure continues to appear almost entirely as a function of their willingness to accept colonialism, as in the 1986 film *The Mission.* Those who fight against white people tend instantly to be transformed into violent savages, without pity or other "civilized" sentiments. Melanesians are rarely presented as kindly primitives; rather, their territories, like Africa, appear to be riddled with headhunting and cannibalism. Dean MacCannell has recently written on the exemplary status of New Guinea in anthropological discourse for precisely this reason.[6]

Sublimity appears in representations of China, Japan, and India. This trope seems to be used primarily for Asia, fabled lands of wealth and mystery (a somewhat different version of the trope appears in representations of Islamic countries, especially with respect to Sufism). For instance, China has traditionally been described in terms of luxury; rarefied elegance; commodities such as silk, jade, and ivory ornaments; and other exquisite objects. (This luxury can be ambivalently valorized as a sign of degeneracy, as in the treatment of the Anna Mae Wong character in the 1934 film *Java Head,* in which—as Butterfly would have it—the silk-clad Manchu princess obligingly kills herself as a favor to the wholesome English girl.) Asia has historically been seen as a source of wealth. The trope of sublimity combines a notion of luxury with that of religion, particularly the rarefied forms of spirituality thought to exist in Asia. The European interest in Buddhist thought, along with Confucius and Taoist philosophies, can reflect this notion. Japan, which is to say the old Japan of the prewar era, tends to be seen more in terms of the aesthetic purity of the Zen tradition. India is described as an almost mythical place characterized by immense wealth, as exemplified by enormous rubies and tiger hunts, but has more recently been thought in the West in terms of complicated (and possibly vulgar) spirituality amid squalor. This mixture of luxury, poverty, and spirituality seems to function as a source of excitement for some Westerners, which might also have something to do with the availability of hashish.

Passivity and timelessness are notions that have been utilized to characterize nearly all societies outside of the Western tradition and carry with them an assertion of the supposedly inherent dynamism of European cultures. Although speed is a characteristic of modernity, all societies are dynamic and adaptable. The assumption of passivity informs a range of venues, from the different social theories that make arguments about the inability of traditional societies to change until European influence forces them out of their torpor, to the idea that some version of "the past" can be visited in a traditional culture, to the view that traditional people do not have histories (and, indeed, in many North American history textbooks the section on Africa still begins with the period of European colonialization). In articles on Canadian Native issues appearing in the mainstream media the months prior to the 1990 Oka standoff, we see a peculiar tendency to attribute substantive issues facing Native communities, such as land rights and poverty, to abstract entities or causes such as "change." [7] According to these articles, Native communities are forced to wrestle with change rather than with the effects of land theft, particular government decisions, pollution of specific rivers, and the like. This device underscores what appears to be the inevitability of change (and the notion of progress that underlies this) as well as the supposed passivity of Native communities in the face of new conditions. In reports of the standoff, the trope of violence was always lurking in the background, to be trotted out when required.

The notion of timelessness can be valorized and used to underpin a romanticized view of non-Western people, but more commonly it appears as a sign of inferiority and stasis. This has obvious political implications, as it ignores both the transformations that occur and have always occurred within traditional societies and the reality of what change means in a colonial or neocolonial situation. There are very good reasons for being suspicious of change. This trope also overlooks the extent to which Western consumerist culture and economic structures systematically weaken land-based economies.

We can see how many of these tropes come together in a recent ad for Cašmir perfume, which evokes sublimity, timelessness, and luxury. The lotus flower logo refers to unnamed Asian religious philosophies, whereas the name of the perfume itself (pronounced Kashmir/cashmere) refers both to a geographical site and a luxury product. Timelessness is evoked by the image of the river.

Eroticism has been used as a way of framing most of the world but has perhaps most frequently been associated with the Muslim world, nearly all of Asia, and Polynesia. This is one of the most persistent tropes of exoticism and indeed floats through and informs the other four. The notion that sex is somehow more interesting in a colonial setting, particularly if accompanied by accoutrements the Westerner finds unusual, such as colorful clothing or oddly shaped furniture, is extremely persistent. Exotic accoutrements of sex have always titillated the colonist, which fits in with Malek

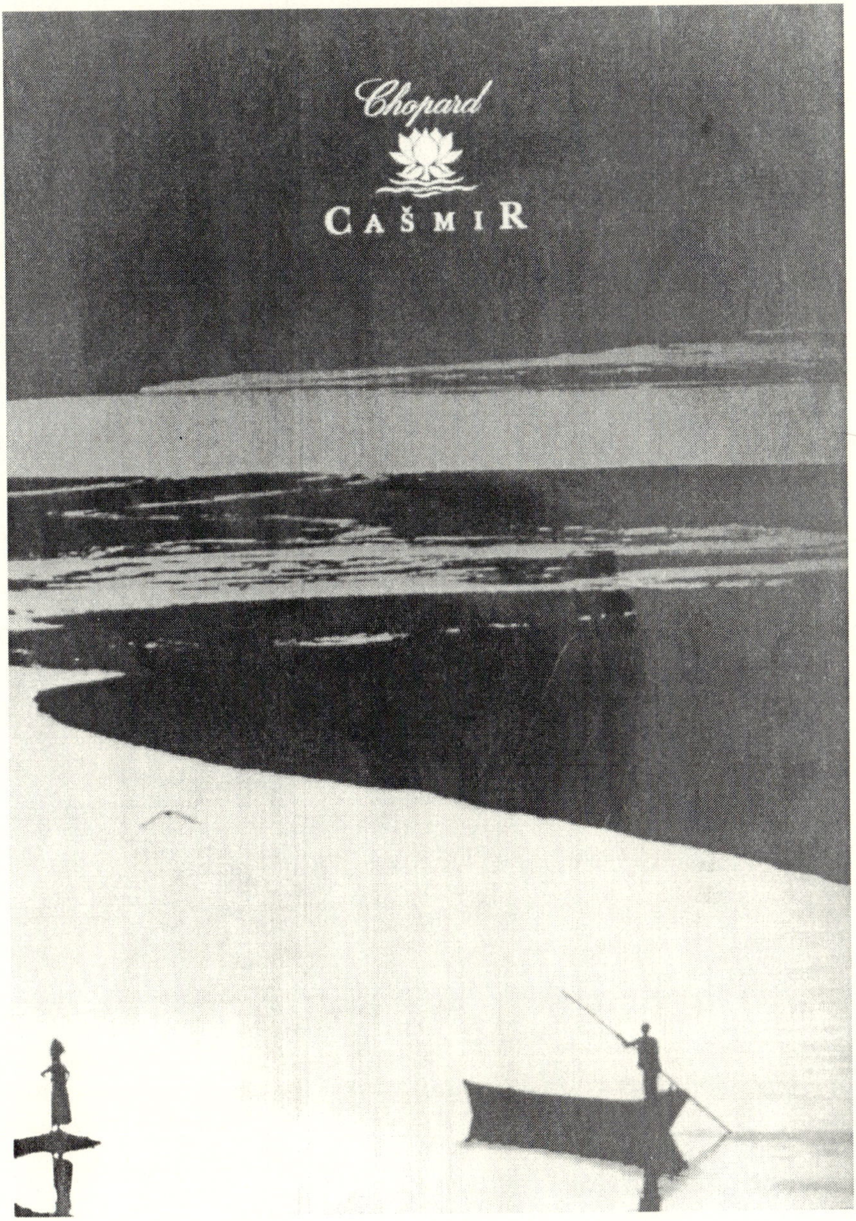

FIGURE 2.4 *Cašmir perfume advertisement*

Alloula's study of erotic postcards in French colonial Algeria in which he observes that French colonists wanted to see Moorish women behind bars.[8]

The sex tour industry in Bangkok and Manila explicitly uses exoticism as a selling point in the flyers circulated in Western Europe; the industry also mixes exoticism with an evocation of what is forbidden in the West by promising access to extremely young women and boys. The point of these flyers is to arouse sexual curiosity by suggesting that sex is somehow different with twelve-year-old Thai girls and to promise the Western male the fantasy of absolute power over foreign women once enjoyed by his grandfather in the colony. Many Asian airline companies also combine sex appeal and exotic images in advertisements directed toward the presumably male business traveler. The particular site of eroticism can shift and is dependent on historical factors. For instance, until the fifteenth century African women were used to represent sexual desire in European paintings but then seemed to disappear from such art. Somewhat later African women became the source of a particularly nasty strain of the European sexual imaginary in which absolute authority was eroticized and plantation scenes became sites of erotic adventures for white men. I include the Muslim world as a locus of European erotic desire primarily because of its status in this regard for the last two hundred years, from the fascination with the harem to Rudolf Valentino's sheik. More recently, however, this locus seems to be changing as the attractively seductive Arab is increasingly replaced by the figure of the terrorist, who is always shouting or shooting someone and hence is too "fanatical" to be appealing. Polynesia remains a site of Western desire if tourist advertisements are any indication. Also, films such as the 1980 adolescent sex fantasy *Blue Lagoon* draws on notions of the South Sea islands where all is permitted.

One of the most persistent tropes of exoticism is the fascination with the erotic possibilities of the colony, which in effect becomes the eroticization of racial power. Exoticism always seems to pertain to sex in some way, even if it focuses most obviously on violence or sublimity. This interest in sexuality links up in fairly obvious ways to how authority is articulated in colonial situations. Exotic images of women have to do with colonial fantasies of power, and the sexual availability of women classified as exotic is for the most part dependent on the ability of the colonist to coerce, that is, to militarily and economically control the colony. At some level colonial power ensures the sexual availability of colonized women. It seems that difference equals danger equals excitement, but still the colonist remains in control, or at least this is the way the story is supposed to go. I believe this is the source of the notion that sex is somehow better, freer, or more interesting in the colonized world: Again, if we keep in mind the self-referentiality of power, the excitement for Western men seems less to do with a desire for exotic women than with a (false) belief that finally, at long last, Western men are in charge. In other words, authority functions as mood enhancement, a phenomenon also apparent in the West.

These tropes are able to work as efficiently as they do because, in extremely subtle and complex ways, they refer to what is lacking or expelled from Western culture. Projecting certain qualities onto other societies permits people to talk about what cannot otherwise be talked about. Violence, primitivism, sublimity, and sexuality are reformulated within an aesthetic of cultural difference and displaced onto specific communities in order to legitimize them as an area of interest for Europeans. For instance, the trope of primitivism and savagery probably draws on European pagan histories and legends of the Green Man and transfers these to colonized people. Similarly, the trope of sublimity seems to draw on old legends of far-off lands of unimaginable wealth, for example, the Prester John stories of the Middle Ages. Examples of this reformulation and displacement are in some cases very close to the surface: For instance, in nineteenth-century European painting, sexual or erotic themes were permissible in scenes of Orientalism or antiquity but not in contemporary settings. This has continued well into the twentieth century, with *National Geographic* being the only acceptable venue for bare female breasts in the 1940s and 1950s (as long as they were not white, of course), and the sex and violence spectacle *Caligula* (1979) almost achieving mainstream acceptability at the end of the 1970s because of its cast and classical theme.

Fragments of Culture

David Henry Hwang's depiction of Rene Gallimard in *M. Butterfly* reveals what in the long run is the key failure of colonial thinking and the failure of exoticism, as it has been constructed in some streams of Western thinking. Gallimard decided in advance what Asia was going to be like, and he assumed he would understand China because his privilege and status as a European man gave him access to a universal and supposedly superior knowledge of the world. (Of course, he lacked basic cultural knowledge, such as the fact that many female roles in Chinese opera are sung by males.) Indeed, because of his relationship with the opera singer Song Liling, he further assumes knowledge of all Chinese and confidently informs his ambassador, "The Orientals simply want to be associated with whoever shows the most strength and power."[9] Because Gallimard's supposed comprehension of difference is based on an illusion of universalized European authority, it can function only as an attempt to aggrandize his own position. Gallimard is thus seduced by a notion of the exotic in which he mistakenly assumes he is in charge by virtue of his European identity. This anticipation of difference leads to closure and blindness and, in the end, to Gallimard's own undoing, disgrace, imprisonment, and death.

Exoticism is multifarious and works, not through single images or stereotypes, but through entire complexes of notions that evoke, bleed into, and reinforce one another. "Asia" has appeared to Westerners not only as a fantasy of submissive and beautiful women but also as a place of luxury, philosophical sublimity, and exquisite manners. These qualities can be evoked through objects and through fragments of objects: In Puccini's opera the evil American Pinkerton speaks of Butterfly as being "like a figure on a painted screen" who frees herself "from her glittering background of lacquer."[10] Song Liling's seduction of Gallimard is made possible because the Frenchman expects China to conform to certain expectations and to be "exotic" and for this exoticism to play out erotically and aesthetically, saturating the events he experiences and the objects that surround him.

For Gallimard, as for so many other Europeans, difference is connoted by signs he can recognize because they were part of his conceptual framework long before he arrived in Beijing. The particular signs used to represent difference rarely constitute a cultural whole, yet are made to stand for entire concepts and cultural categories. Cultural, ethnic, and sexual difference is connoted by fleeting, fragmentary images. Each fragment evokes another—the fluttering silk scarf refers to the downcast eye, which refers to the smoking incense burner—and these together make possible the European's seduction of himself through the illusion of the exotic Chinese woman. This fragmentary nature of exotic signification contributes to Gallimard's willful ignorance. Because the Westerner both devises and experiences exoticism through a structure of recognition in which particular objects or fragments connote difference, the woman in the story is identified with the objects that have come to signify her cultural background. The objects that evoke certain cultures, as have painted screens and lacquer for China, further permit a shortcut to the exotic experience desired and anticipated by the Westerner. I return to the question of experience in Chapter 5, but the type of exoticism that is manifested as a desire to possess foreign objects or bodies seems increasingly represented in experiential terms: The Westerner desires a unique, authentic experience in which he or she remains firmly in charge. Vacations are experienced in this way as well, becoming a fragment in time that is imagined and experienced as separate from the everyday experience of real life and in which anything is possible.

Exoticism, then, works through a process of dismemberment and fragmentation in which objects stand for images that stand for a culture or a sensibility as a whole. Exoticism is synecdochal, and fragments of culture work to exemplify and evoke a larger whole. Cultural and aesthetic fragments refer to and express tropes, and in this respect exoticism can be thought of as a system of appropriation of fragments that symbolize, or substitute, a given cultural totality. In his excellent article "The Museum's Furnace," Eugenio Donato quotes a remark by Gustave Flaubert that exemplifies how fragmentation works: "Is not *all of China* contained in a Chinese woman's slipper decorated with damask roses and having embroidered cats on its vamp?"[11] We can question Flaubert's fascination with sexually charged, exotic images, apparent in his writings about Egypt and in the novel *Salammbô,* but at some level the images he uses are extremely evocative precisely because they are fragmentary and concerned with eliciting an emotional response from the reader. This process of fragmentation of culture is apparent in other venues as well, for instance, in discourses that make claims to truth and to scientific objectivity. Ethnology fixes on certain cultures and on certain cultural institutions within a larger whole (such as the kula ring of the Trobriand Islanders) because these minutiae are believed to exemplify cultural wholes and to elucidate scientific problems.

Connoisseurs of Ambivalence

As the millennium approaches, and as the victory of the New World Order becomes increasingly apparent, many living at the heart of Western culture continue to fix on cultural difference as a source of pleasure, excitement, and authenticity. The colonial relationship between the West and the rest of the world has merely changed its shape, but what people in the West sometimes forget is that the multinationals are now in charge. These corporations follow the money and have no particular loyalty to past structures of authority. At the same time, the pleasure in difference is not quite as easy to come by for the Western subject as it was one hundred years ago and indeed has become the source of a certain anxiety.

In *M. Butterfly* things do not work out as Gallimard expects; indeed, they break down entirely for him in the end. But colonial misperceptions do not usually end quite so disastrously for most Westerners in their sojourns in former colonies because their continued relative wealth and authority cocoon them from unpleasantness and ensure that those with whom they have contact will behave as if they know their place, at least for the time being. Certainly many, many Westerners have not abandoned the notion that experiencing a colonial-style adventure provides a particular kind of pleasure, one dependent on the aggrandizement of cultural difference through a structure in which the would-be colonizer continues to articulate cultural and racial authority. The expensively produced musical *Miss Saigon* can be thought of as a rear-guard action to enforce closure on the issues of race, identity, and imperialism that Hwang called into question.[12] The story line says it all: After the American man fulfills his dream of an erotic adventure in the exciting war-torn soon-to-be-former colony, the Asian woman sacrifices herself so the white lovers can be together. She makes sure to give her child to the Americans to raise because a "better life" is possible in the United States. As in the opera *Madame Butterfly,* the story ends disastrously, but not, we note, for the American. In other venues, for instance, the films *The Sheltering Sky* (1990) and *A Winter's Tan* (1988), interest seems to be shifting to the Western female's quest for intense erotic experiences in colonial contexts, maintaining the notion of exotic adventure within a rhetoric of women's liberation. These stories, however, never end well.

We are confronted with what at first glance seems a paradox. On the one hand, the colonial narrative decrees that the Western man subdue colonized women, sometimes to the point of aestheticizing and deriving pleasure from their deaths. On the other hand, these stories often call for the degradation and death of the Western male himself, seemingly as a consequence of having experienced sexual desire in a colonial situation. Why do so many of these stories insist that someone must suffer a tragic fate?

The story of the Westerner confronting a false image of the other, and being seduced by this construct in such a way that leads to his (and, more recently, her) mental or physical dissolution, is an old, old colonial tale. Europeans visit the colony and promptly die, go crazy, go native, drown in alcohol or sex—the list goes on. Potential disaster has always been a subtext of colonial tales, and these often operate as cautionary tales for Europeans, who have to negotiate their position with respect to the ubiquitously treacherous and unreadable natives they are supposed to have under control. It seems that Westerners are safe only if they strictly maintain their position of colonial or racial authority, a position that is in some instances fictive. It is because the story is an object lesson that it so often has a bad ending for the Westerner, despite all the Butterflies and Miss Saigons. We can think of example after example of movies and novels where something unpleasant happens to the white person after she or he actually comes to love someone from a different background or culture (something unpleasant tends to happen to the person of color as well, but this is rarely the focus of the narrative). This can be seen most emphatically in the "miscegenation melodrama" films of the 1930s, 1940s, and 1950s that played with interracial fascination before quickly rendering it tragic, as in *The Chinese Bungalow* (filmed three times, in 1926, 1931, and 1940) and *The Rains Came* (1940).[13]

The former colony continues to be presented as a place of disorientation and danger, where nothing is as it seems. Rene Gallimard desires a woman who turns out to be a man, and the truth of Gallimard's desire—to live out an Orientalist fantasy of power—lies precisely in the falsity of his perception, his inability to read the situation in which he finds himself. Again, the Frenchman is undone, not (as ideology would have it) by the treacherous Asian, but by his own expectations. The notion of authentic desire and truth raises a number of issues because increasingly truth comes to be located in falsity or, more precisely, in false desire, particularly as it pertains to the intersection of sexuality and cultural difference. At the moment there seems to be a great deal of interest in how sexual ambivalence intersects with culture, particularly in popular culture; if recent movies are any indication, cross-dressing is no longer presented as merely titillating or transgressive but as revelation of truths otherwise concealed (as, for instance, in the 1993 film *The Crying Game*). Certain truths are exposed through the play of shifting, ambivalent images, but at the cost of evacuating questions of power and politics from the construction of desire.[14] The complex issue of sexual ambivalence can draw attention to the way appearance is able to generate its own truth, which in turn has its own internal logic. This interest in appearance is not always able in itself to call into question the larger political issues, however. Sexual ambivalence continues to be presented as something transgressive and dangerous, but many representations of these issues ultimately reinforce the status quo.

Although exoticism claims to be about difference, it ends up being almost wholly self-referential, which is why in *M. Butterfly* Gallimard exists in a perpetual state of anticipation, unable to see past his own fantasy of China or his puffed-up image of himself. We are reminded of Franz Fanon's remark that the colonist is an exhibitionist,[15] which suggests that because the colonist is so preoccupied with his or her position and authority, s/he remains blind to the people around. When desire is constructed within a self-referential framework, it is not really concerned with its object of interest, and therefore the imbalance in the power relation between the observer and the observed is easily overlooked or ignored. The object is not supposed to talk back and shatter the illusion. Certainly the object is not supposed to make any claims or interventions about the representations being constructed. This is one of the main reasons that exoticism tends to occur within colonial relationships, whether the colonialism of the nineteenth century or the contemporary variety.

The self-referentiality of exoticism is also apparent in the way it, again, depends on a European aristocratic ethos. The rare and exquisite exotic object refers not only to the society that produced it but also to the aristocratic collector and traveler of means, whose taste for the unusual produces a properly sophisticated palate. The exotic is, after all, not to everyone's taste. Thus, the consumer of fragmentary, equivocal images of difference is ennobled in advance.

The ability to sample a variety of experiences and cultural phenomena on the basis of a rarefied, dilettantish sensibility has historically been possible only for the elite, particularly the aristocracy, which was not constrained by bourgeois notions of work and duty. The figure of the aristocrat is itself ambivalent, evoking both decadent desires (like the vampire counts) and the ability to live out a dream of pure desire, as is indicated by the continuing interest in Sade and Gilles de Rais. The increasingly extreme images of difference that have begun to appear in advertisements—for instance, in Benetton ads—draw upon a fascination with aestheticized squalor. These also allude to sophisticated, aristocratic taste, as did the images of gilded poverty popular in some streams of French Orientalist painting in the nineteenth century. The aristocrat is supposed to be able to observe or experience the most dangerous or agonizing situation while manifesting absolutely no affect, a skill typified by the legendary stiff upper lip that we see again and again in old movies about the British Empire (and mocked in more recent films such as the appallingly comic *Carry On Up the Khyber* [1971]). Exoticism, then, in its aristocratic mode is concerned not only with beauty and sexuality but also with spectacle and the excitement generated as much by the spectacle of abjection as that of luxury. The spectator is, of course, another manifestation of the unitary, Cartesian subject, who exists outside and often above the action, coolly observing the surrounding chaos.

A somewhat different version of this aristocratic ethos is apparent in Vietnam War movies, with stories of American men going off to a strange, exotic land to learn what they are made of—that is, to address questions of courage and cowardice in between sessions of aestheticized violence and exotic sex. It is precisely the possibility of violent death—their own or someone else's, American or Vietnamese—that heightens the experience for them. How much spectacle can they take before cracking? Does the movie-like effect of war on acid make it more or less bearable? Thus, exoticism does not work solely by referring to the people who are being exoticized but also by referring back to and linking up with exotic, glamorized (and, I think we would have to say, *wétiko*) elements in Western history.

Western culture continues to manifest a great deal of ambivalence about cultural and sexual difference, as indicated by the way these tropes can be differentially valorized. We see how quickly they can move and exchange elements: For instance, Western representations of China rapidly shifted from a focus on luxury and imperial decadence to images of violence and barbarity, most recently connoted by Mao Zedong's cadres during the Cultural Revolution. Again, the turn often seems to be a function of anti-imperialist activities on the part of the people being exoticized, and continuing to use China as an example, we can see this in the way the so-called Boxer Rebellion of 1900 was represented in the West both at the time and subsequently as a wave of pure, faceless violence. Even those elements that at first glance appear positive, such as gentleness or sublimity, are part of a system of representation that objectifies difference as a way to justify racial and cultural supremacy. In colonial systems the apparently positive judgments are always underlain by an ambivalence that can ultimately have political implications as harmful as those implied by wholly negative characterizations.

This ambivalence seems to be a function, in part, of the self-referentiality of exotic images—which is to say, they speak to European concerns and obsessions—but the potential for tropes to be ambivalently valorized also ensures that all volition comes from the Westerner's desire. The power to represent is arranged so that it always appears to remain in the hands of the European, who at least in theory permits no backtalk or reciprocity on the part of the people being exoticized. The result of any dialogue is decided in advance. The ambivalent reaction the Westerner often feels when encountering exotic images is usually experienced as a kind of pleasurable unease, which has more to do with his or her relationship to power and difference than with his or her relationship to the people being exoticized.

Some ambivalence is normal and inevitable when we encounter new experiences, people, or places. The familiar implies a certain ease and comfort, whereas difference necessitates a conceptual adjustment, a constant undecidability with respect to the phenomena perceived. This is not peculiar to Europeans and North Americans but seems to be a way of mentally coping with unusual or disorienting situations. To a certain extent ambivalence seems to function as a mental escape route of the "I hate them, so I just might go home" variety many people seem to experience from time to time while traveling. And, of course, always knowing what to expect *is* boring and can reinforce a sense of the pointlessness of life. Maryse Holder, the bulimic antiheroine of *A Winter's Tan*, says, "If only winning weren't so boring and being bored so terrifying," a way of thinking that leads her to increasingly extreme situations in her search for sexual adventure in Mexico.[16] Yet part of the pleasure in travel occurs when the strangeness breaks down in small, unexpected ways. After a certain point it is very difficult to sustain the level of objectification necessary for the exotification of foreign places and people. This is what Marguerite Duras recognizes in so much of her work. The eccentricities of the foreign inevitably fracture and reconstitute themselves into something familiar, unless a person deliberately maintains the experience of strangeness and affirms this as an end in itself. At the same time, strangeness can appear in mundane, unexpected locales. If a place can be read only as exotic, this disintegration of meaning will never happen. Again, the problem occurs when it is decided in advance what is going to happen and what the experience of difference will be like.

Colonial Desires

Eugène Delacroix's *Femmes d'alger* (1832) was, because of the exotic subject matter and shimmering colors of the room and clothing of the women, seen as the beginning of a new aesthetic sensibility in French painting, but one obvious question is, How did a French painter gain admittance to the women's quarters of an Algerian house in order to locate and reproduce his image of Algerian women? France had militarily conquered Algiers only two years before the celebrated harem scene was painted, an event rarely discussed in any detail in commentaries on Delacroix's work. In the case of this particular painting, the new colonial rulers of Algiers employed a certain amount of coercion to arrange for these women to sit for Delacroix. To pay attention to the context in which the work was created is not to negate the aesthetic interest or value of the painting but rather to open up the terms of the discussion.

By linking the development of an aesthetic of exoticism in the West to colonial power, I am not suggesting that cultures or aesthetic forms exist in isolation, untouched by contact from the outside. Cultures are never pure, and there have always been contact and exchange of ideas between peoples. Notions of cultural purity can, as with ethnic and gender identities, imply fixity and suggest that we all are supposed to remain wholly within an abstraction imagined as our own culture.

Notions of exoticism relate to the colonial process in one extremely obvious way: The aesthetic codes of former colonies tend to be appropriated and rendered exotic in the West, as we saw in the Théophile Gautier quotation in the last chapter. A central pretext for the interest in colonized societies is that these cultures—and their aesthetic forms—are somehow less contaminated by modernity than Western culture, although what this might mean with respect to questions of modernity and of culture is never fully explained. (At the same time, of course, colonized people continue to be presented in a range of Western media as inherently trickier and more treacherous.) In a certain sense I think it is true that traditional, land-based societies have found ways to solve some of the problems that plague Westerners, particularly with respect to organizing authority.[17] It also seems true that the interest in these societies reflects what is probably an understandable desire on the part of Westerners to escape the modernist horror show, especially if the events of the twentieth century are borne in mind (it also reflects a nostalgia for the good old days of imperialism). But the desire to escape will inevitably fail because the way exotic images are made available to the Western spectator-subject means that the culture or part of it being exoticized is already inserted into a commodified, colonial system. We—and here I mean Westernized, urban, probably white people—are thus unable to learn anything from other societies because, like Gallimard, we believe we already know.

Again, at some level the images have nothing to do with the people being exoticized. The constantly reiterated image of the Asian woman who sacrifices herself for a white man because he no longer desires her is an extremely disturbing manifestation of this self-referentiality. The Butterfly fantasy links up, but in an intensified way, to the general problem of how women tend to be represented. This explains the tone of outrage and anxiety in stories about exotic dragon ladies and other evil and unruly women who refuse to conform to this sacrificial model and in articles in the Western press about supposedly treacherous women, such as the reports about Sandinista Nora Astorga, who utilized her sexual charms to entice a Nicaraguan Somozista to his death during the revolution. A gender reversal is apparent in more recent films and literature in which Western women are encouraged to have colonial-style erotic adventures, with the underlying message being "Better late than never. Girls, you, too, can objectify people!" This message, of course, seems somewhat contradictory when we bear in mind all the advertising directed toward white women in which we are encouraged to be, or rather to construct ourselves as, alluring, exotic objects through the purchase of certain commodities. Are white women to act as insensitive white men or as the attractive, dangerous, yet frequently suicidal woman of color of colonialist fantasy?

Exotic Sites: Blood and Flowers

Mexico occupies a peculiar place in the imaginary pantheon of exotic sites. Consider the bizarre equivocality of Mexican exoticism and the high level of ambivalence apparent in so much Western writing on this part of the world, which often seems to become an end in itself. Extreme ambivalence has been typical of the European response to Mexico since the time of the Spanish invasion, when the conquistadors entered Tenochtitlán and encountered the thousands of carved rattlesnakes that decorated public buildings, the Aztec national emblem that just happened to be the Christians' nightmarish symbol of satanic evil. The Spaniards were simultaneously overwhelmed by the wealth and luxury of Tenochtitlán-Mexico and repelled by the blood sacrifices. Early accounts of Mexican arts focused on the alien peculiarities of the images as much as on the skills of the artisans. The ability of the seemingly strange and exotic elements of Aztec society to fascinate Europeans appears early—for instance, in Voltaire's writings he emphasizes the supposedly bizarre juxtaposition of blood and wealth and utilizes the Mexican "paradox" as a way of exemplifying European questions of power and despotism.

The conception of Mexico as a paradoxical, profoundly contradictory site where beauty and brutality exist side by side is apparent in European writers and artists between the two world wars, when the elements of Mexican culture considered most negative in the West—violence, sacrifice, dreamlike states of mind—came to be valorized as qualities Westerners had lost, with unfortunate effects. For many intellectuals who embraced what can be loosely described as a surrealist aesthetic, Mexico continued to be imagined as a fantastic, violent enigma, which was precisely its appeal. This new way of looking at Mexico never seemed intended to question the characterizations that had always structured European conceptions of the country because the sensation of ambivalence generated by the apparently conflicting elements was considered part of what made Mexico interesting. The old tropes persisted but were simply valorized differently.

Mexico *is* physically and culturally different from North America or Europe, and to the outsider it is a visually compelling and intense place, filled with what appears as disturbing images. Here what is concealed in Europe is brought out into the open, perhaps most notably death in the images of skeletons and Day of the Dead ceremonies. Certainly one reason Mexico is able to fascinate Europeans and North Americans is because Western, corporate, and consumerist ideologies have not quite, or at least not yet, won the culture wars in this part of the world.[18]

The surrealists were not completely wrong to notice what to Western eyes appear as contradictory images, although similar juxtapositions can be seen in, say, Paris—only with different content, this time perhaps the clochard next to the imperial monument and so forth. The question that never seems to get asked is whether Mexico is somehow inherently more bizarre and disturbing than other places or if it has been rendered exotic through a process of aestheticization that would not be possible in a more familiar environment. Certainly preexisting tropes operate as a kind of conceptual shorthand; for instance, in the introduction to the paperback edition of Malcolm Lowry's *Under the Volcano*, the essayist speaks several times about Mexico's "tragic fatalism" and "tragic despair" without ever explaining what he means by these terms either culturally or historically.[19] If we assume in advance that a place is going to manifest existential tragedy, then any signs of joy or pleasure we encounter will seem very curious.

Cultural differences can be aestheticized and artificially exaggerated to provoke and prolong a sensation of unease and ambivalence. The other can be made to titillate. I tend to think that the only time anyone really affirms extreme anxiety is when they imagine that they are ultimately in control of the process, so the recognition of difference becomes an aestheticized game in which the experience of discomfort becomes interesting in its own right. It is this operation of aestheticization and making strange, and the way it functions within a structure of appropriation, that is at issue here. The deliberate focus on the alien and bizarre as a way of generating affect enables writers and artists to produce and make use of exoticized, fragmentary images of Mexico (or any other place) as a way of maintaining authority over what has been deemed the exotic—in other words, to stay in control of the operation. This ensures the failure of any attempt to move beyond or outside of the certainties of rationalist Western thought, which in some cases is the ostensible point of the exercise. I am not suggesting that the tendency to romanticize difference is always and by definition corrupt and to be avoided, only that the process has some very definite dangers for all concerned.

The experience of visual and physical dislocation is not peculiar to Mexico, as anyone who has traveled knows; indeed, this is one of the reasons people travel. So in this sense of affirming dislocation there is very little difference between the evil Westerner who exoticizes difference and thus reproduces a colonialist dynamic and the visitor who finds the experience of dislocation interesting and stimulating. Sometimes ambivalence is no more than another name for exhaustion and language difficulties. But when dislocation, disorientation, and delirium become the raison d'être for visiting another culture, and when everything and everyone a person encounters are run through a conceptual machine in which all experience is coded as bizarre and incomprehensible, a great deal of objectification is taking place.

Exotic Imaginaries

The Mexico of the Western imagination tends to come in three basic varieties, all of which share certain repetitive and stereotypical characteristics. It is worth paying attention to how these have been constructed because of the ability of such projections to disguise the very tropes on which they are dependent. The first imaginary is Aztec Mexico, since the first days of the Spanish invasion forever depicted as a place of sacrificial blood and the immense quantities of gold that were of such interest to the conquistadors.

For those who find the Aztecs a bit too vivid, there are alternatives. A quite different projection concerns Mayan Mexico and Central America. Mexico is a huge country, and the Mayan Yucatán and Chiapas regions evoke an entirely different sensibility from Aztec central Mexico: The Yucatán has elicited a particular exoticism of dense jungle, mystery, and lost cities. The apparent contradiction lies between the luxuriant, yet unruly vegetation and the extremely refined court culture of the classic Mayans—in other words, the hoary culture-nature dichotomy so beloved in Western thought. We are supposed to imagine gold, emeralds, and jade; a fantastical congregation of pyramids emerging from the mists; and, of course, extremely large and unpredictable snakes. The Yucatán and Guatemalan Peten region immediately brings to mind the heroic archaeologist, and it is here that the archaeologist appears most as an adventurer, the twentieth-century conquistador bearing the flag of science. (Stories circulate in archaeology departments about graduate students, armed only with machetes, being abandoned in the snake-infested Yucatán jungle by hateful, laughing professors. Such stories always seem to be related in an approving tone and function as a professional rite of passage in themselves.)

Exoticism's self-referential structure plays out in this evocation of the machete-wielding explorer, in which Mayan temples and people appear as a backdrop to the Western adventure story. Gringos in the Yucatán hope to experience the real explorer adventures, which somehow refer to other, earlier "explorers" who also had the wherewithal to hack through the jungle, that is, the Spanish conquistadors. In this way the word *explorer* (or *military adviser*) becomes an alibi for *conquistador,* with this affinity concealed by the adventure story. The twentieth-century fortune hunter, armchair or otherwise, is thus able to identify with and rehabilitate the Spaniards, sometimes with no more effort than reading the archaeology articles in *National Geographic.* The Western agenda in this part of the world still seems to revolve around gold, which this time around is headed for national museums instead of royal treasuries; in a certain sense the "gold" of beautiful, exotic images ends up going back to Europe even if the actual artifacts remain in Mexico or Guatemala. Indiana Jones always retrieves the treasure. Even though the Mayans of the present are rarely acknowledged by Western aesthetes, the Mayans of the past are promoted as mysterious aristocrats who were good at mathematics, and the European collector of Mayan artifacts is believed to have unusually refined tastes. In this way aristocracy becomes contagious.

Despite the ongoing fascination with the pre-Columbian past, Aztec or Mayan culture per se does not figure in the romanticized images of Mexico in the popular culture of Europe and Anglo America. Aztec Mexico fascinates but is not easily rendered sentimental. Rather, the explicitly romanticized images are almost always postconquest and involve European and North American white people in the starring roles, usually as various kinds of adventurers who must confront the unpredictable and dangerous world south of the border. There are few, if any, romantic stories of life under the Aztecs in Western narratives, particularly those in which actual Aztec people are the subject of the narrative.[20] We have yet to see, in North America at least, historical romance novels with an attractive, amorous protagonist going off to fight the opaque and cruel Spaniards or being unavailable to a lover because he has to sacrifice a prisoner of war or be sacrificed himself to a deity. Aztec culture is just a bit too strong for most Westerners' tastes, particularly as exemplified by the exotic romance genres, which tend to avoid excessive unpleasantness (strangely, there does seem to be a subgroup of romantic story in which the hero dies horribly in the Roman arena—but the violence of the arena is familiar territory).

The Mexico of recent history is a different story. Unlike the Aztec empire, modern Mexico definitely manages to be romantic, but it is the romanticization of failure. The failure is the Westerner's, but one that is mirrored by the Mexican backdrop. Mexico is the place the Westerner goes to fall apart, escape from the law, or come to terms with his or her own degradation. This idea of degradation revolves around the question of how much farther a person can actually sink than he or she ever imagined; the true message is that Mexico is identical with the degeneracy and dissolution of the North American or European.

The Mexico that appears in North American popular culture has to do with lawlessness and alcohol. Embedded in the consciousness of a generation is Jimi Hendrix's version of "Hey Joe," in which he replies, "Mexico" when asked where he is going to run to. Thelma and Louise were heading for Mexico. In *The Night of the Iguana* (1964) and similar films Mexico is where the broken people end up. Both the film and text of Malcolm Lowry's *Under the Volcano* frame the hero's alcoholic dissolution through the Day of the Dead and the violence of the cantinas. Within this imaginary, Mexico becomes the site of escape from or absence of law, the place way down south where order breaks down. This suggests that without the law to keep people in line, the characters' identity as Norteamericanos will collapse, and they will become no better than Mexicans, a state of affairs that seems to generate considerable anxiety. Mexico, then, is the place where a person journeys to go to seed; to reach the end of the line and discover that none of the northern melodramas really matter after all. There is a subtext to this anxiety that seems to involve the extent to which the United States has been unable to control the lands and peoples south of the border, despite its various attempts and oft-stated trumpeting of its cultural superiority. Many do seem to remember the Alamo. Much in the same way that Mexico is thought to engulf the visitor, the country exceeds North American attempts to master the south and bring it under U.S. purview.

The constant positioning of Mexico as a dangerous, lawless land seems to refer conceptually to the Aztec past through the focus on violence and disorder. Again, this construction can be valorized in a range of ways, all of which are predictable: Mexican-American writer Richard Rodriguez speaks of being approached by an undergraduate in California who informed him that "it must be cool to be related to Aztecs."[21] In a complex way this has something to do with the recent interest in Frida Kahlo's work, particularly the way this interest has been fueled by Madonna's promotion of the Mexican painter. Is it possible to separate the appeal of Kahlo's images to a new generation of North Americans from Madonna's accumulation of as many of these paintings as she can buy (and can we separate this accumulation from the pop star's interest in packaged versions of transgression)?

Surrealist Dreams

If we think of surrealism as an oppositional aesthetic that focused on or produced unexpected juxtapositions of aesthetic and cultural phenomena, we can see how Mexico came to be framed in terms of radical difference and disturbing affinities. Surrealist thinkers were continuing to imagine

Mexico as it had always been imagined in the West, but they now invested the supposed strangeness of the country with a redemptive function. Many postwar Western intellectuals were anxious to locate the origins of culture and society, which they thought they could find outside of Europe.[22] Mexico came to be thought of as an outside that held out the promise of escape from the disaster of Western culture and the limits of Western consciousness. Mexico attracted the attention of post–World War I Europeans because of its particular history as much as its different cultural and aesthetic traditions, and because of the way this historical specificity could disclose possibilities that had been excluded in Europe.

This attention had more to do with the different valuation of the traits thought to be associated with Mexico than with a radically new interpretation of the culture or with the binary conceptions of cultural difference that continued to influence surrealist thinking. There were still only Greeks and *barbaroi,* Christians and infidels. The interest in Mexico was a result of the influence of "primitivism" on French art and letters of the period, which derived from a fascination with unconscious experience. This meant that intellectuals turned not only to exotic cultures such as those of Africa and Mexico but also to categories of people in Europe who seemed to exhibit this psychic innocence and general lack of Hegelian self-consciousness. For instance, the art and utterances of the insane and of children would evoke a response in many French intellectuals similar to that of Aztec or African art, and although all these were of interest because they were believed to be free from the burden of consciousness, this freedom always seemed coextensive with being under some kind of authority, whether colonial, state, institutional, or parental. Because Aztecs, children, Africans, and mad people manifested a partial relation to (European) authority, they could exist in a state of full presence and heterogeneity.[23]

As we have seen time and time again, appreciation of another cultural tradition can still be framed within a hierarchical system of cultural value and indeed one that made conquest possible (and thinkable) in the first place. If rationality is believed to be the Western disease, then any outside to European culture would have to be framed as profoundly irrational. This was decided in advance of any actual encounter with different people, much like the Christian interpretation of other religious traditions was decided in advance. I have said that exoticism involves the exaggeration or production of cultural differences, the appearance of which come to be charged in certain ways. The surrealist interest in Mexico did not call exoticism into question, nor did it particularly want to do so; indeed, in some respects the surrealist project was precisely about intensifying and aestheticizing difference rather than about challenging Western conceptions of cultural superiority. Surrealist, cubist, or academic painter—none of these really sought to look outside of Western culture, despite their claims, because they still needed an other to generate affect and excitement. This problem of the aestheticization of radical dualism has not been solved, and this production of difference continues to recur in and inform Western culture and aesthetics.

Sergei Eisenstein, Georges Bataille, and Antonin Artaud were all very different thinkers, but they shared an uneasy fascination with the bizarre in their attempts to come to terms with Mexico in their work. French writer and philosopher Bataille wrote on the art of Aztec Mexico and the economics of human sacrifice but never managed to visit the country. Russian filmmaker Eisenstein traveled to Mexico in late 1930 to make the film *¡Que Viva Mexico!* with the initial financial support of American writer Upton Sinclair. The film was never completed for a range of financial and political reasons, but a version continues to be screened in art house cinemas from time to time. He remained in the country for a little over a year before being recalled to Moscow by Joseph Stalin. Poet and actor Artaud went to Mexico in 1936, when he was forty years old, and gave lectures on art and revolution in Mexico City before attending a peyote ceremony in Sierra Tarahumara in northern Mexico.

Bataille

The past can be exoticized as much as a contemporary society or event can. Dissident surrealist Georges Bataille offers an extreme version of Aztec Mexico and the Spanish invasion in which these are almost completely aestheticized and transformed into a bizarre and enigmatic object lesson for Europeans. Bataille's work shows some of the implications of approaching a culture such as Mexico as a conceptual schema, an aestheticized series of alluring, yet ambivalent fragments, for the interpretation of colonial history: Exoticism places culture outside history. Although he broke with André Breton's circle in 1926, he continued to be influenced by surrealist aesthetics.

Bataille's interest in Aztec and other "archaic" societies because of their ability to elucidate universal needs and fantasies was in many respects typical of his generation. In the Parisian milieu of the 1920s and 1930s in which Bataille worked, two broad intellectual or theoretical streams were apparent. The first was sociological and in general derived both from Marxist writings (such as Alexandre Kojève's reading of Georg Hegel's philosophy) and from ethnological theory, such as the work of Marcel Mauss. The second was an ecstatic primitivism most strongly evident in the arts; here a certain primitive energy was cultivated, as is apparent in the influence of *art negre* on French aesthetics (for instance, the well-known effect of African art on such artists as Pablo Picasso and Georges Braque). The sociological and aesthetic currents were linked theoretically as well as socially. For instance, both surrealists and ethnographers were influenced by the work of Émile Durkheim. Bataille's strong connection to ethnographic circles are well known: He was an enthusiastic reader of Mauss, a close friend of ethnographer Alfred Metraux, and a founding member of the College of Sociology (1937–1939). He also helped found the journal *Documents* (1929–1930), which brought together the work of ethnographers and artists.

Bataille first articulated a fascination for pre-Columbian, particularly Aztec, culture in his brief art review, *l'Amérique disparue* (1929). Pre-Columbian art has tended to appeal to equivocal, rather decadent tastes precisely because of the kinds of images manifested in this tradition, and it is not surprising that this art caught the eye of Bataille, who wrote on slaughterhouses, the dirty drawers in Salvador Dalí's *Lugubrious Game,* and Sade's writings. *L'Amérique disparue* was written for the first major exhibition of pre-Columbian Mexican art and artifacts in Paris, "Les Arts anciens de l'Amérique" at the Louvre. French writers and critics such as Guillaume Apollinaire had been interested in Mexican art since before World War I, but a major show could not be mounted until the late 1920s. Twenty years later Bataille developed the themes expressed in his earlier piece on Mexico in *La part maudite* (1949). Bataille is fascinated by the Aztecs because they appear to him as an enigma, civilized, yet engaging in mass human sacrifice, offering "air and violence . . . poetry and humour."[24] He is certainly right in describing Aztec art in these terms, but he gets carried away by his ideas of radical difference and the specificity of violence. For Bataille, the intensity of the Mexican "sacrificial madness" renders this society more seductive than any other aboriginal culture in the Americas, but also more capable of provoking dread and terror. Thus, the stage is set for extreme levels of ambivalence.

The strength of Mexican art attracted surrealists and other jaded Parisians. Pre-Columbian Mexican art occupied a somewhat unique position in the European-based aesthetic taxonomic system in that it was not quite classified as primitive, but tended instead to be placed in the category of archaic art, along with Khmer sculpture. This category stressed luxury and a refined court culture and could thus draw on certain elements of nineteenth-century romanticism, such as an interest in decadent empires. It also suggested a moribund quality to the work. At the same time, Aztec art could be subsumed under the category of *negre,* along with modern jazz and Oceanic art, all of which were believed to be sources of primitive, unconscious, or dreamlike experience. The 1928 exhibition was a huge success and provoked an interest in Mexican ethnography among French artists and writers. For instance, Antonin Artaud visited the exhibition and, as might be expected given his obsessions, became fascinated by the (to

Parisian eyes) bizarre images of death and violence of Aztec art, a fascination that ultimately impelled him to travel to Mexico in 1936.

The title of Bataille's review of this exhibition, rendered in an English translation as "Extinct America," sets the tone of the article: Aztec America has vanished from the face of the earth; it has disappeared. Indeed, in the first paragraph Bataille speaks of the "instantaneous disappearance" of Aztec society, a statement that we (and Bataille) know to be historically inaccurate, but one that underlines the apparent incomprehensibility of Mexico. This elision of historical fact is symptomatic: For Bataille as for so many other Europeans, the Aztecs' "bloody eccentricity" (as he calls it) does not bring to mind history in the sense of the development of institutions over time and an intelligible progression of cause and effect. Rather, Mexican culture exists as a nightmare, an insane society that haunts the European dream of the well-ordered polis.[25] Mexico is forever outside history. Bataille describes Aztec culture: "Continuous crime committed in broad daylight for the mere satisfaction of deified nightmares, terrifying phantasms, priests' cannibalistic meals, ceremonial corpses, and streams of blood evoke not so much the historical adventure, but rather the blinding debauches described by the illustrious Marquis de Sade."[26]

Bataille seems to be suggesting that the Aztecs are comprehensible through Sade. For Bataille, the sacrifices of the Aztecs resemble Sade's bloody orgies, and the Aztecs both evoke and exemplify the Sadean libidinal investment in what Bataille believes to be excluded by modern society: blood, corpses, cannibalism, and other heterogeneous, apparently transgressive forces.[27] In this way the nature of traditional Mexican society is rendered visible through a structure of resemblance and analogy: The Aztecs are like certain passages in a Western literary text; their heterogeneity is similar to the heterogeneity of Sade. Bataille refuses to engage Aztec culture on its own terms, so what initially appears as similitude becomes reinforcement of the radical difference of Aztec society.

Bataille insists upon the "amazingly joyous character of these horrors": Tenochtitlán was a "human slaughterhouse," yet beautiful, wealthy, a city of flowers as much as of flies.[28] The flowers provide a counterpoint to the sacrificial horror; Tenochtitlán was above all filled with gardens, and flowers were everywhere, even and especially in the sacrificial temples. Again, we see the juxtaposition of apparently bizarrely contradictory elements. This association of flowers and death is not accidental. For Bataille, the beauty of flowers and the love they represent are always attended by a certain perversity; the ideal beauty of a flower's petals is "spoiled" by the "sordid," "satanic" stamens, the "filth of its organs."[29] He is saying that the loftiest human ideals—love, beauty, art—contain perverse and squalid elements, just as the perversity of human sacrifice is surrounded by the beauty of flowers. Bataille's apocryphal description of Sade throwing rose petals into manure recalls his evocation of Sade's orgies and the Aztecs' religious sensibility: By having flowers at their sacrificial ceremonies, the Aztecs, like Sade, seem to have recognized and affirmed the way in which the sublime and the noble are rooted in filth. But this description works only if the Aztecs are read through Sade.

Bataille's juxtaposition of blood and wealth, flowers and flies, seems at first glance to disrupt traditional categories of civilization and barbarism by combining the apparently antagonistic elements of an elaborated, urban civilization and a bloody, barbaric ritual. It is disingenuous, to say the least, to suggest that sacrificial violence is somehow peculiar to Aztec Mexico or to evince surprise that high culture can exist side by side with extreme violence. The link between civilization and barbarism (in Bataille's sense of bloody spectacle) seems evident, as does the fact that these two have always gone hand in hand. Blood and wealth are no paradox at all, whether in Aztec Mexico or at home in Europe.

As I noted, the juxtaposition of bizarre, contradictory elements was a feature of surrealist practice but had been present much earlier in European writings on Aztec society, in which Mexico appears as a kind of collage, both violent and luxurious, barbaric and refined. This aestheticized construct evokes a delightful ambivalence and provides lessons to a European audience without, however, calling into question the hierarchical relationship between European and Mexican societies or the notion that cultures may be divided into contradictory elements that exist in opposition. Accordingly, a trope of the Aztec "paradox" was available to be taken up by writers such as Bataille. Mexico was able to function as a locale of authentic, intense experience precisely because it appeared as a paradox: on the one hand, an inversion of Christian values and on the other, an exemplification of internal disorder and violence. Through the device of juxtaposition the strangeness and poetic delirium used to characterize Aztec society are underlined or, better, constructed. Human sacrifice becomes a poetic experience, and the apparent heterogeneity and difference of Aztec society are intensified and rendered more Sadean. The flowers seem to make the sacrifices both less and more horrific; somehow a society described wholly in terms of brutality or of sublimity would be less aberrant and disturbing to Bataille's modern reader.

The failure of this kind of approach to Aztec sacrifice has to do with a blind spot about Western culture: When Bataille associates violence and wealth in his description of Mexican society, he does not seem to be making a point about the violence and madness that accompany production in *all* imperial societies, including those of twentieth-century Europe, or about the extent to which capitalism shares *wétiko* principles with other, more explicitly sacrificial economies.

Bataille retreats to European rationality after exhausting the Aztec metaphor, but he first produces and then drains the society of images to illustrate a tableau of excess and death. For Bataille, the Aztecs were savages because they went too far, carrying the sovereign affirmation of death to unimaginable extremes, worshipping gods he describes as having been "the bloodiest ever to people the clouds of our earth."[30]

And this is where we approach the end of the line, the ultimate political implication of exoticism and the way it is used to generate an aestheticized ambivalence: Bataille's insistence on the extreme nature of Aztec sovereignty leads him to inform us that "death, for the Aztecs, was nothing," as if the sacrificial ceremonies presuppose an unmediated will to death in every sphere of Aztec life. For so many Europeans, the institution of human sacrifice connotes a literal affirmation of death, which becomes a will to suicide and disappearance. Bataille is less astonished by the Aztecs' presumed disregard for death than by the fact that, despite this, these "savage warriors" seemed to enjoy life and everyday activities such as visiting with friends. His astonishment that Aztecs were more or less like anybody else leads him from asserting that "death ... was nothing" to claiming that the Aztecs had "an excessive taste for death,"[31] which led directly to their conquest and disappearance: "They surrendered to the Spaniards in a sort of mad hypnotic state. ... As if this people had vaguely understood that once they had reached this degree of joyous violence, the only way out ... was a sudden and terrifying death."[32]

Even if we leave aside the implications of the words *vaguely understood,* in reading the European conquest of Mexico through a notion of an "excessive taste for death," Bataille suggests that the Aztecs were in some profound way responsible for the Spanish invasion because their sacrificial violence demanded that they sacrifice themselves to their own sovereignty, their own will to death. In this sense their defeat was the inevitable result of Aztec conventions of religious representation and the institution of human sacrifice.[33] It seems that the Spaniards only obliged the Aztecs' desire to affirm death, and to this extent the conquest was inconsequential, if indeed "death was nothing."

Bataille closes *l'Amérique disparue* with this requiem: "They died suddenly, like crushed insects."[34] I think again of the way he evokes the sacrificial altars, swarming with flies and blood; the violence repeats itself in conquest, with death and flies now affirmed by a different hand. For the Aztecs, an excessive taste for death could lead only to conquest and massacre and crushing defeat by a superior military force. Bataille does not seem particularly troubled by the conquest of Mexico; the crushing of such insects is of no real importance.

Bataille is by no means a stupid man, which is what is so frustrating about his work on Mexico. He is generally quite careful in his analyses of

European culture, which, although idiosyncratic, are usually philosophically rigorous. However, when it comes to Mexico, or indeed any other different culture, Bataille never lets social or historical facts get in the way of a good idea. He is certainly aware of Mexican resistance to the Spanish invaders, from the street fighting in Tenochtitlán to the uprisings in the provinces. He has read, at the very least, William Prescott and Bernardino de Sahagun by 1929, and although these are in many respects problematic sources, they nevertheless describe in detail the months of bitter resistance to European encroachment and conquest. But Bataille is not atypical, and his error is to be so enamored of the exoticized notion of sacrificial sovereignty that he must "disappear" the Aztecs to support an argument, a discursive conquest that operates as a repetition of physical conquest. What seems a deliberate oversight remains difficult to understand, given Bataille's general insights about violence and power in society. It is here that we see the link between a certain objectification of societies such as Aztec Mexico in European writing and the systems of colonial authority that make these writings possible.

The production of images of radical difference is based on a selective use of mythological and aesthetic fragments, itself the result of an abridgment or pruning whereby elements that are not useful to the story are excised and made to disappear. A particular version of difference is produced so that it can be used to support the argument Bataille is making, an argument that continues to manifest a blind spot about the extent to which Western culture is itself based on violence and mass death.[35] Several readers of Bataille have assured me that he knows that European empires are as permeated with violent institutions as the Aztec state, but I am not convinced. Bataille takes entirely too much pleasure in his construction of Aztec violence as completely beyond anything seen before or since, and his tendency to aestheticize Mexican sacrifice means that we can only wonder at its incomprehensibility rather than see how it puts the certainties of the Western polis into question.

Eisenstein: Mexico as Redemption

Eisenstein spent over a year in Mexico filming *¡Que Viva Mexico!* and circulated with people such as Diego Rivera (whom he had met in Moscow) and Frida Kahlo in the leftist intellectual milieu of Mexico City. The Russian filmmaker supported the anti-imperialist agenda of many Mexican artists and attempted, to a greater extent than many, to come to terms with the foreignness and cultural history of the country and to do so in a way that left some room for a Mexican aesthetic to emerge. Yet even Eisenstein could go only so far, and although he sought to create a socially engaged art, he shared with the Parisian aesthetes a tendency to focus on—or to produce—the fascinating oppositions and excesses as a way of constructing an intense, aestheticized Mexico. This happened despite a political and intellectual agenda that was very different from that of people like Bataille and Artaud and despite spending a fair bit of time in the country. Eisenstein manifested the peculiar Western blind spot about cultural difference, one that crosses ideologies and is apparent in so many otherwise unrelated Western characterizations of different cultures and traditions.

Like the French surrealists and many others before them, Eisenstein construes Mexico in terms of the juxtaposition of apparently contradictory, paradoxical elements. He visualizes a constant clash of opposites and is fond of comments like "Mexico—lyrical and tender, but also brutal," a sweeping characterization that at first glance seems evocative of a particular place but that could actually describe anywhere.[36] Although this describing of Mexico in terms of vivid oppositions is typical of Western intellectuals of whatever political persuasion, in Eisenstein's case this interest in contradiction may be intensified by his commitment to dialectical materialism, which, as Hegel would have it, views contradiction as inherently creative. Eisenstein continually frames Mexico as a series of contradictions. For instance, in his memoirs he describes Mexico as a contrast between "monumental simplicity and unrestrained Baroque (in each of its aspects, Spanish and Aztec)" and insists that the opposition between the plain white clothing of the farmer and the wildly embroidered coat of the matador exemplifies the ethos of a nation.[37]

One of the four sections of *¡Que Viva Mexico!* is set in Tehuantepec in southern Mexico, and Eisenstein's attempts to describe this area fall into a time-worn convention of colonialist writing. This is not the same as saying Eisenstein is a colonialist, but rather that certain Western literary protocols have become so naturalized as to be almost invisible. For instance, in attempting to render the feeling of the scene, Eisenstein first compares the Tehuantepec marketplace to India, then to Baghdad, and finally to the South Seas.[38] In this way he collapses several exemplary sites in the Western imaginary into one exotic locale. Difference circulates and refers to other differences rather than to the West, which is assumed to be universal and transparent. Describing Mexico in terms of other exotic places becomes a way to enforce a notion of this country's radical difference.

The gaps in Eisenstein's thinking are most obvious in his writings on Tehuantepec, when he is far from the intellectual climate of Mexico City and the Western certainties he brings with him no longer quite work. Some of the failure of his attempt to come to terms with Mexico has to do with the intellectual climate of the time and the confidence of the Left. This confidence that the socialist project would ultimately succeed, especially when combined with clichés of revolutionary thinking, at times meant that intellectuals were ill-prepared for reality and unable to see the extent to which aspects of the revolutionary project were based on the privileging of Western notions of progress and industrialization.[39] For Mexican intellectuals the interest in indigenous cultures that emerged after the 1910–1920 revolution was linked to concrete practices and a specific political agenda (at least in theory), but for foreigners such as Eisenstein this interest could easily fall into romanticized, utopian abstractions.

In his memoirs Eisenstein recalls Tehuantepec:

> The tropics responded to dreamy sensuality. The intertwining bronze bodies seemed to incarnate the latent rovings of sensuality, here in the over-saturated, overgrown grasping of the lianas, male and female bodies wreathed and intertwined like lianas; they looked in the mirror and saw how the girls of Tehuantepec looked at themselves with black, almond-shaped eyes in the surface of dreamy tropical creeks, and admired their flowered arrays, reflecting on the golden surface of their bodies.[40]

The tropics again become a site of pure sensuality, perhaps a bit too lush and overblown, but one in which the inhabitants are identified with the natural world of luxuriant growth and fecundity. Some of Eisenstein's language seems rather breathless today. For instance, he writes of the "marvellously feminine dark-coloured girls" of Tehuantepec and speaks of them as if they exist suspended in a voluptuous dreamworld.[41] In this sense Eisenstein recalls Paul Gauguin's fantasies of utopian innocence in the Pacific, in which the demands of colonial reality are not permitted to interfere with pleasure. The imaginary primitive allows unfettered sensuality, without guilt or the constraints of culture, because it exists outside of historical time and space. Western rationality nevertheless intrudes in this dream in Eisenstein's tendency to describe the south in terms of extremity: The terms *over-saturated* and *overgrown* imply a standard of measurement in which Europe is the norm. The absence of temporality has always been a characteristic of the trope of primitivism, and Eisenstein, too, is quite clear on this point, boldly asserting, "Time is unknown in Tehuantepec" (which assumes we all mean the same thing by time).[42] Tehuantepec is undoubtedly different from Moscow or New York, but it is a mistake to imagine this difference as something that can be calculated in advance or indeed as something that is in any way definitive. It is all too easy to imagine that the other exists outside of the everyday demands and conflicts that exist in any society.

Tehuantepec is beautiful, but to insist on a utopian natural world is yet another way to enforce a notion of radical difference. This can obscure the extent to which all people must construct their social and cultural worlds, in Mexico as in Moscow. No culture exists in a state of nature, although some may pay more attention to the earth than others. There might be another reason for Eisenstein's interest in tropical sensuality: He had been working in the puritanical postrevolutionary Soviet Union, and the Isthmus of Tehuantepec must have seemed appealing when he contemplated returning to Moscow in February, especially the Stalinist Moscow of the 1930s. If Mexico is seen in terms of absolute difference, it will always be incommensurable with Western experience, and it will not be necessary to call the cultural or political orthodoxies of the West into question, which might be a relief to some.

Eisenstein is not alone in imagining the aboriginal Mexico of the south as a place free from politics or conflict, an attitude that continues to be typical of many Westerners. The idea that certain cultures exist as gardens of innocence is extraordinarily persistent, as are the notions of what this innocence might mean. This is, I think, one reason for the success of the New Age appropriations of Native spirituality; the New Age sees these cultures as inherently timeless and apolitical. A fascination with Native spiritual activities can become a way for non-Natives to elide the profoundly political issues of land rights and cultural survival. Traditional, land-based societies may appear as a place of escape that remains free of the demands of Western politics, but when we consider that the survival of traditional ways is itself a profoundly political act, Eisenstein's sensibility takes on a different implication. These societies have been under immense pressure, from all points on the political spectrum, to assimilate, Christianize, industrialize, become civilized, relinquish their land. As I write these lines, aboriginal people in the Chiapas region of southern Mexico are dying in the struggle to maintain their traditional ways in the face of a Mexican government committed to free trade with the north. For whom are the tropics a dream?

Artaud: Redemptive Madness

Artaud presents us with a different kind of extremity. For him, Mexico is not the site of benign sensuality but "the land of speaking blood."[43] Artaud visited the country because he sought a certain intensity of experience that he was unable to locate in Europe. Artaud believed that the modern societies of the West were deadened to the truth that comes in visions and dreams. Although he was probably right about orthodox forms of Western thought, his expectations of Mexico made it impossible for him to find the kind of difference he was looking for. Mexico existed as a fantasy for Artaud long before he disembarked in Veracruz, and he seemed to expect a constant stream of extraordinary, visionary revelations to accompany him on his travels in the country. Artaud hoped to achieve the hallucinatory state of mind accessible through magic mushrooms and peyote, states that ultimately would redeem him from his alienation and show him the way out of the impasses of modernism. (This project is in keeping with the tradition of all the Westerners who have gone to Mexico to get high.) An interest in unconscious, fantastic experience was in the air in the Paris of the day, but whereas Bataille wanted to play with difference and ambivalence in his writings and in the contained atmosphere of the Trocadero museum, Artaud wanted to experience these states of mind as intensely as possible. With these kinds of aspirations, it was predictable that he would be extremely likely to crash and burn.

Artaud had high hopes for Mexico, as the trip constituted something of an escape from a bleak situation in Paris. He was unwell when he set out from Europe and left a string of failures behind him. His association with surrealist orthodoxy had ended badly after he was purged from the movement by André Breton in 1926.

Artaud's letters from Mexico suggest that he believed—or at least hoped—that the Mexican government would be truly revolutionary, which in his terms meant revolutionary enough to accept his message that hope for the future lay in indigenous cultures and their relationship to the land. It can be difficult today to grasp the extent to which Mexico, whose revolution was still recent, appeared to many European intellectuals in the 1930s as a site of revolutionary potential. During his stay in Mexico City Artaud lectured and wrote impassioned newspaper articles about the necessity for contemporary Mexicans to retrieve the spiritual vision of the indigenous past of the pre-Columbian era. He explicitly sought to convince people that the revival of aboriginal religious experience was the only way to renew revolutionary Mexican society. He was not particularly successful and was surprised at the resistance of urban intellectuals to his message (their indifference no doubt stemming from several sources, an obvious one being that Artaud was a foreigner telling Mexicans what they were doing wrong, which must have irritated some people). Mexico City was not what he had hoped or expected; in some ways it was like any other big city, which is to say, not quite alien enough or far away enough from the problems he had left behind in Paris.

Then came the experience Artaud was waiting for: He visited the Tarahumara nation for peyote ceremonies (a visit that may have inspired Ken Russell's treatment of the peyote ceremony in *Altered States* [1980]). French novelist J.M.G. Le Clézio raises the question of whether Artaud actually traveled to Tarahumara Sierra and participated in peyote ceremonies as there is very little evidence of his presence there.[44] This question makes a certain amount of sense. There is a tone to Artaud's descriptions of Tarahumara that sounds strangely like something out of the Apocalypse of Saint John. Some of his descriptions are extremely unlikely—for instance, the Tarahumaras who supposedly threw dirt clods while simultaneously lying down, masturbating, and staring fixedly at him. (Artaud was withdrawing from heroin at the time.)[45] Given that Artaud spoke neither Spanish nor the Tarahumara language, we may wonder how much he could have understood if he indeed was there. Bearing all this in mind, we can see that Artaud's travels are of a poetic nature and existed in the realm of the imagination rather than in a particular site or culture. As part of his general project Artaud tends not to distinguish between reality and fantasy, which is not a problem in itself. The problem is that he thinks he has to defend his poetic practices by associating them with the proper names *Mexico* and *Tarahumara,* which refer to real people and societies. These in turn have particular historical relationships with the West that, like it or not, Artaud manifests in both his presence and his aestheticized treatment of Mexico.

In 1947 Artaud wrote a poem entitled "Indian Culture." He wrote this very near the end of his life, and its feeling is very different from the optimism (however misguided) of the work he produced during and just after his return from Mexico. An excerpt reads:

> *I came to Mexico*
> *to make contact with the Red Earth*
> *and it stinks the same way as it is fragrant;*
> *it smells good the same way as it stank.*
> *Caffre of urine*
> *from the slope of a hard vagina,*
> *which resists when one takes it.*[46]

There is something extremely twisted about this poem, a bitterness and anger that go beyond the obvious rape metaphor. Artaud feminizes the Mexican landscape so that he may rape it, but more insidiously, he deliberately produces and then collapses the time-worn opposition between sublimity and foulness. The predictability of this juxtaposition of opposites undermines any new understanding: Mexico remains a paradox, no more, no less, incomprehensible to the end. And perhaps that is what Artaud is trying to say, assuming we can get past the privileging of rape: Mexico is what it is, and all the projection in the world cannot change that. Contemplating a work such as "Indian Culture," I have to ask what Europeans such as Artaud wanted from Mexico. The poem seems permeated with resentment that Mexico did not freely give him what he thought he needed, that the other did not in fact exist to heal the Frenchman. There was no escape, after all.

Artaud believed that traditional peoples—particularly the "interesting" ones, such as shamanistic cultures—manifested a higher truth than Western rationality and science. He was another who could well see the failures of orthodox Western culture, and for him the consequences of this understanding were to be madness and incarceration. It is difficult to say precisely what caused Artaud to slip into a kind of insanity (or to allow the authorities to define him as such), as the vision-as-madness story has been so consistently romanticized and collapsed into his interest in drugs and shamanism. I feel a certain impatience with Artaud. He clearly understood that the real limit of the rationalist Western mentality is its tendency to negate things that cannot be measured. Yes, many other realities exist, and to repudiate these is to lose deeper ways of understanding the world. But Artaud seemed unable to break past his expectations of what these different realities would look like. Part of the problem is imagining two binary, exclusive categories, one called "rational thought" and the other "magical thought," with the latter constantly and conspicuously exhibiting exalted levels of hocus-pocus. Shamanistic approaches to reality seem to me to be essentially based on common sense, achieved by noticing nuances of cause and effect and connections that a faster, cruder eye would miss. It takes a great deal of patience and discipline to hear what the spirit world has to say. Even hallucinatory states of mind are concerned with paying attention to things that are present all the time, even in the banal, everyday world. To expect something too strangely magical from ceremonies such as those of Tarahumara is to miss the point.

Artaud was, I think, reasonably sincere in trying to come to terms with a relation to the land and spirits that is extremely difficult to locate in modernist Western culture. Ronald Hayman remarks on the lack of a patronizing manner in Artaud's approach to Mexico and to Mexicans, including indigenous people, which was unusual in Europeans of the time (although breathless enthusiasm can certainly be patronizing in its own right).[47] But, like Bataille, Artaud's mistake was in expecting Mexico, traditional people, or hallucinations to be weirder or only really trusting the message when the world was grotesque enough to generate the affect that had become the sign of shattering Western rationality.

Mexico did not save Artaud, but it was his own fault. His love of the grotesque, as much as his ambivalence about the country, turned on him in the end. For so many Europeans, Mexico can be no more than a tease, promising delight and redemption but unable to deliver on the promise, or worse, offering a kind of moral and spiritual degradation to the Westerner foolish enough to believe in the possibility of rescue from the Western nightmare. The problem lies in expecting redemption and in expecting another culture to be more different than it is or to be different in ways that have been decided in advance. Thus, there can be no movement, no way out of the box in which the Westerner has placed him- or herself. Again, I think of the sad people in *Under the Volcano* and *Night of the Iguana*.

3

Conquest, Appropriation, and Cultural Difference

It is a rainy day in Victoria, B.C., as I walk the tourist strip. Next to the authentic English woolen shops and the stores selling genuine Scottish tartans, I encounter shop after shop of "authentic Indian" arts and crafts. Killer whale prints, silver jewelry, Tsonokwa masks, Cowichan sweaters, large carvings of grizzly bears, all are available to the visitor with the right credit balance. As I wander around in the drizzle, I notice one artist—a printmaker—trudging from shop to shop with his portfolio in an effort to sell his work. He is being refused every time. The designs look pretty good, clan emblems in a very traditional Northwest Coast style, I observe, looking over his shoulder as he shows his prints to an unsmiling white shopkeeper. Now artists everywhere have their problems, and tensions between dealers and artists are nothing new, but the way this incident cuts so clearly along cultural and racial lines is disturbing. The printmaker is Native;[1] all the shops selling Native art are white owned.

What is now called British Columbia is the traditional home of the Nuu'chah'nulth, Haida, and Kwagiutl nations, among many others. These nations have always lived on this land and have created distinctive aesthetic and theatrical traditions. The provincial government, like the rest of Canada, has an abysmal record of settling Native land rights disputes, and there is an unsavory history of racism in the province that has yet to be addressed by the government in any credible way. Despite the antagonisms between the government and the Native communities, the provincial tourist industry explicitly markets Native cultures as one of the principal reasons to visit the province. Victoria is a bit less self-conscious than Santa Fe, but as a tourist spot it is the same general idea of a fascinating, yet safely colonized Native culture, this time with a British colonial overlay. The mix is part of the charm: After gawking at the enormous collection of nineteenth-century Native carved poles at the Royal British Columbia Museum, the visitor can attend high tea at the Empress Hotel. Americans love it. The

British Columbia tourist office recognizes that Native arts and cultures are one of the province's prime selling points, after the scenery, of course, and it comes as no surprise that in tourist advertisements Native cultures appear as an integral part of the natural beauty of the landscape.[2]

The Native culture marketed to tourists almost always appears in its past or apolitical incarnations and spotlights traditional arts and crafts. We have yet to see tourist brochures exhorting visitors to come to British Columbia and meet Gitksan land rights activists. With the bizarre telescopy peculiar to tourist board advertising copy, Native culture is presented as something that continues to live, yet is nonetheless anchored firmly in the past.

Many municipalities in the province display totem poles (more properly, family or clan crest poles) in local parks, and traditional-style ravens and thunderbirds abound on souvenir objects such as mugs and tea towels. Complex political and spiritual questions circulate around the buying and selling of these images, and indeed one issue is whether outsiders should have any access at all to traditional images and symbols, completely apart from whether non-Native individuals or institutions should possess actual ceremonial objects. Although it seems obvious that ceremonial items should belong to the people who use them (or who would like to), the majority of museums and private collectors continues to resist this idea.

For the moment I want to focus on the larger context in which such images are bought and sold, specifically the way Native art enters the national or international market through the mediation of the tourist industry. The white-owned shops in Victoria and Vancouver make a great deal of money selling works of art by Native artists, many of which are executed in the most traditional styles, as is the work of the unlucky printmaker. Although the contemporary Native carver of a commissioned crest pole is usually paid reasonably well for the work, as are the artists creating upmarket sculpture and jewelry, Native people are not as a rule consulted or compensated when clan designs are used on tourist or other objects. The traditional design forms are considered by many non-Natives to be part of the broader, universal, but ultimately white heritage of British Columbia and so available for appropriation. These designs appear all over public buildings in Vancouver and Victoria (and in Seattle, Portland, and Anchorage) as a way of symbolizing the regional character of the area. Sometimes, as in the Alaska Airlines tail decoration (see Figure 3.1), it is the Native body itself that is appropriated and used to evoke regional identity.

Appropriation occurs because cultural difference can be bought and sold in the marketplace. One hundred years ago people in the colonizing nations were taught to fear difference because of the potentially contaminating qualities of other ways of life. Although many Europeans found other cultures interesting and mined these for objects and images considered to be of aesthetic value, this was strictly a minority taste, as most Westerners viewed

FIGURE 3.1 Alaska Airlines promotional postcard

the world as a source of raw materials and labor rather than of ideas. The British officer who went native was the object of pity and ridicule, which may have been a way of drawing attention away from the reasons for this phenomenon. International systems of exchange have subsequently broken down some (but certainly not all) of the anxiety around difference in the West, and the conceits of European high culture are not necessarily the most useful means for maintaining economic and political dominance and justifying capitalist consumption. It is now possible to find at the very heart of the empire (for instance, at Bloomingdale's department store) a wide range of commodities that sell the look of different cultures. This new appreciation of cultural difference is all done with mirrors, however, and, as in the past, what is usually available are the morphological forms that connote difference, which is to say, alluring commodities—difference in effigy, as it were.

Notions of Western cultural superiority continue to obtain but are now articulated in a more insidious manner, for instance, in how questions of aesthetic value are organized around consumption. To consume the commodities that have come to stand for other cultures is to neutralize the ambivalence cultural difference is able to generate and to extract excitement precisely from this ambivalence. Not a lot has changed since the nineteenth century after all. In order to work, the objects, events, and experiences that are commodified and marketed as cultural difference are dependent on concepts of cultural and aesthetic authenticity. In other words, difference has to be seen as real. Native designs manifest and refer to what many non-Natives see as the inherent cultural authenticity possessed by Native people, which is one of the main reasons Native cultures have been commodified. Non-Natives want to consume this authenticity and are willing to pay for the privilege. This desire takes many forms. An ad for the province of Saskatchewan (see Figure 3.2) seduces the tourist with a promise of ancient Indian ways, such as that evoked by the man and the teepee in the photograph. Some entrepreneurs (both Native and non-Native) go even further than the souvenir vendors and offer Native spiritual experiences to non-Natives for large sums of money. In this way the spirits and their ceremonies are marketed along with images. As with exoticism, the cultures from which aesthetic or ceremonial forms are obtained are usually deemed more interesting, weaker, or moribund, more authentic or exotic by those who are doing the taking, usually the politically or economically dominant societies.

That the provincial tourist industry appropriates Native imagery and traditions to encourage visitors to the province seems evident. But simply identifying the process that occurs in British Columbia and elsewhere is insufficient because the term *appropriation* encompasses so many different issues and questions. What is cultural appropriation? For one thing, the term signifies not only the taking up of something and making it one's own but also the ability to do so. People have always shared ideas and borrowed from one another, but appropriation is entirely different from borrowing or sharing because it involves the taking up and commodification of aesthetic, cultural, and, more recently, spiritual forms of a society. Culture is neatly packaged for the consumer's convenience. Because of the political implications of appropriation and the way such concepts link up to institutions such as museums, art galleries, and universities, the term has recently been appearing in discussions of the politics of voice and in the field of cultural studies. In some instances appropriation has been the subject of bitter debate.

In Canada many First Nations writers are looking at questions of cultural appropriation and arguing that the theft of cultural forms is coextensive with land theft and the confiscation of ceremonial objects and human remains by museums and university anthropology departments. For instance, critics such as Marcia Crosby are suggesting that difference, especially that represented by Native cultures, has itself become a salable commodity. Artist Joane Cardinal-Shubert writes succinctly, "Money, that is what appropriating is about. Whether the issue is land or art or iconography or ceremonial reliquiae, the focus of the deprivation is money. Something to be gained by imitation, copying, stealing. Where do ethics enter this issue, where does the law intervene?"[3]

SASKATCHEWAN
Where you belong
1-800-667-7191
Saskatchewan

FIGURE 3.2 Saskatchewan tourism advertisement

Is appropriation simply another word for theft, as some suggest? At base, appropriation seems to involve a profound sense of entitlement on the part of the person or institution doing the appropriating, which behaves as if the desired objects or images *already* belong to it. This attitude parallels the imaginary relationship a person tends to have with any object of desire, but here the dynamic is extended to images and sensibilities that are part of, and already belong to, living cultural traditions. Appropriation reduces the living people and culture to the status of objects. If the person who is appropriating imagines that he or she already possesses whatever happens to catch the eye, then the source of all the fascination can have no say in the terms of the exchange. If we think we already own something, why would we ask anybody's permission to take it? Moreover, in places such as British Columbia these living cultures continue to be repressed by the same dominant elements that oversee and profit from the process of appropriation. The provincial government never seems to put the same amount of effort into, say, supporting the survival of Native languages that it does into promoting Native arts to tourists; rather, the government's approach is just a continuation of the colonial attitude in which artworks are coveted and praised at the expense of the people who make them.

The argument that appropriation is theft focuses on two points: one, that the people from whom the material is taken are not consulted about the appropriations (or that these consultations take place in a dishonest manner); and two, that the primary motivation for appropriation is financial, with few, if any benefits accruing to the creators of the material. The company manufacturing the thunderbird key ring neglects to ask permission from the Native community in question; this tends to be equally true of the white craftsperson making "authentic" medicine wheels or beaded earrings. (The latter seems particularly apt to cry reverse racism when the issue is raised.) Within many Native societies a variety of symbolic and aesthetic forms are subject to internal systems of copyright; for instance, in many cases only certain members of a clan have the right to use a design and then only at particular times. In these communities, as in any society, the wearing of symbolic regalia communicates very precise social information to other members of the society, and there are consequences to disrupting the system. Such internal conventions of use and copyright are generally ignored by the larger marketplace.

Because the people from whom the material is taken are not compensated, they by definition are treated as objectified, passive sources of inspiration rather than participants in an exchange of ideas. This practice has several unpleasant implications. For instance, a white town councilwoman who selects a Haida design for a municipal seal is at some level treating Native cultures as if they were dead because if she imagined a living people, she would consult them and respect internal conventions of ownership and copyright. Despite the councilwoman's presumed admiration for the design, her willingness to view it as available to be used at will is another manifestation of the colonial relationship, which all the art appreciation in the world cannot shift by itself. Is the incorporation of a Haida design into a municipal seal really a way of demonstrating British settlers' colonial domination of the Haida nation? Whether intended or not, this is how such images function; they both reflect and produce colonial space.

Salvaging Culture

Within a capitalist economy culture—by which I mean songs, stories, images, emblems, ceremonies, techniques—has been inserted into a system of exchange in which any element can be abstracted from its social and ceremonial context and assigned a monetary value. Because cultural material sells, more and more cultures and components of cultures enter the marketplace as commodities. Indeed, culture itself has become a commodity, provided it can be marketed as authentic and hence interesting (and it can sell even when it is inauthentic). Until fairly recently racist fantasies of cultural superiority kept African or Native cultural and aesthetic forms from having a mass audience in the West, especially among those who imagined European high culture to be more sophisticated or interesting than the arts of other peoples. (A quick glance at the curricula of most art history departments, at least in Canada, makes it abundantly clear that this historical prejudice has yet to be laid to rest.) The non-Western art that did get taken up tended to be framed within an explicit colonial narrative. For instance, classical Mayan sculpture was carefully situated within a rhetoric of discovery in which the archaeologist figured as the heroic explorer, if not a new, improved conquistador. But today as many in the dominant culture are increasingly uneasy about the emptiness and commodification of mainstream, "white-bread" culture, there are attempts to look elsewhere for meaning and cultural and aesthetic integrity—hence the interest in other cultural, aesthetic, and spiritual traditions.

This interest has two main problems. Art appreciation does not take place in a purely aesthetic, apolitical space, regardless of what we have been taught, and the process of appropriation tends to displace the local social, ceremonial, and political contexts of the cultural forms being appropriated. The availability of the arts of another culture in the West means that somebody—entrepreneur, collector, academic specialist—has decided that these forms should be available to Western consumers. In this sense the aesthetic forms have been captured by the market in advance of their availability to a mass audience, which means that potential consumers will tend to see the commodified versions of the culture first (this tends to be true of

most new aesthetic fashions as well). Consumers may imagine that the representation they encounter is all there is to the cultural tradition in question and reject other versions as inauthentic. Because value has been determined in advance, cultural phenomena enter the market in a preassigned manner, and the presence of non-Western aesthetic forms in the larger marketplace rarely calls the premises of the Western market economy into question. (This occurs despite the ability of some cultural paraphernalia to stand for alternative values. Even good political intentions do not necessarily preclude appropriation. London-based Survival International markets both a traditional design and the proper name *Yanomami* on the T-shirts worn by two white models [see Figure 3.3].) Wealthy collectors of so-called tribal art may decide to appropriate a particular tradition and insert it into a system of capitalist exchange, but this practice can itself continue to reinforce the hegemony of Western art and the idea that art objects are dead commodities.

For instance, non-Native collectors can be interested in Northwest Coast art (or the arts of other Native traditions), but this interest can be underlain by the insidious salvage paradigm, which assumes that Native cultures are being overwhelmed by Western culture. In other words, the societies in which Northwest Coast art is produced are again treated as if they were dead. Marcia Crosby writes, "Predicated on the concept of a dead or dying people whose culture needs to be 'saved,' those doing the saving choose what fragments of a culture they will salvage. Having done this, they become both the owners and interpreters of the artifacts or goods that have survived from that dying culture, artifacts that become rare and therefore valuable."[4]

This notion of the supposedly inevitable disappearance of Native societies can affect not only how Native arts are taken up and interpreted but also how stylistic, symbolic, or cosmological elements from indigenous societies enter Western art. The attitude seems to be, if they are already dead, it does not matter what we do; if they are dying out, then we are doing them a favor. The salvage paradigm is extremely pervasive and apparently able to overdetermine historical and contemporary realities. For instance, in a critical article on contemporary German artist Lothar Baumgarten's use of the proper names of Native nations in his work *Feather People (The Americas)* (1968), Marie-Ange Brayer writes that the "language and cultures of these peoples only now survives in their names on our maps—names which are falsified on them."[5] Even if we leave aside the way terms such as *our* and *their* function to universalize one version of Western culture, Brayer seems to be informing the international art world that Native cultures are dead, that they "only survive" in Western texts such as maps. The names of the supposedly dead cultures that appear in *Feather People* include Cheyenne, Hopi, Navaho, Omaha, nations that are very much alive. There is no excuse for not knowing this, regardless of whether one is white or Native, North American or European. Brayer's secondary question of whether these proper names are in fact colonial designations (for instance, Sioux as opposed to Lakota) gets lost in the assumption of the disappearance of these nations.

The second problem with the fascination with other cultures concerns the refusal of many of the most cherished institutions of Western culture to come to terms with the continuing consequences of colonial histories, here with respect to the way they privilege and universalize particular approaches to reality. Ontological assumptions affect not only how other traditions are interpreted but also how questions of culture and national identity are approached in the society whose traditions are being appropriated. This is an extremely complicated and nuanced subject, but an immediate example of this problem might be the imposition of a linear notion of time on a story or poem that was conceived of as existing within a cyclical system. Many in the West assume that the linear approach is real (or in any case more real than the other) and hence real for everybody everywhere, but there are other approaches to the paradox of temporality.[6] Indeed, there is a faint memory of cyclic time in the disorienting quality of Christmas carols heard at other times of year.

The universalization of Western ontological notions can mean that the commodified version of the story will also be universalized and through marketing become more widely available than the version used in ceremony. In other words, the story is abstracted from the cyclical system of meaning (so someone can cash in, let us not forget). This wider availability of recorded versions means that the story or poem will be heard differently. Part of the problem of the transformation of tradition into commodity is the general problem of mechanical reproduction that so concerned Walter Benjamin in the 1930s. The recorded, commodified poem or song can be played at any time, again and again if the listener wishes, whereas the original was tied to a sacred cycle that had little to do with individualized desire. The recorded version can eventually usurp the local version of the song or poem not only among outsiders but also within the culture itself. Every mall has a music store. In other words, in this example the universalization of a Western view of time parallels the universalization of a market economy in which everything is for sale.

Advertising presents the world as a vast warehouse and seduces us with an abundance of choices. The myth of the free market produces a fictional equivalence between a plethora of cultures and cultural phenomena, an equivalence based on a notion of culture in which fragmentary elements float through time and space, available to all equally (at least in theory). Anything may potentially be commodified, but the extent to which the availability of the product is dependent on money is absent from this discourse of individual and individualized freedom.

Here is a squash blossom design from the Southwest, there is a Northwest Coast thunderbird, and there is an Anishnawbe petroglyph image; any would look good on a CD cover, to attract the eye and let the buyer know that there is something a bit different inside (even if this difference has nothing to do with Native people per se). The free market tells us that all we have to do is choose. But there is an asymmetric power relationship between a system that has billions of dollars behind it and one that does not and is being squeezed out both economically and culturally. It is not a question of give-and-take between equal partners but rather of the way money is able to promote and make available to consumers commodified versions of cultural phenomena. Appropriation—which is to say, commodification and use that overlook both the cultural context and the desires of the people of that culture—is generally possible only in an economic system that is more powerful than the one subject to appropriation. This economic power does not exist in an abstract universe but rather is based on guns, armies, and dead bodies. Rome appropriated the aesthetic codes and objects of Greece only after it had established military and economic hegemony in the area. French artists took up Orientalist themes en masse only after Algeria had been subdued, and Native people began to be romanticized by white Americans after the former had ceased to be viewed as a military threat.

The relative difference in economic power between the people whose culture is appropriated and the people doing the appropriating determines not only what is available in the marketplace but also how it is available. Southwestern style is extremely fashionable at the moment, and even in northern cities like Toronto this tendency is all too apparent in food, in the insipid pastels promoted by interior designers, and in the Old West–type clothing available in every department store. Some of the appeal of this style for those living in cities has to do with the way it references Native cultures and aesthetic conventions and suggests that authentic Native wisdom—which is part of the attraction of this aesthetic for white people—is simply a matter of selecting the right accessories. Obviously the commodification of Southwestern Native cultures involves varying degrees of appropriation, and because the vogue for this style is currently so widespread, these appropriations are able to evacuate questions of power. This is apparent in arguments that suggest that we take things from their culture and they take things from ours, with the we-they couplet always presented as perfectly exchangeable and based purely on personal choice, something that conceals both economic inequalities and the persistence of the salvage paradigm. But the fictional equivalence between cultures that has been created by the market and promulgated in advertising begins to break down when we consider it closely.

There is a difference between a marketing executive in New York, Los Angeles, or Toronto deciding to use a Navajo design as a theme for a restaurant chain and a Navajo man in Arizona deciding to buy, say, a new chair or a landscape painting for the living room. At some level of pure abstraction each is taking up something from the other culture and using it in "decor" (if, indeed, the objects of Western consumer culture can be thought of as culture at all, even as white culture). But these decisions and purchases occur within a nonabstract system of capitalist exchange in which aesthetic forms can be reduced to money. There is an obvious difference between contemporary consumer culture and traditional Native cultures in terms of which is most likely to decide the terms of the exchange, and neither the Navajo traditional aesthetic nor the American consumerist aesthetic is a pure category that exists in isolation from each other. But the executive is getting his ideas about traditional Navajo design forms from somewhere, probably a design manual issued by a large, non-Native-controlled publishing house. The Navajo householder is making his decisions about what to buy based on the choices available to most North Americans, Native and non-Native alike. His choices may derive from mixed sources, however: neighbors, catalogs, local stores. The point is that the version of Navajo culture available to the marketing executive is highly mediated by what is available in the larger, capitalist market, which is to say, determined by outsiders with little or no cultural investment in the

Navajo community. The version of white, mainstream culture available to the Navajo man is also adjudicated by the market, although his relation to commodity culture is mediated not only by the market but also by his everyday experiences in the community in which he lives.

As with exoticism, appropriation has to do with who decides what is interesting enough to commandeer and reproduce, usually someone from the more powerful group who is in a position to select and use whatever happens to catch her eye. When an outsider decides which aspects of a cultural and aesthetic tradition to take up and emphasize and which to ignore, these decisions may have nothing to do with the internal meanings of the dances, art forms, and ceremonies within the culture in which they were created. As with exoticism, fragments are taken up and manipulated, although there are some differences between appropriation and exoticism. Exoticism evokes a sensibility and uses objects to construct a conceptual line of escape out of Western culture into a titillating, yet manageable other. Appropriation incorporates the objects and sensibilities into the dominant, Western-based culture, sometimes by domesticating and sometimes by erasing the origins of these objects. Although exoticism does the same and to some extent exoticism and appropriation are overlapping concepts, with appropriation it is the taking up that is important.

Authenticity and Cultural Integrity

Authenticity is a tricky concept because of the way the term can be manipulated and used to convince people they are getting something profound and substantial when they are just getting merchandise. A marketing expert has decided in advance which variant of difference will sell best and has attempted to promote this version as the most real and desirable. From the spectator of the museum display believing that she is gaining an understanding of the real Indian, to the urban restaurant-goer in Toronto who seeks real New Mexican dishes, to the tourist who longs to see the real Egypt (properly sanitized, of course), authenticity is the currency at play in the marketplace of cultural difference.

Authenticity functions as an ideal, both for the people trying to sell commodified versions of culture and for many of those who have taken on the project of criticizing consumer culture. But authenticity does not exist in any absolute, pure form outside the endless debates of academics. No cultural practice is or ever has been totally authentic, fully and seamlessly inserted into a social context in such a way that permits the experience of perfect presence. But the fact that things can be made to look this way is not without interest. This *appearance* of seamlessness itself has a pacifying effect and with a conceptual trompe l'oeil effect can decoy attention away from the margins that do exist, something that Louis Althusser recognizes so well in his work on ideology. A cynical approach to culture insists on the collapse of any possibility of cultural or social integrity, which is to say, of cultural practices having meaning in their original contexts, in a living social matrix connected to the people around, rather than the marketed versions experienced by the tourist or consumer. In a cynical world there is only the mall.

But this commodification of authenticity raises another problem. Any notion of cultural authenticity carries with it a notion of inauthenticity, against which the former is evaluated. This distinction seems somewhat artificial, and it is neither possible nor particularly desirable to draw a clear line between the real and the counterfeit in order to decide which aspect of culture is authentic and which is not.[7] Any clear demarcation between the two categories that is decided in advance would have to be based on a universalized—which in this day and age means market-driven—notion of what traditional looks like. It would also presuppose the existence of someone doing the deciding, who presumably is able to stand above the action and choose the good, someone who is likely to be our old friend, the Western subject.

An abstract notion of authenticity can be used as a political tool to legitimize or delegitimize actual people and communities. This is especially obvious when the term is deployed against people who are seen as a source of exotic, authentic, and highly marketable images, yet who also occupy resource-rich land coveted by governments and resource companies. In a recent land rights trial in British Columbia the question of cultural authenticity revealed the extent to which the discussion takes place within a colonial context, with colonial-style authorities continuing to reserve the right to designate a people as authentic or not. Marcia Crosby writes:

> In 1989, government lawyers, in disputing Gitksan-Wet'suwet'en land claims, attempted to establish that Indians who eat pizza, drive cars and watch television—that is, who no longer live as "traditional" Indians residing in some timeless place—did not meet Eurocentrically established criteria for authenticity under which, the courts assert, Indian "rights" were established.[8]

The term *authenticity,* then, becomes a definition imposed from the outside on a living culture so that the community will never be able to live up to the way it has been defined. Deploying a notion of authenticity gives a twentieth-century colonist an appearance of liberality that overt self-interest cannot. The colonist says sadly, "Gee, we really *would* support your claim if only you were authentic, but unfortunately . . ." The motives for this deployment are clear when we bear in mind the agenda of those evoking authenticity in this particular context. Colonial wars are always propaganda wars. The provincial government's logic seems to be that if a particular community is deemed inauthentic, it can then be stripped of treaty privileges and treated like everyone else, which is to say, as if it has no right to exist on its own terms.

In the marketplace authenticity is no more than a merchandising device. I prefer to use the more flexible idea of cultural integrity to refer to autochthonous cultural traditions and to the possibility of aesthetic, social, and ceremonial meanings able to exist outside of the system of capitalist exchange, at least for the most part. Integrity retains an idea of cultural wholeness and of a relatively unbroken connection between the image or object and the culture in which it is made and used. A visitor to Victoria might purchase a Kwagiutl button blanket and hang it on the wall. The same blanket could also be draped around a dancer during a potlatch. Whereas authenticity is dependent on the external form of the object, integrity takes into account how and where the object is used. In other words, I am using the word *integrity* to suggest connection to a social and ceremonial matrix. Certain objects are more connected to their cultural source than others, precisely because of how they are used and the contexts in which they occur. But herein lies a paradox because the appropriated forms of culture tend to be marketed as authentic, which can cause confusion even in the minds of the well-intended.

Questions of cultural authenticity and integrity can become very complicated because any cultural object or practice can still manifest integrity among the people who respect and treat it as such, even if aspects of the form or practice have been appropriated and inserted into a market economy. Someone belonging to the killer whale clan might purchase a $2, mass produced key chain with a killer whale emblem on it and carry it precisely because it is traditional, which in this context is to say that the design is executed in a traditional style that refers to a traditional clan structure. The clan member has a personal connection to the object. Correct ideas do come from practice, as someone once noted, and there is never a nice sharp line between unequivocally authentic culture and market-driven, commercialized culture. Powwows, which can be quite culturally mixed and even play with notions of authenticity, are another case in point because at some profound level culture—whether traditional, contemporary, or mixed—often has very little to do with the market, despite the hopes and dreams of eager MBAs.

Appropriation, like exoticism, is dependent on a rhetoric of origins. This can generate anxiety on the part of the consumer about whether an object or event is authentic, and this anxiety is especially common among collectors of ceremonial items. For instance, I recall visiting a collector of African art who made a point of announcing proudly that his masks "had been danced." For this collector, the authenticity and value of the object were precisely dependent on its having been removed from its formerly meaningful social context. The obvious question was, "If people were using the mask, why do *you* have it?" But this was already framed as irrelevant and, perhaps worse, impolite, which means that there was no preexisting place in the discourse of art appreciation for such questions to be raised. Christopher Steiner makes the point that worries about ceremonial authenticity on the part of collectors of West African art have led to elaborate definitions and subdefinitions of authenticity that circulate in this market and are skillfully manipulated by African art producers and merchants.[9]

The point of owning a ceremonial object seems to be to display ownership or, more precisely, to display the ability to possess something of value to someone else. It is as if the collector imagines himself to have usurped the mask's cultural integrity, which was formerly dependent on the community in which it was danced. That the object is valuable to someone else is precisely what makes it valuable to the collector, who has at some level vanquished the previous owners through the possession and display of the object or, rather, the display of power.

Collectors are much like the tourists who want to experience an authentic ceremony and feel cheated by a noticeably inauthentic event or performance. Consumers want their purchases to be authentic, and tourists want their experiences to be real, even though at some level it must be clear to all concerned that this is not the case, that a genuine, pristine, authentic tradition is an impossible dream in a market driven by capital (if indeed authenticity was ever possible in any society). At some level they must know that precisely because they are in a position to witness the event or purchase the object, it has lost some of its spiritual efficacy. Because of this subterranean comprehension of what appropriation involves, such consumers find the explicit recognition of both the impossibility of authenticity and the unequal power relation inherent in the exchange too unpleasant and go to a great deal of trouble to ensure that the question never comes up. A bargain is struck; a pact of silence is enforced. The organizers of tourist events, much as the carvers of masks for the tourist market, take pains to assure their customers that they will achieve a glimpse, an almost-memory, of traditional, non-market-driven culture. This is why the marketed version of culture explicitly refers to the uncommodified version through a rhetoric of authenticity.

There remains another question: What are the effects of appropriation in the Western culture of the mainstream, which is to say, on the people who haunt the shopping malls and tourist agencies and long for sanitized but believable authenticity? A definitive, programmatic answer may be impossible, but it is important to pay attention to the oddities that lie beneath different kinds of appropriation and to what these say about the culture in which appropriation occurs.

Deterritorialization and Recoding: National Agendas

One of the most immediately obvious forms of appropriation occurs within the tourist industry, and for this reason tourism can clarify some of the processes involved in the taking up and commodification of another culture. As in British Columbia, the tourist industry sells images of the past and images of difference but manipulates these to make cultural difference seem both nonthreatening and available for consumption by whomever finds it interesting. In doing so, the industry creates a space when the tourist is able and encouraged to suspend judgment about what he or she is seeing. For example, an ad for New Mexico (see Figure 3.4) evokes cultural difference but immediately renders it benign—what is more felicitous than a rainbow? The ad certainly does not talk about pueblos being closed to outsiders because of mobs of photo-happy tourists disrupting ceremonial dances.

The tourist industry not only attempts to promote an unlikely equivalence between the past and the present but also engineers particular kinds of folkloric experiences as a way of drawing tourist dollars. These often seem to take the form of dance, probably because such extravaganzas focus on the exotically costumed, different-looking bodies that have always been of interest to colonists. Tourists often claim that folkloric dance evenings are the high point of the trip, but I have never really understood the language of dance. Classical dance forms leave me cold, and folk dancing has always seemed to me a pointless and exhausting activity. Whenever I am traveling in a foreign country and stupidly get roped into some tourist event in which "folk" dancers appear, I experience profound dismay. It is not a question of actually disliking the dancers but of suspending disbelief long enough to imagine I am at a village wedding or other event. I think one reason cultural events such as national dance are sometimes unable to work is because of the way they have been taken up and used to serve a greater, national interest such as tourism.

Here is an example of the way the tourist experience collapses questions of verisimilitude. At Aswan in southern Egypt, actually Nubia, the air is perfect and crisp, the Nile glitters in the sun, hotels crowd the shores. There are islands in the river across from the main part of town, and on one a luxury hotel shares space with a Nubian village. Between the two sites there are a wall and a round-the-clock guard with a machine gun. This sight was a bit unnerving because in the early 1980s when I visited Aswan, tourists were not at risk from the legendary gun-toting Muslims of Western nightmares. Unlike many other tourist destinations, Egypt has never been a particularly crime-ridden or dangerous place. The guard existed primarily as a spectacle for the wealthy tourists, his presence no more than a display of

In New Mexico, rainbows aren't just in the sky.
NEW MEXICO

FIGURE 3.4 New Mexico tourism advertisement

the idea of security and of the putative value of the foreign tourist. Undignified and the source of ill-will in the local community, yes, but the Egyptian government wanted the hard currency brought in by tourists. There were many alternatives to the colonial exhibition at the Hotel Oberoi, which means that those who stayed there did so because they liked the atmosphere of the place.

As a resort town Aswan sought to entertain tourists by mounting folkloric events such as Nubian dance. Assured by all that this was an event not to be missed, I attended. The circle dances and songs flow together at this distance, but one scene has remained with me: the identically costumed dancers pretending to be drawing water from a village well. They teasingly splashed each other, intended (I suppose) to add charm to the scene as a way of lending veracity to the display of village life. It was all very irritating. Nobody in real life wears identical costumes, so why were they part of the dance? More important, however, the dancers were going beyond folk dance in order to construct a simulacrum of village life, complete with nonexistent water from a nonexistent well, a village life that was under pressure from both the tourist presence and foreign agricultural concerns. My mind kept drifting back to the other display that had been mounted for the tourists—the guard and his gun—and to the extent to which that exhibition was connected to the smiling dancers. Certainly both produced a fiction of contemporary life, one a fictional danger, the other a fictional present in which traditional ways of life were able to continue. How many spectators even noticed that on Elephantine Island the residents were kept at bay with M-16s and were consequently angry and hostile to tourists?

The Nubian dance evening not only entertained at least some tourists with its vision of happy villagers, but it also exemplified the displacement of these same villagers, a situation not entirely separate from the presence of the tourists at the dance event. The tourist evening both occluded and bore witness to the massive shifts in the traditional relationship between city and countryside, the shifts in population in which economics forced villagers to move to Cairo slums, and the changes in the meanings assigned to the traditional cultural and aesthetic forms of these villagers.

In the first volume of *Anti-Oedipus* Gilles Deleuze and Felix Guattari identify a process whereby a particular cultural practice can be detached from its original context and subsequently assigned a new meaning. Taking an imaginary folk dance as an example, we can see that the external form of the dance can remain the same, but the reasons for performing it have changed. To deterritorialize a traditional dance is to remove it from its social and ceremonial matrix, which initially can liberate the practice because it is no longer subject to a system of religious or social authority. People can dance whenever they want. Recoding occurs when a new system of meaning is attached to the newly free cultural form or practice and it becomes subject to that system of meaning. Today the main systems of meaning in culture tend to be organized around money, so we can say that the dance has been recoded by capital. For instance, the folk dance can be taken out of a community—which is to say, detached from its local social and religious context—and performed in a capital city for tourists. Festival clothes become costumes (which are usually standardized, as was the case in Aswan), a living cultural practice is subsumed under an abstract notion of folklore, and the performance of the dance is inserted into a new system of exchange dependent on cash payment. The original meaning is decoded or deterritorialized (we can imagine the sense in which this means "removed from its territory") and quickly recoded as something else, according to a new system of meaning determined by outsiders with different values and agendas.

So whereas the local meaning of a dance might have to do with, say, the harvest, which means that the activity is coded through the seasonal cycle, the tourist meaning has to do with the exchange of money. Here the activity is coded through the market economy and a concept of national identity, as defined by the national tourist office. As such, the activity becomes something moribund: It cannot change.

Deleuze and Guattari's formulation of deterritorialization and recoding makes it possible to focus on the affinities between the traditional form of the folk dance (traditional in the sense that the dance is performed primarily for reasons internal to the community) and the capitalist form organized in the cities. What this focus reveals is the way financial considerations are able to link development and aesthetics. The connection between capital and traditional culture, and between the traditional form and the commodified form of culture, is extremely important to the problem of appropriation because the explicit referencing of a traditional system of meaning is the reason cultural difference sells. The original, culturally situated *form* of the commodity is retained, at least enough so that the consumer is able to recognize it as being, in some respects at least, traditional, yet these forms are assigned a new meaning by the larger market, a process that itself elides the specific social and historical context in which all this buying and selling are taking place. The Nubian dance I witnessed in a tourist setting bears some relation to the dance performed in Nubian communities, for and by the people concerned, within a local context.

Yet the links between the local cultures and the quickly recognized, commodified signs of those cultures become increasingly tenuous as difference is marketed in more and more venues. What relation do the vaguely African bed linen designs I see at the department store have to the specificity of the societies in which the designs originated? And how many steps did the design go through before it appeared on sheets the North American consumer could recognize as exotic?

Interestingly, because the recoded, commodified version of traditional arts retains the external look of the original, and in fact explicitly refers to ways of life presented as existing outside of the market, the illusion of seamlessness sometimes breaks down, and tourists occasionally do get a glimpse of something real. Consumers are able momentarily to imagine that the world is not uniform and market driven. Culture turns out not to be completely dead after all, which rather paradoxically means that tourists think they do not have to think about, say, International Monetary Fund policies in the countries they are visiting or their own pointless job back home (some obviously do think about such things and occasionally even transform their lives accordingly). Yet it is this possibility of exteriority that keeps tourists coming back, through all the commercialization of culture inherent in the tourist industry, because vacations are one context in which cultural margins are apparent to people who might never notice that they also exist at home. So this same desire for an outside is also what keeps tourists inserted in a commodified relationship with the cultures they visit, a relationship in which meaning tends to occur primarily through appropriation. Happy tourists laughingly attempt to dance the hula in Hawaii; they could perform this dance at home but are much less likely to do so because it is difference that frees them from ordinary constraints. All this is aside from what indigenous Hawaiians might think of the matter.[10]

The transformation of foods, dances, clothing, art styles, and ceremonies into easily assimilated commodities whose primary function is to be consumed by Westerners (or other urbanized people) is only one consequence of the deterritorialization and recoding of culture. Perhaps even more important is the way the *process* of deterritorialization and recoding makes the marketing of culture seem perfectly natural, part of an absolutely seamless operation that recognizes no disruptions. If nothing exists outside of the market, then cultural identity can come down only to a choice between products, and communication between people of different cultures can come down only to a relationship of buying and selling. If everything is a commodity, if all aspects of culture can be exchanged for money or for another aspect of culture, then culture loses its meaning. The end result of this kind of thinking is that culture can no longer be imagined as something that could exist outside of the marketplace. The only choice—and the only way to survive in such a system—is to adopt the cynicism of the marketing executive. As the New World Order makes it increasingly difficult for land-based cultures to thrive outside of the market, many recognize, sometimes almost unconsciously, that we have all lost something.

The apparent seamlessness between culture and the marketplace means that anything can come under the purview of capital. A bank in Tucson attracts tourist business by offering customers free prints of certain kachina spirits. The kachinas periodically visit this world to instruct the people of the pueblos. What are kachinas to white people? Do we really want to be inserted into a commodified relationship with another people's spirits? Are we so certain that these matters are without spiritual consequences to both the people of the pueblos and the outsiders doing the appropriating? The bank seems to be associating itself with difference and drawing on the authenticity associated with Native cultures by many non-Natives; perhaps it is also attempting to suggest that this bank is protected by the spirits, that it is somehow carrying on the many-thousand-year-old tradition of that land. With the equivalence between the spirits and the financial institutions, we see the perfect marriage of capital and commodified tradition, here in the form of the notoriously corrupt Arizona banking system. Arizona also promotes cowboys as part of its regional character, and everywhere in this state cowboy impedimenta, images of broncos, and the like are for sale. With this sort of appropriation there is a further equivalence produced, this time between cowboys and Indians, with the latter set in a colorful, ahistorical, and apolitical past, one in which white settlers and Native people are strangely separate from each other. For the tourist in Arizona, the two never met and never fought for territory on the land currently occupied by Americans. Just because commodification of culture occurs, and just because the banks market kachina spirits, does not mean that the spirits are not real.

The New Age: Appropriating the Spirit

What precisely is the New Age? The term seems to have many meanings and is able to encompass a vast smorgasbord of interests, from crystal power, to the channeling of ancient extraterrestrials, to a revival in goddess worship. The version of the New Age in which I am interested here explicitly takes up the trappings of Native spiritual philosophies and the ceremonies and regalia that go along with these, but the different variants of the movement tend to share certain characteristics. The New Age generally involves a rejection of middle-class Christianity and mainstream, middle-class culture but in many respects tends to be a middle-class phenomenon. Indeed, the New Age genealogically follows the line from the 1960s and 1970s and the interest in Eastern religion and suppressed Western traditions such as Tarot cards and astrology.

Although much of the New Age movement seems almost deliberately to leave itself open to ridicule, it is not necessarily all bad and is in some ways preferable to the harshly scientistic rationality it seeks to challenge. It is too easy to make fun of the wide-eyed gullibility of anxious suburbanites as a way of avoiding paying attention to what they are so anxious about. That said, the New Age qua social movement does have some serious problems, which I suspect will ultimately bring it down and send it the way of all the maharishis of the 1960s. Generally speaking, the New Age movement has a blind spot about money, and people involved in these practices tend to see no problem with buying and selling spirituality. This may make life easier for the would-be shaman, but not everyone can afford $335 for a Kilaut drum from Maryland, advertised as the "only source" for such an item (see Figure 3.5). Lady Poverty has been abandoned at last by the mystics of the West, and in the New Age we are continually reassured that we can be both rich and virtuous, despite murmurings about the need to "simplify" our lives. The world of the New Age is generally pretty fancy, which seems to be a relief to many of its adherents. (This trend, too, follows a direct line from such 1970s gurus as Baghwan Rajneesh, whose Pacific Northwest ranch boasted a designer clothing boutique.)

Part of the emphasis on money has to do with the venality of New Age entrepreneurs, part with the need for people engaged in spiritual practices to find alternative ways to make a living, and part with the permeation of people's consciousness by mainstream notions of private property and value to such an extent that they can scarcely conceive of another way of doing things. How far does this commercialism go? It seems like almost anything can be made attractive to potential consumers and marketed, particularly if given a spiritual twist.

A few years ago I saw a show on Home Box Office when I was flipping through channels at a U.S. motel. The program concerned the "personal growth" industry and approvingly depicted the antics of a so-called Cherokee sex workshop. In the bit I saw several white couples were instructed to lie down on the ground, bounce up and down, and moan rhythmically. Sex with mother earth, I quickly ascertained. The workshop was led by an extremely confident, beaded, and befeathered white man and assisted by his silent wife, who might have been Native and, to my eye at least, looked rather embarrassed by the whole exhibition. The couples all seemed to be in their midthirties or so and to be more or less prosperous middle class, with an aura of the more intellectual professions clinging to them. They had all paid good money to locate something they felt was wanting in their lives; or rather, they were willing to pay to have their (presumably lackluster) sexuality officially renamed "Cherokee." They believed this would liberate them.

But what precisely made the experience Cherokee, or, to put the matter more accurately, what made it possible for the proper name *Cherokee* to be attached to these activities or indeed to sex? For one thing, the appellation derived solely from the authority of the workshop leader. The leader informed the participants that his particular approach to sexual liberation was in fact *Cherokee* and, in a surprisingly orthodox pedagogical technique, used a blackboard to draw diagrams that purported to explicate the Native attitude toward sexuality. Not unexpectedly, the participants were

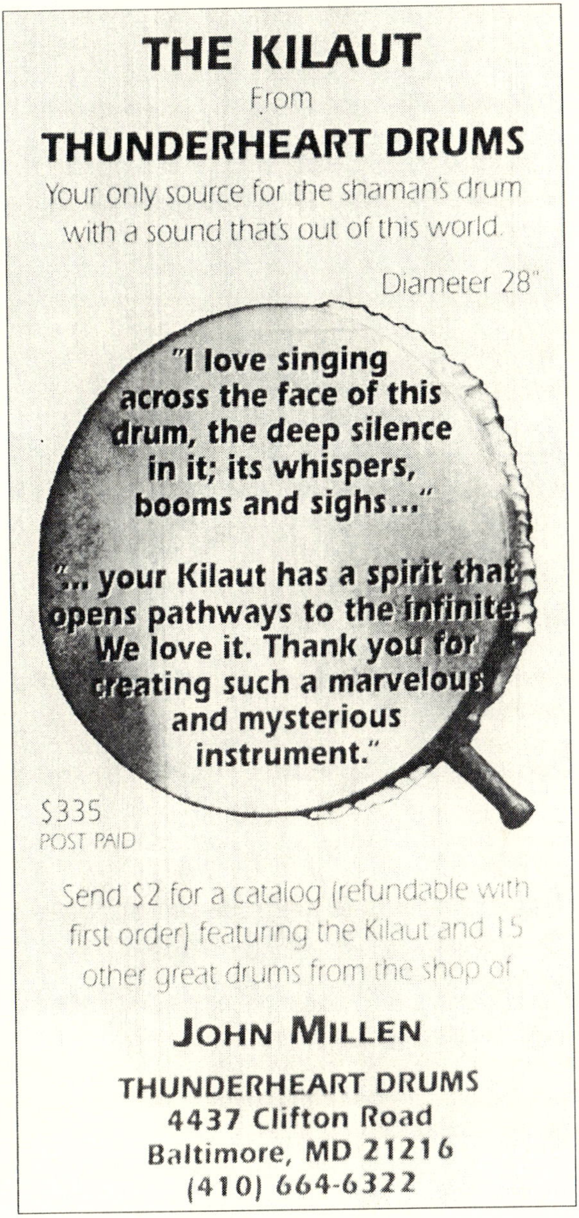

FIGURE 3.5 Thunderheart drums advertisement

informed that for Native people (who seemed to be imagined as a single, ahistorical entity), sex is considered natural. This was what they came to the workshop to hear. Then the organizer used objects associated with Native cultures, specifically smudge sticks and drums, to get the participants in the mood (not an easy task, I would think, with cameras rolling and several other couples making the same noises. I imagine internal dialogue: "Do my noises sound authentic and/or enthusiastic enough?"). A smudge stick is a bundle of sacred medicine plants that is burned at certain times to release the purifying, cleansing, or protecting smoke contained in the plants. People smudge or wash with the smoke before they go into ceremony, and sacred objects are usually smudged before they are used. I have never actually heard of people smudging to have sex, although I suppose there are situations in which this might be possible.

Switching off the television left me with a multitude of questions. What was going on here? Why would middle-class white people want or need something to be called Native for them to experience emotional or sexual feeling? Why did sex have to be coded as spiritual to legitimate desire? How could drums and aromatic smoke heighten erotic experience and the perception that this experience was in fact authentic, both authentic in regard to the Cherokee and authentic with respect to personal life? What did participants imagine they were receiving for their $300 workshop fee? The logic was circular as well as being filtered through several hundred years of colonialist propaganda: Native people are somehow associated with both the wilderness and wisdom; hence they are natural. Presumably Native people have sex; consequently "Native" sex must be natural (and, the participants hoped, wild) as well. Because natural here meant without social or familial restraints, the workshop participants imagined that they could now release all their sexual anxieties and do whatever they wanted: Their desire was legitimized by naming it Native, hence natural and in some profound way authentic as well. The notion that natural somehow implied an individualized freedom devoid of community demands was elided by the circularity of the logic.

The New Age was commodified almost before it was born, as the true lesson of the 1960s demonstrated that alternative lifestyles could be marketed and make resourceful people a lot of money. It took Clairol a while to catch on to the potential embodied in Herbal Essence shampoo, but today the marketing of the natural and authentic is taken for granted. It is perhaps too easy to imagine that the New Age was dreamed up by marketing executives who were determined not to be left in the dust this time around. But now it goes beyond mere commodities, and the emporiums of the New Age sell not only objects such as drums and feathers but also entire experiences such as sweat lodge ceremonies.[11] An ad for portable sweat lodges (complete with 800 number; see Figure 3.6) emphasizes convenience

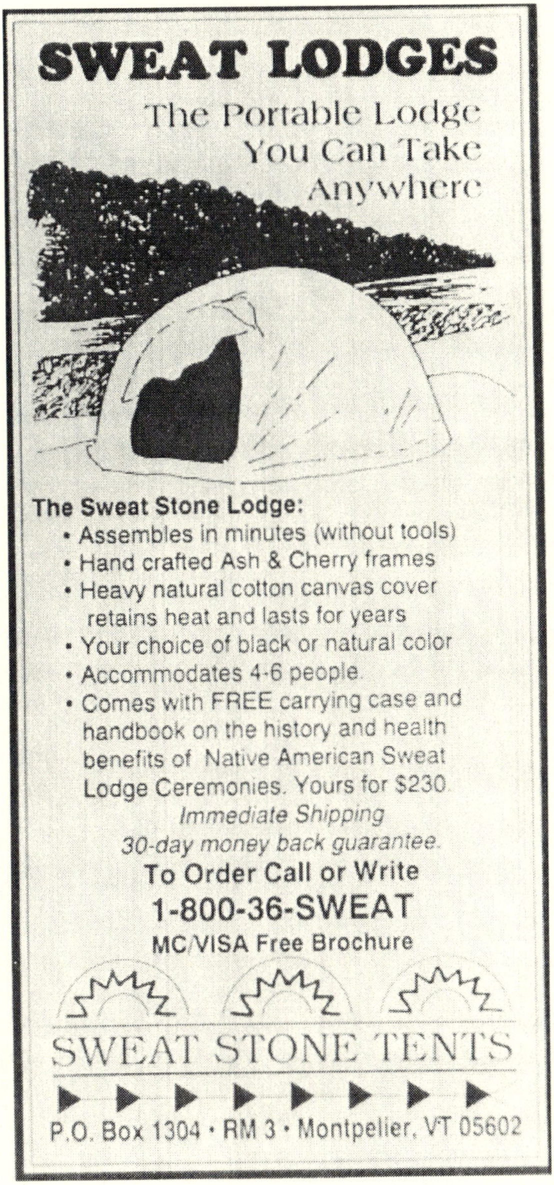
SWEAT LODGES
The Portable Lodge
You Can Take
Anywhere
The Sweat Stone Lodge:
• Assembles in minutes (without tools)
• Hand crafted Ash & Cherry frames
• Heavy natural cotton canvas cover retains heat and lasts for years
• Your choice of black or natural color
• Accommodates 4-6 people.
• Comes with FREE carrying case and handbook on the history and health benefits of Native American Sweat Lodge Ceremonies. Yours for $230.
Immediate Shipping
30-day money back guarantee.
To Order Call or Write
1-800-36-SWEAT
MC/VISA Free Brochure
SWEAT STONE TENTS
P.O. Box 1304 • RM 3 • Montpelier, VT 05602

and includes a free handbook—this is not just a tent but a ceremony, one that consumers can undertake "anywhere." Because at some level the New Age exists precisely to be commodified, spirituality appears first and most intensely in places where elaborate consumption machines are already firmly entrenched. Appalachia might have the snake-handling Holy Ghost people, the Midwest might have various mystical Anabaptist communities, but the New Age proper never comes out of places like these because they are not beautiful or sublime enough or beautiful in ways that can be quickly recognized by people living in cities. New Age people always seem to be glossy and expensively dressed in soothing pastels, and somehow West Virginia cannot be thought of as glossy. I always imagine New Age people to be Californian, or at least occupying a California of the mind, which quickly becomes a nightmarish vision of wealthy suburban shamans performing ceremonies in the nude, or worse.

This, in my stereotypical fantasy, means that the vast majority of New Age people have been so brainwashed by a constant barrage of television and giant shopping malls that they do not believe something is worth paying attention to unless it is tarted up to look like the television version. They expect medicine women to look like the medicine women they grew up seeing on their screen; hence in the advertisements in expensively produced New Age magazines such as *Shaman's Drum* the white women who claim to be medicine women are all dolled up like slightly garish nineteenth-century Indians (think of the costumes in the film *A Man Called Horse* [1970]). The healer-for-hire Oh Shinnah looks very, very wise in her braids and feathers, with a suitably grave, yet compassionate look on her face captured nicely by the camera. I assume that the consumers of the spiritual service industry take their activities seriously (or at least seriously enough to pay money for their experiences), but do they really imagine that community-based medicine people would have any interest in advertising? Do they imagine that the spirits prefer glossy national magazines? There seems to be no end to the effects of television and the movies. The problem, of course, is that when New Age followers do happen to run across the real thing, they reject it because it is not always as immediately authentic looking as the simulacrum in which they have placed all their expectations (I suspect this was part of Artaud's problem). Perhaps this is the idea, after all: Real spiritual people are delegitimized (to some, at least) by the Hollywood versions created by the demands of capital.

Part of the reason New Age followers have turned to Native beliefs is the way Native people have come to stand for an abstract, stereotypical quality called spirituality, in which consumers imagine that they can know in advance what this spirituality would look like. This is the same process that has worked so well in the marketing of Native arts and crafts. This abstraction of spirituality makes it possible to treat spirituality as a commodity, and a prerequisite to buying and selling ceremonies is to name a spiritual tradition as such, abstract it from its social context, and conceptually situate it in the past. Aside from any of the internal meaning of beliefs and ceremonies, the inserting of spiritual practices into a capitalist market economy is profoundly alien to the way Native spirituality is traditionally practiced, and Native elders across nations are explicit on this point: The spirits and their ceremonies must not be bought and sold. A recipient of spiritual aid can give something to a healer (or indeed to anyone who provides help), but the medicine person does not generally ask for payment. If the practices are occurring within a community in which these conventions are understood, everyone involved knows what is expected, and the healer is properly taken care of.

As with the tourist industry in British Columbia, the existence of an a priori category of authentic Native spirituality attracts non-Natives and leads them to expect pearls of wisdom to drop from the mouths of each and every Native person they meet. For the white person, problems of judgment will definitely ensue if she or he assumes that every Native person is wise and everything he or she says is true. These levels of anticipation also make it possible for non-Native New Age followers to take up a disarticulated, fragmentary version of Native religion or culture, which is to say, an image that never engages with the actual people or communities and indeed has no real interest in doing so. In most cases the question never even comes up. When this unwillingness to deal with real people goes hand in hand with a notion of cultural authenticity based on nineteenth-century sartorial and discursive styles, we begin to see the reasons for the success of the befeathered bogus shamans advertising in magazines. Authenticity is not necessarily where people expect to find it and certainly does not always look as pure as they expect.

Exploitation of the public's fascination with spiritual matters can go to extreme lengths. In twists of bizarrely unpleasant reasoning Ken Carey, the white author of the New Age best-seller *The Return of the Bird Tribes,* suggests in an interview that computer-literate white people are the most appropriate heirs to Native spiritual traditions because the poverty of the reservations has "debased" the culture and made it unworthy of the spiritual traditions that have always been part of Native community life. He also insists that this Native-style spiritual enlightenment will take place in a technological utopia in which everyone will be extremely well educated and able to speak to each other via computer (assuming anyone would want to do so). I do not know why I should be surprised at both the effrontery and absolute stupidity of such notions, as this is not the first time people in the New Age movement have expressed distinctly colonialist sentiments. The idea that spiritual knowledge now belongs to any non-Native who happens to desire it is the new version of Manifest Destiny, with the belief that white people are entitled to possess territory now replaced by a belief that white people are entitled to possess any spiritual practice that happens to catch their fancy.

If people assume that spirituality is another commodity, it is also easy for them to imagine that they have the right to take whatever they please, that everything is somehow by definition available to them. If local people seek to put any limits on outsiders' participation as a way of protecting the ceremonies, many become bitterly angry and confused. This anger can live very close to the surface, to be called up and deployed when would-be consumers feel threatened.

A white man from Manhattan informs me in skewed and angry logic that Native people must be taught about spirituality by the whites who join their ceremonies; the Lakota people who will not allow him to participate in a Sun Dance ceremony are wrong, he says, because he knows more than they do. How can he be so sure? Well, he has read some books on Native religion, and most important from his point of view, he really wants his version of a non-Native role in ceremony to be true so that he can attend the Sun Dance. He also believes he has more knowledge than the elders because his is the universalized knowledge of mainstream culture; he views the local specificity of the ceremonies as a parochial limitation on his desire to participate. Again, personal freedom is held up as the greatest virtue, regardless of how it is conceived in other traditions and regardless of the consequences. Again, local is taken to mean narrow or worse, and, as Christianity would have it, a religion has legitimacy only if it can be universalized and open to all. If the frustrated Sun Dancer is any indication, it seems that many New Agers are prepared to go only so far in questioning the assumptions of their culture. Aside from the question of this New Yorker's cultural or ethnic identity as a white man, he seems unaware that part of the reason he has been barred from the ceremony may be that he is not ready to participate in such events, that his willingness to shoot his mouth off angrily may have something to do with spirituality.

Workshops that appropriate and market versions of what they call Native spirituality have been of increasing concern in the Native community. The Cherokee sex workshop seems especially bizarre because of the twist it puts on sexuality, but others offer to locate a person's power animal or transform him or her into a shaman. At a meeting held in Montana in 1980 the Traditional Elders' Circle passed a resolution that addressed the problem of spiritual appropriation and of what Wendy Rose calls "whiteshamanism" and Ward Churchill and others call "plastic medicine men." The text of this resolution, and of similar declarations, has been circulating in Native publications over the last several years and has also been published in magazines with a largely non-Native readership. The Elder's Circle directed the resolution toward those presumably ignorant non-Natives who imagine that they have every right to take part in a generalized Native spirituality, but the resolution focused on the people who make this possible by selling spirituality to the desperate and alienated:

> These individuals are gathering non-Indian people as followers who believe they are receiving instructions of the original people. We, the Elders and our representatives sitting in Council, give warning to these non-Indian followers that it is our understanding this is not a proper process, that the authority to carry these sacred objects [pipes, medicine plants, and other objects] is given by the people, and the purpose and procedure is specific to time and the needs of the people. The medicine people are chosen by the medicine and long instruction and discipline is necessary before ceremonies and healing can be done. These procedures are always in the Native tongue; there are no exceptions and profit is not the motivation. . . . We concern ourselves only with those people who use spiritual ceremonies with non-Indian people for profit.[12]

The elders are, I think, reminding both Native and non-Native readers that spirituality, and the particular ceremonial practices that go along with it, is embedded in the communities in which it occurs and indeed helps sustain the community as such. Ceremony has to be part of people's everyday lives and should be approached with respect at all times. Spiritual practices have real effects on the health of both communities and individuals and carry responsibilities that can be onerous at times. The text of the resolution repeats what the people who have paid attention to these matters have always said: When approaching the spirit world, we cannot be too quick or too eager. We should always be extremely careful of how we speak of spiritual matters. The bridge between the everyday world and the spirit world is fragile. To try constructing a fraudulent version of this bridge for personal gain is not only highly disrespectful to the cultural tradition in which the spirits exist but can also have grave consequences for all concerned. If ceremonies are real enough to play with, then they are real enough to treat with respect.

As with appropriation in the arts, respect for the proper way of attending to such matters continues to be a problem when spirituality enters the marketplace and when non-Natives decide to take up commodified forms of Native religion without recognizing the responsibilities involved. This lack of respect goes back, in part, to the question of universalized ontologies that I raised previously: All the mainstream institutions of Western culture—schools, churches, medical and scientific communities—insist that spirits do not really exist, that the effects of spirit activities are not real, which suggests they have no effects in the world. Others know differently. If we assume something is false, then there is no point in allowing it to affect our plans, hence the proliferation of plastic medicine people. And although there is a difference between the entrepreneur who makes money

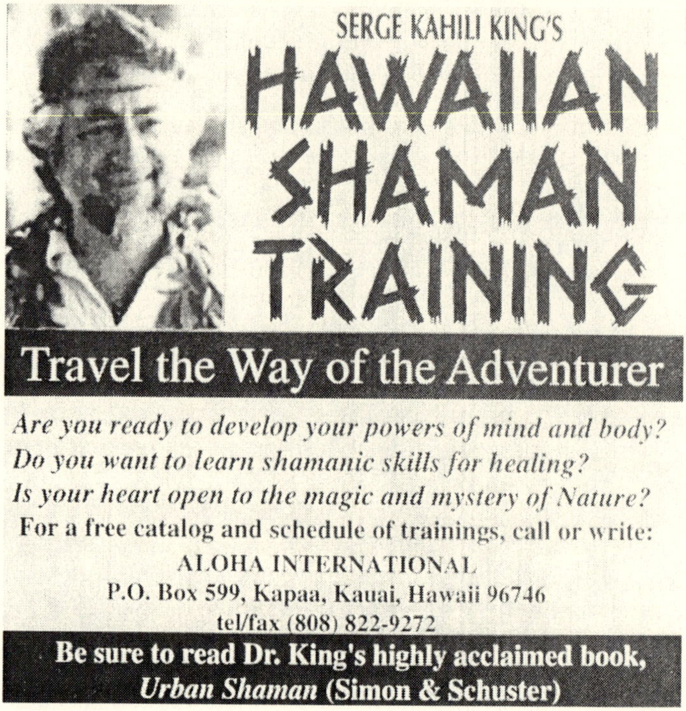

off these traditions and the confused but basically well-intentioned individual who attempts to put meaning into his or her life by any means necessary, both have done damage to the integrity of spiritual beliefs. An ad for Serge King's Hawaiian Shaman Training (see Figure 3.7) bears witness to this damage by presenting spirituality as a question of individualized desire and by reducing a complex cosmological system to a series of training seminars. Some people believe that the greatest threat facing Native survival today is the spiritual appropriation of the New Age movement because it saps and distorts the strength of the culture under siege.

New Age appropriation does seem to involve a kind of necrophilia. Like the manufacturer of souvenirs who summarily utilizes Native designs, the person who attempts to appropriate spirituality imagines Native cultures as something dead and gone. In this way the desire to appropriate and to usurp meaning from another cultural tradition is not just a romanticized nostalgia for supposedly dead cultures but can also be a way of marking death and conquest and doing so on the bodies and communities of living people. Even if New Agers wanted to do so, they would probably not have the same confidence to appropriate conventions from, say, the Catholic

Church because it is alive and well or at least alive enough to make its outrage felt. People apparently do desecrate the Mass from time to time, and this tends to be discussed hysterically on television talk shows as a resurgence of satanism and accompanied by elaborate discourses in which thousands of dead bodies are believed to be hidden, the so-called ritual abuse problem. When artist Andres Serrano suspends a crucifix in urine and calls it *Piss Christ,* a scandal ensues and the National Endowment for the Arts becomes involved. At least people think the issue is important enough to argue over, even if most of the discussion is uninterestingly polarized between Christian fundamentalists and New York artists. When non-Native artists use images from Native spirituality in their work, there either tends to be profound silence in the art world or fancy abstract talk about freedom of the imagination.

Desperate People: Honky Shamans and Wannabe Indians

Some Native elders have explained that spiritual appropriation is a function of the cultural and spiritual dislocation experienced by so many non-Natives and indeed by anyone who has been raised exclusively within contemporary society. There do seem to be a lot of tense, unhappy people in North America today. People no longer know who they are in the sense of being able to imagine a connection to a historical, cultural, and ceremonial past from which they can derive strength and meaning. Because individualized conceptions of the self suggest that this connection is limiting and oppressive, people become confused and can imagine only greater individualism as the solution. What Deleuze and Guattari describe as deterritorialization has left people vulnerable to recoding by capital, which rushes in quickly to fill the void. Traditional spiritual people have described those likely to turn to the New Age as lost people who float through the cultural matrix without feeling like they belong to it and who moreover are used to being able to buy anything they want or need. A consequence is that such people find it difficult to imagine a world that does not work like this, in which culture or ceremony is not subject to exchange value. Because so many people have been taught that the world is a giant warehouse in which everything is or ought to be available, they too easily believe they can achieve enlightenment by paying money. Anything can be bought and sold. When this proves not to be the case, as it inevitably does, people become even more hopeless and cynical.

Although profit seems to be the primary motive of the leaders of bogus spiritual organizations, the motives of the participants are a bit different.

The desperation of non-Natives for something they imagine will reconnect them to a system of meaning has been recognized by many Native people. In *The Almanac of the Dead* Leslie Marmon Silko describes a New Age healing conference in Tucson, Arizona:

> Lecha watched for awhile; she had watched the hands. The hands had gripped the cash feverishly as they waited for their turn; old Yoeme used to brag that she could make white people believe in anything and do anything she told them because they were so desperate. Money was changing hands rapidly; fifties and hundreds seemed to drop effortlessly from the white hands into the brown and black hands.[13]

Silko is focusing on the desperation of the conference-goers, which has reached a new threshold as the environment continues to break down and people find it increasingly difficult to envisage a future. Many non-Native people do long for an alternative to the overdetermined, artificial world of the mall but cannot seem to imagine that exchange could take place outside of the consumption of commodities in a system regulated by capitalist exchange. Many Native people, particularly those who live close to the land, do pay more attention to spiritual matters than suburban white people, but that is not really the point. The issue here is the way the fears and desires of the followers of the New Age overdetermine all other considerations and incite them to move so fast that they will never find what they are looking for.

The feelings of dread and alienation that provoke the willingness of New Agers to take on and make their own the trappings of another culture are not altogether unfamiliar territory if we think back twenty-five years or so. The general cultural climate has shifted considerably since those days (the dread has, if anything, increased), but paying some attention to how Native culture functioned as a symbol of authenticity in the 1960s can perhaps throw light on similar functions in the more capitalistic world of the New Age.

I think most people who actually remember the infamous 1960s also remember when a fantasy of Native people functioned for many young white people as a metaphor for the rejection of mainstream, bourgeois white society. Native culture or, more properly, the bogus version of Native culture that existed in the white imagination came to stand for this resistance. Many of us (and I have to include my adolescent self) appropriated the most superficial and hackneyed marks of this romance—beads, feathers, fringe—as a means of displaying our opposition to our own cultural background and the flatness and airless neighborhoods of suburbia.

It is almost impossible to look back now and imagine what we supposed Native culture to be or indeed if we imagined anything beyond the beads and feathers. Our concerns at the time for the most part had to do with political and social tensions within white society rather than with Native people. It seems obvious now that the images of Native people we mined for our countercultural costumes came directly from television and the movies, hardly sources outside the mainstream bourgeois culture we set ourselves against. And despite the flurry of shows in the early 1970s that seemed at first glance to represent Native people in a "positive" light (*Little Big Man* [1970], *Soldier Blue* [1970], the *Star Trek* episode where Captain Kirk marries an "alien" Native woman), the commodified images we sought to affirm drew on and remained in the same narrow range as those in traditional Westerns, albeit differently valorized.

How was our (ostensible) rejection of the straight world mirrored in these movie images of Indians? In white films and literature Native people usually appear as those who are by definition victims of an inevitable historical fate, executed and enforced by the U.S. government, the army, and the swarms of settlers. It was the movies' racist subtext—that Native people are destined to vanish in the face of progress—that made Native people seem heroic to us and made us want to affirm headbands and fringe as a way of marking our dislike of our parents' commodity culture. Again, the salvage paradigm enabled us to insist that everything had already been decided, that the issues of land and conquest remained in the past (despite the example of Vietnam). There is very little attention paid in these narratives to resistance or the real issues that came up during the colonial invasions of Native territories. Of course, this oversight is not accidental. We were exposed to colonial tales that reinforced the notion of Native people as heroic victims or, perhaps more accurately, as people who are heroic precisely because they have been victimized. At the same time, we were presented with the old stereotypes of cruelty, savagery, and, more equivocally, closeness to nature, which in traditional Christian thinking is always an ambivalent quality. It is no accident that the word *savage* means "of the forest," that wilderness where the devil lurks.

In westerns and similar narratives that claim to describe encounters between Natives and non-Natives, white people tend to have limited roles. There is no real deviation from the party line. With a very few exceptions, I have rarely seen white people challenging Manifest Destiny; rather, they are made to embody this doctrine even in movies that show white Americans being defeated (as in John Wayne's *The Alamo* [1960]). Such losses appear as no more than temporary setbacks to the final, inevitable victory and indeed make that victory even sweeter. The soldiers and cowboys and, to a lesser extent, the dance hall girls all have an agenda of nation building and acquisition of wealth, which is the reason for all the outlaw activities in the western narrative. The cowboy loner appears from time to time, enigmatic and often cruel, but always looking out for himself, a state of mind that hardly calls American values into question. The movies assume that white people are the ones who are going to win, despite internal squabbles over fencing the range, robbing a bank, or whatever. There are no real victim roles for white people in these narratives, except in the most individualized way (which is also no accident). In this way white histories are also emptied of meaning, and an alternative to the colonizer role becomes almost impossible to imagine, which seems to be part of the problem with the way white kids took up fragmented, Native-style identities in the 1960s.

Why would relatively privileged white people, both in the countercultural delirium of the 1960s and in the more corporate milieu of today's New Age, identify with people who are presented as victims time and time again? Deborah Doxtator makes the point that it is precisely the image of Indians as doomed victims that some white people identify with; she calls this the "I'm a victim too" complex.[14] Indeed, Nietzsche conceives something like this complex as the very core of Christian culture, underlining the link between pity and contempt. Thinking of someone else as a victim is a way of displacing one's own pain; in reactive Christian thinking, the individual imagines himself as less of a victim than someone else because the latter is more of a victim than he is. White hippies do tend to recognize some of the oppressive aspects of industrial, consumerist society but express this understanding by focusing on and identifying with people who seem to be even more oppressed, thus reproducing the 1970s movie version of Natives as defeated victims.

Western culture is permeated with the duplicitous, Christian notion of victimization, which, on the one hand, implies a moral or spiritual superiority and, on the other, a weakness that must be overcome through various kinds of spiritual struggle. Martyred saints are represented as suffering physical torment with a heroic steadfastness of faith. Yet the body, whether sinful or suffering, is thought to be inherently abject. Thus, to be a victim is to be both heroic and abject. White representations (both sympathetic and explicitly racist) of colonial wars tend to maintain this definition and underline the view that Native heroism derives from and is the consequence of defeat.[15] The white fascination with the romantic, abstract heroism of Native people is thus able to function as another means of colonial pacification because it presupposes the inevitable defeat and disappearance of the nations. Colonialism adds a new twist to the Christian view that people are victims by their very nature or essence, and here the relation between aggressor and victim becomes wholly static and cannot shift. Thus, appreciation qua appropriation of the arts and ceremonies of Native societies never quite calls into question the reasons for this constant reiteration of Native defeat.

And, of course, conceiving of an enemy nation as heroic also makes the oppressors look good because they have defeated a truly worthy and valiant enemy. This, too, is nothing new in Western culture. We recall the famous Roman sculpture of the dying Gaul, an image of a heroic, yet defeated enemy.

Here we approach what everyone forgot in their eagerness to embrace the representation of Indians as heroic victims: If Native nations are portrayed as inherently abject and doomed to defeat, the white viewer will not feel any connection to colonialism, either in the past or in the present. This is why the phony Native culture of movies, Edward Curtis photographs, and television is so appealing to white people: If, as Hollywood and capitalism would have it, the nations are foreordained to assimilate and vanish, then the white viewer need not question racism or face the discomfort of interrogating our continuing position as members of a colonizing nation. Any sense of connection to events occurring on the ground today is lost, and Native becomes another empty category that can be mined for its trappings and images. And the "love" of Indians professed by counterculture old and new continues to have nothing to do with Native people and certainly nothing to do with supporting such contemporary Native struggles as land and treaty rights.

Westerns and other colonial narratives are in the business of producing binarisms, which have affected all of us. Those of us who are white (or who come out of mainstream, consumer society, which can mean almost anyone) need to rethink and recover the histories erased by popular culture and school textbooks. There were always alternatives to John Wayne. We also need to think through the nature of power and its relation to culture. Native activist and poet John Trudell says that there is a difference between being oppressed and being powerless: Native people may be oppressed, but the traditions have power; white people may be in charge, but Western culture has lost its heart, soul, and life—its power.[16] It is up to us to look into how our traditions were taken over and distorted by a destructive, soulless ethos and to find ways to heal these diseases of culture (and to figure out how to do so without turning into fascists or nationalists). This is where both the countercultural and New Age approaches break down: Some non-Natives think they have to turn themselves into some version of Native people because they cannot find a way to transform and comprehend their own tradition. Because of elided histories, they are unable to identify with white people who have resisted various kinds of oppression over the centuries. And because so many imagine that Western culture is one thing—the dead, shopping-mall culture of our time—appropriation becomes the only escape, and with this it becomes impossible to imagine standing side by side with Native people as equals.

Part of the problem lies in how the desire to display affiliation enables white people to insist on being the center of attention. Proclaiming alliance with First Nations people in a visible, emphatic manner has a performative quality that demands instant recognition and approval of the white person. It manifests a certain impatience; rather than demonstrating affiliation over time with actions, many people want immediate recognition of their good intentions (this insistence on recognition is, I think, one reason for the anger that emerges when some are asked to leave ceremonies). Displaying the fringe and jewelry can become a way of attempting to seize discursive space from Native people, and to the extent that it functions as a demand, such display constitutes an endeavor to extend and underline the authority of the white person. We are reminded here of Franz Fanon's observation that the colonist is an exhibitionist who seeks constantly to "remind the Native out loud that he [or she] alone is master."[17]

This issue can cut very close, especially on those days when everything seems charged with political significance. Whenever I go to powwows or Native solidarity functions, I see white people dressed in fringed jackets, beaded and turquoise jewelry, sometimes feathers. This can produce twinges of embarrassment in other white people as well as a particular form of shopping anxiety, which ultimately has to do with a certain self-consciousness as a white woman that can come into play at such events. The jewelry and clothing are both beautiful and available because people set up booths at these events to sell their own work and the work of other Native artists. They obviously want to sell their art work and make some money. But what about the problem of consumption? They are selling, and sometimes we buy, but is this really a good idea? What about the appropriation factor? People have given me gifts of traditional beaded jewelry even though I am not Native. But when should I wear it? There is a very fine line between appreciation and appropriation, respect and self-aggrandizement, a line that is always shifting and impossible to decide in advance.[18]

Appropriation goes hand in hand with colonialism and the display of authority. In the New Age the old colonial "We want it, so we'll take it" mentality has been rendered a bit more complex in that appropriation can function as an ostensible mark of sensitivity to another culture. What has caused this turn? Or is it a turn at all or simply a reiteration of the colonial moment, now utilizing a different grammar? Many non-Native people seem genuinely sensitive to Native issues (which I guess is a start), but they may be unwilling to take their sensitivity further, to relinquish authority, which begins by questioning everything, including their right to do and demand as they please.

Grey Owl and the Problem of Identity

Wendy Rose suggests that the problem of appropriation can be thought through as one of integrity and intent, of presentation of self and project. Thus, the question becomes one of what kinds of claims are being made, which moves it away from notions of cultural purity and bloodlines and back to practice. Rose writes:

> As an Indian person who was deeply impressed with the oral literature of the Catholic Church during my childhood, I might compose verse based on

> this poetic form. I might go on to publish the poems. I might also perform them, with proper intonation, as in Mass. All of this is appropriate and permissible. But I would not and *could* not claim to be a priest. I could not tell the audience that they were actually experiencing the transmutation that occurs during Mass. At the point I did endeavour to do such things, a discernable line of integrity—both personal and artistic—would have been crossed.[19]

There seems to be a continuum that contains taking up an art style and taking up a ceremony, but an entirely new threshold is crossed when a non-Native declares that he or she is in fact an Indian. It happens more often than we might think, in different versions that range from the so-called Indian grandma syndrome, in which people identify themselves with reference to a probably fictional, unnamed Native ancestor, to case after case of outright fraud. Identities are housed in the same conceptual warehouse as other objects and images. Identity can be a mask, and this particular mask has truly been danced before; hence its value increases. The point is not that someone decides to shift or upgrade her or his identity into a new, improved form; to some extent we all do this at different points in our lives. Rather, what is important is the way that "Indian" has been one identity at play in the marketplace of cultural difference, and for a certain type of non-Native it becomes the identity of choice.

Archie Belaney, an English writer and lecturer who marketed himself as "Grey Owl" in the 1920s and 1930s remade himself into precisely what white people expected to encounter in an Indian man, which came down to fringed buckskin, a feel for nature and wild animals, and enough of that whiff of unpredictability and anger to make people think they were getting the real thing (see Figure 3.8). (This still works. At a powwow in Ottawa the master of ceremonies periodically jokes, "Soon we're gonna scalp all the white people—just kidding, folks," which is precisely what the tourists want to hear, of course, another fabled danger like the one at the fancy hotel in Aswan.) Belaney lived too soon to offer sweat lodge ceremonies for $299, but he did present himself as an example of the authentic Native mind and of the natural, traditional way of life of the northern woods. Again we see the salvage paradigm at work, again with the white person acting as cultural translator and medium.

It seems that Belaney had always been obsessed with the Canadian north and emigrated from England as soon as he possibly could. He headed straight for the Ontario bush and did actually manage to live out his adolescent daydreams of the great northern woods. At the same time, however, he made a point of publishing articles about Canada in London's *Country Life,* in some respects a rather odd choice for a man of the wilderness. But he was extremely successful because city people in Britain and North America responded to his stories and were able to imagine a world where

life was simple and very beautiful. At a certain point he seems to have decided that he could speak with more authority if he did so as a Native man, although this was a fairly complex decision given the lengths to which he carried his new identity. His publisher suggests that he took on a Métis persona to convey a message about the necessity to preserve the natural world; also, he says, Belaney was drawn into the deception by the expectations of his public. But Belaney did seek in a fairly calculated manner to present his writing and his dramatically stoic stage personality as an example of the authentic Native voice.

The popularity of Grey Owl was enormous and is a good example of how actual cultures and communities of people can be overdetermined by preconceived expectations of what a Native person ought to sound like. The point of this discussion has little to do with Belaney himself or with his relations with Native communities (no doubt people in these communities drew their own conclusions about his background), but rather concerns the enthusiasm of his audiences, which included the king of England, along with crowds of ordinary people. Grey Owl's claim to authenticity still worked years after he had died. I had his stories read to me by a third grade teacher in Oregon, in which we city kids were solemnly offered the true inside story of what it was like to be Native, as presented by an authentic Canadian Indian. The story involved baby beavers and a Native brother and sister (I think), and I can vaguely remember a canoe trip through the city of Ottawa, which seemed rather exotic to us. I do not remember any residential schools.

People were willing to believe Belaney's Grey Owl persona and what he had to say about the natural world in part because his message was nonthreatening: Let us live in peace; let us be kind to animals, he told them. But there was a rather unpleasant political background to his performances: In the years Belaney was filling lecture halls, it was illegal for Native people in Canada to work for land rights. This means that a person could go to jail for even talking about treaty obligations. On the prairies a Native person could not leave the reserve without a pass. It was illegal in Canada for Native people to dance, and in British Columbia in the 1920s people went to jail for dancing (others were forced to turn over their ceremonial regalia to the police). The Canadian government maintained a strict assimilation policy and in 1924 dissolved the traditional Iroquois system of government by force and confiscated the wampum belts that recorded Iroquois history. All this happened while Grey Owl was talking about beavers. And how many people had heard of Deskaheh, the great Cayuga speaker who in the 1920s argued for Iroquois sovereignty at the League of Nations?[20] Deskaheh spoke eloquently of land and justice and sought support from non-Natives for treaty rights. White people undoubtedly preferred to listen to Grey Owl.

Grey Owl's popularity with the white public begins to appear in a different light. Again, individual acts of cultural appropriation do not float in space but are underlain by very precise systems of authority. In a society where land theft is legitimated by law, and where communities and individuals are repressed to facilitate the colonization of territory, the taking up and popularizing of the culture under seige are not neutral acts. In effect, Belaney told non-Natives what they wanted to hear, which was that Native people did not actually concern themselves with politics and indeed were quite content with the colonial status quo. There may or may not have been anything wrong with the Grey Owl stories themselves; the point is that Belaney felt it necessary to lie to achieve a certain credibility and to feel better in his skin (which, incidentally, he dyed). Was it so impossible in the dominant society of the time for a white man to write perceptively and powerfully about the natural world? Or was Belaney's appropriation about money after all?

Belaney's publisher writes of the disappointment Grey Owl's readers experienced when his true identity was revealed on the eve of World War II: "Suddenly everything that had been built up—the hope, the moral compunction that people had felt for the first time—seemed empty and foolish. We had been duped. There was no Arcadia. The machines were our masters, and we had been deluding ourselves into thinking we could defy them."[21] This quotation illustrates one of the unhappiest consequences of pinning hopes and dreams on people like Belaney and on the plastic medicine men of the New Age. When faced with the inescapable fact that the "wise" guides are charlatans, people quickly become disoriented and lose their sense that other possibilities can continue to obtain despite the existence of quacks. They forget that they set themselves up to be duped by imagining that they knew in advance what they would hear. They wanted to be in charge. Another consequence of such appropriations is that both Grey Owl and the contemporary fake shamans conceal the realities of Native survival and continue to tell non-Natives what they want to hear. This can overwhelm the contemporary Deskahehs, who have rather different stories to tell.

As an Indian man Grey Owl could keep the machines at bay, but as a white man Archie Belaney could not, even though he spoke the same words and lived the same life in the natural world of the woods. And this is the paradox of the Grey Owl phenomenon: Native people carry a certain moral weight among non-Natives despite and because of history, oppression, and continuing racism, yet non-Natives are hungry for that glimpse of a different system of morality, if not for the history that goes with it. Part of this hunger involves a desire to contain the questions raised by land-based moral and religious systems—to domesticate these questions and place them among those other people, the Indians. But part of this hunger is a recognition of something real, much as the tourist dances can give visitors a moment of something real, something that is lacking in their lives. The problem arises when people think they can decide in advance that truth will look a certain way, that they can acquire the knowledge they so badly need by buying it.

4

Art and Taxidermy: The Warehouse of Treasures

The first time it truly struck me that there is a stream of Western culture that seeks to consume people's spirits was several years ago when, on a tourist museum visit in Rome, I saw a Lakota ghost shirt on display at the Museo Preistorico ed Etnografico. The museum was, somehow unsurprisingly, built as part of a Fascist architectural project during the 1930s and had encased the shirt in a Plexiglas cube and pinned it down with intense beams of light. This treatment reflects a trend in museum techniques of display: The "artifact" is decontextualized and treated as pure form or aesthetic object, which is to say, as a European art piece. The shirt was old, and I could see sweat stains. It was so obviously somebody's shirt rather than an exquisite objet d'art created for anonymous spectators. I think it was the shirt's status as an everyday object that made viewing it so disturbing; suddenly it seemed unbearably cruel that this building in Italy should have captured and displayed as a trophy an article of someone's clothing. That this particular shirt was one used in ceremony, and moreover a ceremony that was bloodily suppressed (something else not talked about at the museum), made the entire process worse, legitimating and mystifying the seizure of the Lakota shirt in the name of science.

As we near the millennium, it has become increasingly clear, even to some of us at the heart of Western culture, that there is something not quite right about the idea of large buildings stuffed with the booty of formerly conquered people. This was always obvious to the people whose culture was being carted off to Europe, New York, or Toronto, but only recently have many in the West challenged the ability of Western experts to represent the rest of the world or the desirability of their doing so. Museums exist to display booty and power and in this sense constitute what Louis Althusser calls ideological state apparatuses. I say this, not to disparage the endeavors of each and every person involved with such institutions, but to draw attention to another way *wétiko* psychosis is manifested in a mainstream, commodified culture. Colonialism has always involved the transfer of objects as much as the control of human beings and territory. People subject to cannibal economies were transformed into units of labor, and their bodies were moved around and set to tasks not of their own choosing. People died for no good reason. Their possessions—some of which belonged to individuals, others to associations and communities—began to move toward the European centers of power. The colonizers decided for reasons of their own which objects would be moved: Some were taken because the objects were worth money to the colonizers, some because they were considered grotesque, and some because they were classified as "beautiful." Many of these objects found their way into museums, to be classified and defined according to current scientific orthodoxies and to be examined by the public at large.

Museums are founded on several extremely eccentric and questionable assumptions about life and death and about the relation of these to representation. If we think the matter through carefully, the concept of museums—particularly ethnographic museums and museums of "natural history"—quickly dissolves into strangeness and necrophilia. Museums can truly be thought of as cannibal institutions: large edifices containing stuffed animals and the paraphernalia of cultures believed to be dead or dying, all organized according to the current scientific theory. Here the process and display of consumption are played out in one of their purest forms, the consumption of culture supposedly taking place for lofty motives rather than for the market, at least according to the myths of science. In a very emphatic sense the museum is the institution where the colonizing nations seek to display their power over life and death, over the past and over all former empires, and over those they have conquered. It is one of the most important sites where the archons of Western culture seek to concretely demonstrate the validity of their claims to cultural and moral superiority over the rest of the world.

Life and death: Death is displayed as life or, rather, is transmuted into life by the objects that vivify the people and animals they display and impersonate. The now-extinct quagga exists only in the museum, but through contemplation of its anatomical form the spectator perceives the living animal or, more precisely, some version of the living animal. Possession of the stuffed animal suggests that thanks to science and modern techniques of representation, the living animal is not "lost." Essence is collapsed into morphology, and a lifelike appearance draws attention away from the fact that these animals are not real (hence the common reaction of small children, which wavers between delight and the tearful question "Why did they have to kill them?"). By making dead things look alive, taxidermy not only strives for and normalizes the godlike powers of the expert but also displaces life through an ability to represent the living. Like the zoological garden, which offers a representation of animals that live, yet whose captivity permits only an approximation of their existence, taxidermy substitutes appearance for the real, for what exists in the world on its own terms. Taxidermy forces the animals to speak, but it is only ventriloquism.

A taxidermal aesthetic suffuses the museum. Because the museum is able to manipulate life and death, ways of life believed to be dead or dying are resuscitated in ethnographic exhibitions. The notions that other cultures exist as objects of study, that the museum has a responsibility to salvage aspects of cultures under pressure from colonialism, that the spectator's perusal of this display of culture constitutes some form of understanding, and indeed that understanding must be mediated by experts enforce the separation between them and us. This separation makes it extremely difficult to approach other cultures respectfully or indeed even to imagine doing so, which at times seems to be at least part of the intention. Most exhibitions of so-called ethnographic cultures elide colonialism altogether, preferring an idealized space untouched by capital and bad taste. In some instances photographs are used to verify that some bodies are still alive and that traditional arts and technologies, like the people themselves, are not facing pressure from multinational interests. Again, morphological accuracy functions as an alibi. The remnants of traditional, land-based societies are usurped and treated as living fossils and, like the quagga, assumed to live if possessed by the museum. Land-based societies continue to exist as a metaphor, and the techniques of representation used to make these societies accessible to the Western viewer become another way to subdue and supplant them. The question of how all this has come to be is obscured.

In the last few years there has been a flurry of critiques of museums. Books with titles such as *Exhibiting Cultures,* Sally Price's *Primitive Art in Civilized Places,* and a plethora of critical articles call into question some of the assumptions on which museums and related institutions are based. Many of those who write these works are in the business. For example, Michael Ames, director of the Museum of Anthropology at the University of British Columbia, has written a book about problems of representation and cultural difference in contemporary anthropology museums.[1] The attempts by many of these writers to rehabilitate the museum and render it postcolonial are often the result of a genuine unease with the colonial history of ethnographic museums, but few suggest a wholesale dismantling of museums and a return of ceremonial and other objects back to the people who made and used them and who need them to survive spiritually. Few still are even prepared to let this come up as a question, which reveals the limits of good intentions. Most museum people, no matter how critical of the colonial history of the museum, continue to subscribe to notions of science and of expertise, which continue to maintain that objects are best off in places where they can be seen by white people, even if certain objects were not intended to be displayed. Most contend that the museum is the site where these objects can be properly looked after. And most continue to maintain a notion of the authentic object, which precludes in advance the substitution of reproductions in museum displays and the possibility of return of ceremonial objects to the people to whom they belong.

Resacralization of the Authentic Object

No matter how elaborate the exhibition, in the final analysis museums display *objects*. Museums presuppose a particular approach to the problem of the object in itself and maintain a set of assumptions about the relation of objects to culture. Notions of originality and authenticity, and of the relation of detailed information to "truth," underlie museums' presentations of the objects they administer. One of the most cherished convictions of high culture concerns the primacy of the authentic object, which is believed to provide an experience that a reproduction cannot.

In medieval churches and early museum collections the language of objects was part of a religious discourse. Isolated objects were displayed to signify socio-religious abstractions and, like the total environments of contemporary museums, to represent the real, here by their ability to concretize classes of concepts. The object was intrinsically part of a sacred order of meaning, regardless of whether this meaning was apparent to human beings. For example, the ostrich eggs displayed in medieval churches drew people to the building and referred to the Christian's relation to God:

> Again some say that the ostrich, as being a forgetful bird, leaveth her eggs in the dust (Job xxxix:14), and at length when she beholdeth a certain star returneth unto them, and cheereth then by her presence. Therefore the eggs of ostriches are hung in churches to signify that man, being left by God on account of his sins, if at length he be illuminated by Divine Light, remembereth his faults and returneth to Him, who by looking at him His mercy cherisheth him.[2]

The rather convoluted logic of this passage nevertheless firmly and explicitly ties the object—the egg—to a sacred order and an entire complex of ideas. Ostrich eggs, along with the stone tools, kayaks, and other objects exhibited in European churches, embodied entire canons of faith and, like the relics of saints displayed with them, possessed in their substance spiritual and medicinal qualities. Similarly, the unicorn's horn found in every noteworthy museum of the sixteenth and seventeenth centuries testified to the existence of the animal and illustrated the power of God to perform miracles through the healing power of the horn itself.

Today there seem to be two approaches to the display of objects in museums. Unless an object from another culture is explicitly identified as art, it tends to be presented in such a way that it serves a didactic function similar to the animals in natural history dioramas. The object is important insofar as it is part of a larger whole. Once an object is named as art either by the relevant specialists or by the market, it tends to be exhibited alone, displayed as an aesthetic form rather than a source of cultural information (as has occurred with Native American items, hence the boutiquelike display of the Lakota shirt in Rome). Art universalizes the object and places it beyond culture. Another distinction occurs among the types of societies being displayed: Whereas ethnographic museums tend to assimilate the object into an educational whole, utilizing mannequins and reconstructed villages, displays referring to imperial societies almost always treat the object in a manner analogous to the presentation of European art pieces. The artifact of ancient Egypt, Greece, or Rome enjoys a particular prominence and is exalted both as fine art and as an expression of imperial power. Although these objects may be framed by elaborate exhibitions that offer cultural information, as for the Tutankhamen grave goods in the 1970s, it is the objects themselves that are celebrated, and the display serves primarily as backdrop. Authenticity is contained in the object itself rather than being signified by didactic displays.

Ancient and modern empires come together through a manipulation of a universalized notion of aesthetic value, because imperial art is interpreted according to ideas concerning the nature of the "masterpiece" applied to Western art. Contemplation of the original masterpiece is believed to provide an emotional, quasi-religious experience. For example, for many, many people the genuine Mona Lisa or Venus de Milo provokes sentiments that a reproduction does not (others, expecting transcendence, experience disappointment at the sight of an oft-reproduced original art object). Similarly, the Parthenon Marbles or the bust of Nefertiti is exhibited to enhance its status as a unique masterpiece of the European cultural heritage (the absorption of Egypt into the Western tradition is one reason this country has habitually been treated by the latter as if separate from Africa proper). The sensation derived from contact with a famous ancient object is revealingly described by museologists: "Looking at the original [Rosetta Stone], the least informed visitor comes to feel that his personal experience has been extended to include this famous piece, and he thereby begins to sense that the intellectual triumph of Champollion . . . in first deciphering the mysterious, ancient Egyptian language has become a part of his personal background of awareness."[3]

What is seen as irrelevant, of course, is that Champoillon's "intellectual triumph" (itself an odd turn of phrase) was made possible by Napoleon's invasion of Egypt, during which huge amounts of material were carted back to Europe and housed in state institutions such as museums and in various other public sites. Edward Said has made the point in his seminal work *Orientalism* that Napoleon's expedition was "in many ways the very model of a truly scientific appropriation of one culture by another,"[4] which places the self-congratulatory remarks of the museum document in a rather different light. Here, as with ethnology, scientific objectivity seems to mean that the focus on the object of study interdicts any discussion of power. (The British Museum's presentation of the Rosetta Stone is in fact a marketing triumph. Although very few people can actually read any of the three languages inscribed on the stone, representations of this object consistently outsell any other souvenir of this museum.[5])

Temporality and Writing

When ethnology constituted itself as a science in the nineteenth century, it appropriated as its object of study traditional, generally land-based people living outside of European and North American cities—in other words, people classified as nonwhite, defined as un- or semicivilized, and incidentally subject to European colonial authority (to a somewhat lesser extent, people speaking minority languages in Europe proper were also considered appropriate subjects for anthropological study). Because supposedly scientific notions of cultural evolution meant that many Europeans took their right to rule the rest of the world for granted, questions of colonialism were excluded from the ethnographic discourse. "Literacy" was the term used to delimit ethnology from other scientific fields. People who preferred to maintain an oral culture were considered to be profoundly different from people living in a written culture (by which I mean writing in the narrow sense, as we have learned to say since Jacques Derrida).[6] The differences that do exist between the oral and written approach to knowledge were not necessarily the ones that ethnographers decided were important and hence stressed. Orality was viewed as a lack of writing rather than as a system of transmitting knowledge that has certain advantages and strengths in itself. There are some very good reasons for refusing literacy that have to do with conceptual agility and flexibility of knowledge transmission.[7]

The arts of oral people fell under the purview of ethnology and were seen less as aesthetic objects than as objects of scientific inquiry. Thus, the Gilgamesh sculptures are elevated to fine art and displayed in the Louvre because they were made by specialist artisans who lived in an imperial society that used writing. Dyak bis-poles are exhibited in the Musee de l'Homme with wooden mallets used to prepare food. The Royal British Columbia Museum speaks of Native history prior to white contact as a "12,000 year gap—a reference to the gap in our knowledge that occurred between the end of the last ice age and the arrival of the white man,"[8] which not only suggests that knowledge is not knowledge unless white people possess it but also negates the value of songs, stories, and other indigenous ways of recounting histories. The privileging of writing disarticulates individual societies as well; aristocratic arts such as Hindu temple sculptures are included with the high aesthetic traditions of the West in the British Museum, whereas village India is classified as an ethnographic culture and exhibited in the Museum of Man. The Western tradition is thus able to absorb the social and religious aristocracies of other ages and pose itself as inheritor, but the tradition displays objects in such a way as to constitute a subtext of class: Imperial art imposes and evokes humility from the spectator, whereas village societies are transformed into playpens through the construction of model huts that the spectator may enter to inspect the arts and utensils of these cultures. "After all," whispers the colonial official to the spectator, "they are like children."

There is one rather strange anomaly in the institutional distinction between high and low cultures. The arts of imperial Mexico are generally housed in ethnographic museums rather than with the other empires in the national museums. Assyria and China go with Greece, Rome, and medieval Europe; Mexico goes with Polynesia in a building that is usually way across town, at least in London and Paris. This is not that surprising given the frankness of Aztec imperial representation and the extent to which the state is explicitly linked to violence and the production of mass death; the lofty idealism of the state-polis so cherished in Western high culture is difficult to sustain. The wicked Aztecs went entirely too far and so must be expelled from the imperial club, but this expulsion must be justified. Consequently, great pains are taken to inform spectators that the Aztecs lacked true writing, even though they used a complex writing system that included imperial histories, religious and calendrical texts, genealogies, economic records, almanacs, and books on medicine.[9] This somewhat convoluted excuse for the exclusion of Mexico from the category of world civilization seems to derive from the long-standing fear and horror that this society has been able to provoke in the West, particularly the subterranean dread that the Aztecs might be able to tell us too much about ourselves.

The privileging of writing as the central criterion for classifying societies in the museum deserves a closer look because of what it can do to temporality. Museums contain objects from cultures widely separated in time and space, yet time is manipulated in a peculiar telescopy whereby the past is made to converge with the present, which in turn both assimilates and disarticulates the past at varying rates. This relativizes both time and space, in effect obliterating both, but the museum conceals this absence by references to concrete historical instances. Retrospection becomes a way of decoding and naturalizing the present, and the present becomes the lens through which the past is constructed.

Millennia collapse as ancient empires seem to advance in time and coalesce with the present. The construction of continua draws the past closer as correspondences and a series of primal events are "discovered." Each time classical Athens is declared to be the "first democracy" or Inkhaten the "first monotheist," the fifth century B.C. or even the second millennium B.C.E. is transformed into familiar terrain as these societies are made to mirror contemporary, Western preoccupations. This can be done because ancient empires recorded their histories and museums can therefore name and date specific events, wars, royal smitings, and so forth. Again, the use of writing qua detail is valorized and comes to stand for a kind of authenticity in itself. The presence of dates ratifies these societies' possession of time, which in turn validates their presence in "history" and their insertion into the classificatory construct designated as "civilization." It is this inclusion into the time-history-civilization complex that permits the right sort of ancient empires to signify contemporary empires and that dissolves the time separating their societies from the present.[10]

Ethnographic and natural history displays are less likely to focus on the individual object than art museums are. The role of the ethnographic museum is to make these objects speak to the spectator by placing them within total environments and complete systems of representation in which the objects are articulated with one another to reproduce a visibly complete world. The original object is still the basis of the museum's ability to create evocative displays and of the display itself, but the object's primacy is camouflaged by the increasing sophistication of techniques of representation and the emphasis on total displays.

Contemporary museology warns against displaying depersonalized objects, so mannequins are constructed to breathe life into surrounding objects. Although the detail of the displays can be impressive, the mind still eventually turns to zombie movies. Dressed in clothing once worn by living bodies, these synthetic bodies authenticate the object by performing the frozen behavior of the people to whom the things once belonged and by representing living humans. The mannequin always defers to and is overshadowed by the object, which in turn is animated by the presence of an ersatz, lifeless body in the display. Some mannequins achieve anatomical perfection through having been cast from living human "specimens"; transformed into objects by museological techniques, real people now live only as plaster of paris, offering an illusion of themselves and of the living. But what is being displayed is the ability to construct the real. Again, morphology rules and authenticity becomes a question of technique.

The spectator enters a coastal rain forest in the Royal British Columbia Museum and confronts a reality created by techniques of display: Trees, a running stream, and live crustaceans are juxtaposed against stuffed animals and recorded birdcalls. Fascinating, but do not the trees and shoreline imitated indoors exist just outside the walls of the museum (if the forest has not been clear-cut)? What precisely is being legitimized by the museum? In the Rijksmuseum voor Volkenkunde in Leiden a north Afghan market town is recreated in fastidious detail, with streets and teahouses peopled by life-sized mannequins and market sounds piped in to reinforce authenticity. Films and slides run continuously to reveal additional data not furnished by the model. In these total displays what is represented is not the market town or the rain forest but the art of display itself, revealed through a taxidermy that has as its object the social body or the body of the earth.

Ethnographic exhibitions construct a past that is both temporal and spatial; traditional societies are displayed in something called the "ethnographic present," a term referring to an imaginary time prior to colonial contact as reconstructed a posteriori by ethnologists. The ethnographic present is based on notions of cultural authenticity and purity, and when combined with an exclusion of local histories, this concept suggests that oral societies exist only in stasis and are moreover imprisoned in the past. Cultural authenticity becomes something that is determined by experts but that can exist only as a chimera and as a way of silencing contemporary issues faced by traditional peoples, who can never look as authentic as the mannequins of the ethnographic present. This construction of a past authenticity has effects: So many young (and not so young) white kids seem to expect the contemporary First Nations people they meet to wear war bonnets and live in teepees,[11] which can delegitimize the experiences of actual Native people. And, of course, these white kids can always buy the impedimenta of the exotic culture of choice and create their own displays of difference and authenticity.

To recognize that oral societies exist in time and have their own histories is to begin collapsing the ultimately empty and uninteresting distinction between societies classified as primitive and those deemed civilized. Specific historical instances, such as migrations, federations, or acts of resistance against colonialism, are displaced, and traditional societies seem to vanish once they enter Western history. The Royal British Columbia Museum's linear progression of provincial history begins with a mammoth and ends with modern cities: Northwest Coast Native societies, defined here primarily by traditional arts and architecture, seem abruptly to disappear around 1880, although a small corner mentions smallpox, land claims, and the banning of the potlatch. The museum draws a veil over how it acquired the objects on display, alibiing this question by focusing on how it now consults Native people about such displays. This elision of both the historical and contemporary effects of colonialism, of course, also has to do with the larger issue of tourism and the way places such as British Columbia market sanitized versions of Native histories and cultures to draw tourist dollars to the area.

Ethnological displays present the "real" Native as uncontaminated by contact with modern society. The exhibitions of contemporary "Third World" problems that have become popular in Holland and Germany (for instance, the Tropen Museum in Amsterdam, formerly the Ost Museum of the Dutch colonial empire of the East Indies, now apparently rehabilitated) also suggest a notion of cultural stasis and a view of time in which a never-quite-defined change is assumed to have wrenched the supposedly passive Native out of a primeval state. Present-day exploitation is construed by allusion to a happier past, and the future is presented as an ominous question mark, again referring to a way of life—an ethnographic present, this time implicit—that no longer exists as well as to an underlying conviction that these traditional ways of life will inevitably disappear against the juggernaut of Western culture.

The assumption that nonurban, land-based cultures are by definition moribund can operate as another means of neocolonial pacification because it makes Western culture appear absolutely seamless, in effect erasing margins, resistances, and points of survival (both in the West and elsewhere, as it happens). By presenting cultural authenticity as something that only occurred prior to colonialism, such displays allow the spectator to dismiss contemporary struggles and syncretic elements of traditional cultures as inauthentic.

Necrophilia

One of the most monstrous aspects of museum collections, and one that renders most explicit its cannibal nature, are the drawers full of skulls and bones of dead colonized people. Cannibals consume human bodies. That this is done in the name of science and in what purports to be a spirit of objective inquiry does not change the fact that what the museum contains are dead bodies.

Despite the fine talk about science and contribution to human knowledge, the museum maintains its collections of human skulls and skeletal remains to demonstrate science's mastery over life and death, much like the taxidermy and natural history dioramas in many museums. Possession of human remains signifies the conquest of the dead through the ability to interpret and recreate life in the showcase. As with religious relics, the dead are used to naturalize the discourse of the living. The repatriation of bones to Native communities continues to be the subject of debate in archaeological and museum circles, despite the continual attempts by Native people to explain to these "experts" why there are problems, both political and spiritual, with maintaining collections of skeletal material and grave goods. There is nevertheless a fair bit of resistance among white academics to the idea of Native communities having a say in what happens to the bones of their ancestors. The requirements of scientific inquiry continue to be invoked as an alibi for grave robbing despite the many accounts of supposedly scientific desecrations, some of which have been documented in stomach-turning detail.[12] Even though some Native American skeletal material is now being returned to the communities from which it was removed, there are vast numbers of bones and skulls that were "collected" so haphazardly that museums have no idea where they came from. The use of skulls and bones to demonstrate physical and cultural superiority also occurs at an interspecies level, with the crania in "Early Man" exhibitions providing a text of evolutionary theory written by physical anthropologists that, as has been pointed out by many, places us at the so-called top of the evolutionary chain of being.

There are signs of a new unease on the part of white liberals with the collection and display of physical anthropology "specimens." The PBS docudrama *Ishi: The Last of His Tribe* (1992) is symptomatic of this unease.[13] *Ishi* (title role played by Graham Greene) tells the story of the relationship between the famous anthropologist Alfred Kroeber and Ishi, the so-called last wild Indian of California, who lived in the anthropology museum at the university from his capture in 1911 until his death in 1916. Kroeber is presented as a refined man (something like the viewers of PBS) who knows better than the average white person the value of the Native cultures that are supposedly being lost, yet he is unable to act or act effectively. In the story he acts too slowly to keep his promise that Ishi would not be autopsied after his death. The viewer of *Ishi* is treated to lengthy scenes of the white man's horror at what he has done as Kroeber contemplates the rows and rows of Native skeletons in his museum. This film really is unremittingly bleak; everybody is rigidly trapped in their roles, with no room to even question their position, much less move. Kroeber's rather condescending realization that Ishi is in fact a human being is visually contrasted with the skulls and bones that are part of the anthropologist's career, but Kroeber never feels quite guilty enough to question his own position or academic discipline. In fact, the question never even comes up, which is presumably of some comfort to the viewers of the movie.

The *wétiko* fascination with body parts has always underlain certain kinds of museum displays as well as certain streams in physical anthropology. Techniques of inquiry pertaining to the body have allowed intimate inspection and appraisal, and the stereotype of the nineteenth-century anthropologist with calipers for measuring Native skulls and a suitcase full of glass eyeballs for comparing eye color is not entirely without relevance today. The particular and persistent interest in steatopygia and related physical phenomena in Western medical and ethnological sciences seems to be a function of nineteenth-century beliefs about sexuality and of the displacement of the categories of female desire and sexuality onto Africans and European prostitutes.[14] The genitalia of Saydie Baartman, the so-called Hottentot Venus, are on permanent display at the Musee de l'Homme in Paris. The interest in body parts has influenced conventions of museum display, with authenticity functioning as the pretext for the casting of human bodies and placement of these into what may best be termed *human habitat groups*. Sometimes museums have colluded with the police, as in South Africa, where taxidermists have made casts of people in detention. The following anecdote (which, astonishingly, seems to be intended by the author to be amusing) from the 1920s is extreme but exemplifies the usually concealed, implicit institutional links in an explicitly colonial situation such as South Africa:

> A Bush-Hottentot woman had been taken in charge for soliciting and as she was extremely steatopygeous the police telephoned the museum to enquire whether a cast was required, so Drury [the taxidermist] and the Director went down to Calendon Square. ... They offered her a fee of ten shillings, the usual payment in country districts. With every appearance of injured pride she pointed out that she could get two pounds any night in Buitenkant Street. So the Museum had to pay an enhanced fee![15]

Although the museum was, in a rather neat turnabout, forced to "rent" the body of the prostitute, the museum functionaries never actually wanted the woman's body as a living body; rather, they wanted an imprint of this body, something that was by definition dead long before the woman herself died.

Authentic Details

Museums invent a version of reality by suggesting that authenticity is dependent on systematized, realistic detail, something that is true in other milieus as well. The identification of authenticity and truth with detail not only occurs in the context of museological thinking and in museum displays but also seems to structure Western attempts to account for cultural differences and analyses of colonial history in general. A version of reality is constructed through the repetition of facts, names, and dates, a practice we see in museum displays of imperial histories, where the presence of specific dates renders tangible and inserts into history the society in question. The use of detail as a device to connote historical accuracy and authenticity can draw attention away from questions of representation and power: The spectator or reader is so overwhelmed by factual minutiae that s/he believes that the story must be true.

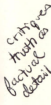

A brief example of how a version of truth can be constructed through detail can clarify this process, and I have selected one that loops back to a question I briefly raised at the beginning of this text concerning Aztec culture and the extent to which it is possible for us to know it in any meaningful way. My example is textual rather than visual but also utilizes the minutiae of cultural difference to draw the reader into believing that s/he is apprehending another culture. Most European writers dealing with the Spanish conquest of Aztec Mexico rely on Bernal Díaz del Castillo's *The Conquest of New Spain* for descriptions of the Spanish invasion as well as the city of Tenochtitlán prior to its destruction. The account contains lengthy descriptions of what used to be called manners and customs of the Aztecs and of material culture. As such, this text is considered to be one of the most important sources of historical and ethnographic information. It is a fascinating narrative, but is it true? *The Conquest of New Spain* maintains its authority as an "objective" chronicle because Díaz was an eyewitness to the events being described and provided detailed descriptions of what he saw. He named names, recalled dates, gave list after list of objects along with their value in Spanish currency, and so forth. Although written more than fifty years after the conquest, the text includes verbatim speeches and conversations (including one purporting to be between Mexicans in the Nahuatl language). Díaz was a Spaniard—which is to say, on the winning side of the battle for Tenochtitlán/Mexico City—and moreover wrote *The Conquest of New Spain* as an attempt to extract a pension from the Spanish crown. Mesoamerican scholar David Carrasco's call for a textual "hermeneutics of suspicion" here toward the truth of the descriptions and story narrated by Díaz seems to be in order.[16]

Despite the circumstances under which the text was produced, Díaz's account has for the most part been accepted as accurately and truthfully representing the facts of the conquest. Díaz has become the main source for the majority of textbook accounts of the Spanish conquest of Mexico. Certainly Díaz uses a descriptive language later appropriated by ethnology, which has bolstered his claim to truth for contemporary readers. But *The Conquest of New Spain* has consistently enjoyed the confidence of its readers. According to William Prescott, the influential nineteenth-century historian of Mexico and Peru, Díaz "transfers the scenes of real life by a sort of *daguerreotype* process." Furthermore, the authenticity of the narrative is affirmed by its apparent innocence: The narrative has a "natural, unpolished style" and was written in vernacular Castilian.[17] But all this praise draws attention away from the problem of the construction of truth. The text's status as authentic chronicle or real life is suspect not only because Díaz wrote it years after the events for personal and financial reasons but also because it is a text of conquest written by the victor and is structured according to certain literary conventions. *The Conquest of New Spain* establishes its authority through a particular rhetorical style that refers to

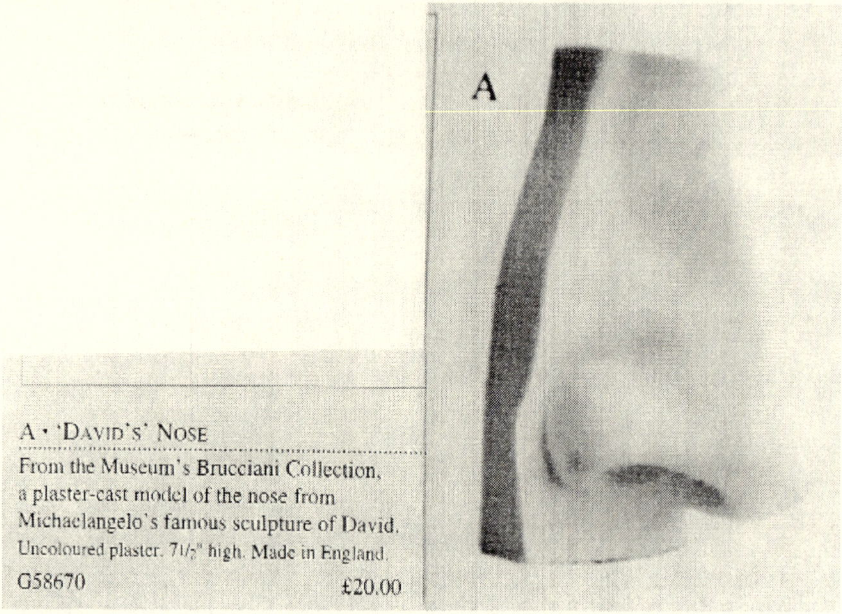

FIGURE 4.1 "'*David's' Nose*" *British Museum reproduction*

Castilian epic poems and romances, including the conquest epic *Poema de Mío Cid.*

We can see again how detail is utilized to construct a version of authenticity, thereby collapsing understanding into morphological accuracy. The issues of representation and colonialism raised by colonial texts such as *The Conquest of New Spain* and by certain kinds of museum displays, and the specific elements that go into producing such versions of reality, occur in a range of different contexts and tend to share key characteristics. I think we may be most suspicious when cultural and historical material is arranged into taxonomies that are not themselves called into question, with these organizational schema ratified by detailed information, such as names and dates. Similarly, when an object displayed in a museum comes to stand for a vast range of social and cultural phenomena, we can inquire whose versions of truth are contained within and attested to by the facticity of the object.

Commodity Fetishism

For £20 it is possible to purchase from the British Museum a plaster cast of the nose of Michelangelo's *David* sculpture (see Figure 4.1); $150 buys a velour "Incan" bathrobe from the Smithsonian Institution. Why do people buy such things, and how is the yearning for a particular object or type of object produced? To what extent are rather prosaic items such as bathrobes ennobled by their association with the museums that market them to the public? Although people do have to be educated to a certain taste—in the case of high culture, the word is *cultivated,* like a flowerbed—this suggests a leisurely process whereby a consumer is carefully taught how to recognize the so-called finer things. Today the process seems much more frenetic than it used to: Commodities swirl around and around, all announcing their desirability and value through sophisticated techniques of advertising, all operating as the means through which a particular mode of desire is constructed, all dissolving and recombining time-honored social and aesthetic codes and systems of value.

European fine art has always been subject to commodification, both in products such as calendars and art books and, more recently, in the blockbuster shows that have become typical of the way European masterpieces are made available to the public—the Picasso and Matisse shows are examples of skillfully marketed, hugely popular exhibitions, and in Toronto the advance ads for the heavily promoted Barnes exhibit focused on the fact that the show had sold out elsewhere. Art appreciation and connoisseurship have entered the mainstream through the marketing of fine art's status as cultural currency, which elevates everything it touches. Thus, what was once the exclusive province of elite culture is taken up within popular culture in a way familiar to most North Americans, which is to say, as a product.[18]

The objects that refer to the aesthetic of Western high culture can be marketed like any other product, but the process is a bit different from the marketing of beer or cars. The commodification of elite culture is dependent on a manipulation of some of the most cherished ideals of Western culture. These include notions of racial and cultural superiority, the belief that various kinds of aristocrats are the true guardians of the European artistic heritage, and the ambivalent position of white women as consumers of images of difference.

The task for people trying to sell products is how to make a particular object shine brighter than all the other objects competing for the attention of the consumer. The particular luster associated with art museums can be transferred to particular objects and mediated through a fascination with notables or through colonial fantasies. The commodity becomes attractive to the consumer precisely because it stands for different assemblages of ideas.

For instance, it never fails to surprise me how things continue to be marketed through a nostalgia for the old days of colonial adventure, when Westerners ostensibly did precisely as they pleased. The pleasures of the colony are an extremely persistent myth and for the white consumer bring to mind attentive servants and languid, sentimental encounters on veran-

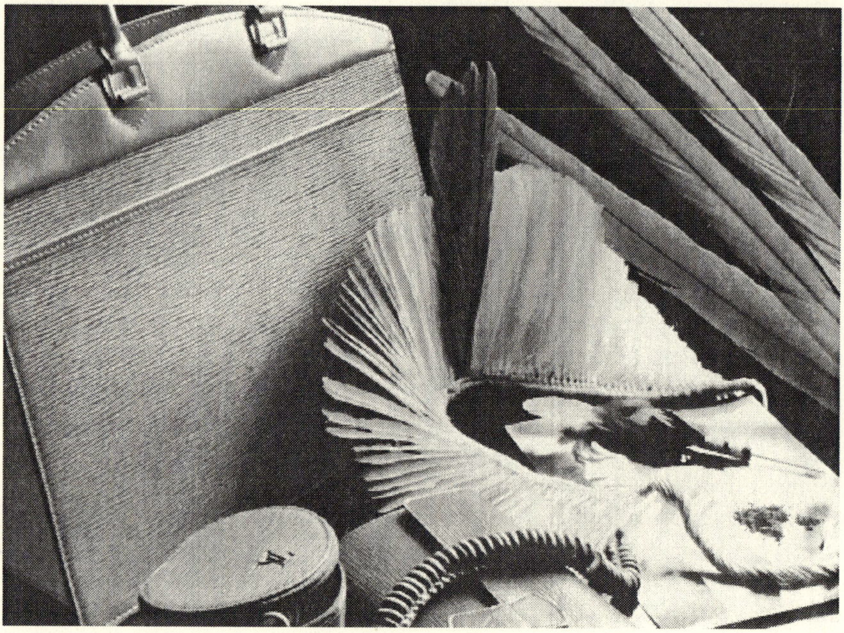

FIGURE 4.2 Louis Vuitton luggage advertisement

das. In ways that might (or might not) be challenged if they appeared in mainstream narratives such as television or film, the colonial romance is marketed in ads for Ralph Lauren's Safari perfume, Vuitton luggage (see Figure 4.2), and other luxury goods. In one sense this link between luxury and colony is obvious: The Vuitton ad blends aristocratic exclusiveness with colonial adventure by juxtaposing its product against the artifacts of Amazonian travel, a destination clearly not to everyone's taste but one of the few places where the tourist can observe actual befeathered "natives" as their great-grandparents presumably did in the old colonial days.[19] The Vuitton ad copy refers to "city lights and Amazon blooms" and "the magic of great journeys," evoking the wealthy sophisticate who is at ease anywhere in the world.

I suggested previously that exoticism works through a process of fragmentation. The commodification of cultural difference is also dependent on a fragmented presentation of culture, but here this works by producing equivalences between objects (luggage) and experience (a trip to Amazonia), which is to say, the experiences the objects are designed to evoke. Things and "lifestyles" and the past and the present are collapsed together into an appealing package, which can be purchased by the consumer worldly enough to recognize what the object's codes refer to. In this identification of luxury object and exotic experience, a particular relation between parts and whole is created: Exotic and nonexotic, high art and popular art, and art and experience all become stylish accessories. Although within advertising everything has been decided in advance, the illusion of difference remains and is indeed the means through which the consumer is seduced.

Museums and art galleries have traditionally been the province of the upper classes, but given the economics of the day, they have had to enter a broader marketplace to survive. The larger museums have been able to do so by skillfully drawing on their association with scholarship and expertise as well as with precious objects. The lofty ideals associated with scholarship have veiled the extent to which capitalist economics has turned these ideals into commodities as well. To be considered viable, these institutions must pay their own way (as the saying goes) and generate wealth. Knowledge for its own sake is no longer enough.

The phenomenon of museum shops and mail order catalogs indicates how the trappings of elite culture are marketed and made available to the broader public. The museum shop phenomenon involves the reproduction and sale of objects, but because the museum contains important art treasures, the reproductions borrow cachet from the original objects and from the expertise embodied in the institution of the museum. The original object is one of a kind, and the museum is the site where it traditionally has been housed; therefore, if the museum magnanimously offers a copy to the public, the commercial process appears less mercenary than if an ordinary company reproduced the object. When museums decided to promote their collections through catalogs and reproduction boutiques, the edifying function of the museum merged with the commercial activity of shopping. In recent years this merging has become even more convenient for the consumer, first with catalogs and then with so-called satellite stores in nearby shopping malls, such as the Royal Ontario Museum store in Toronto's Eaton Centre. When the colonial romance merges with archaeological adventure fantasies and museum shopping, the marketing process becomes a bit trickier because of the way scholarship can be valorized and identified with a disinterested, objective truth.

Museum catalogs and advertisements for archaeologically related products employ a rhetoric of discovery that links back to the nineteenth-century explorer and, before that, to the conquistador. This device is extremely pervasive. The subscription ads for *Archaeology* magazine exhort the potential reader to "make a startling discovery," explaining that the magazine is "required equipment for armchair explorers." Other ads in the magazine utilize similar language. For instance, Far Horizons archaeological tours entices with "Explore Ancient Ruins!"; a Turkish tourism ad says,

"Discover the undiscovered Europe"; Thames and Hudson flogs popular archaeology books by evoking adventure in the fabulous cities of the Aztecs, Mayans, and Incas, exhorting the reader to "Rediscover Ancient America Again and Again" (see Figure 4.3); and the Archaeological Institute of America's ad solicits memberships with

> Now that you have EXPLORED *Archaeology* Magazine
> Begin a new adventure—
> DISCOVER an AIA Membership

which uses capital letters and boldface type just to make sure the reader gets the point. The contemporary reader is encouraged to consume both the past and the experience of the archaeologist-explorer-conquistador and to do so as a nineteenth-century gentleman-scholar.

For instance, a private company called Indigenous Art Inc. offers limited edition reproductions of pre-Columbian and other art objects. Many of these items do stand on their own as aesthetic objects, but the ad copy borrows the prestige associated with archaeology and with museum collections. The catalog explains the company's role in the preservation of a world archaeological and aesthetic heritage: "Throughout history widespread looting and desecration of sacred sites has eradicated vital information concerning the truth about our ancestors and the purpose of the art they created. The demand for this art has been the direct cause of the looting problem. We intend to offset this problem by making these re-creations available to everyone." Indigenous Art sells a Toltec column lamp for $145, which will appeal to a certain kind of consumer because it evokes both the capital cities where famous museums are located and the private collections of wealthy collectors. As a pre-Columbian-style object the lamp also refers to the robust activities of the adventurer and the tourist who visits interesting locales such as Tula. The professional cachet of the archaeologist also increases the desirability of the lamp. The codes used to market commodities such as the Toltec lamp are often mixed, and the ascribed value of a particular object can be based on an association with European high art through reference to colonial past and colonial lifestyle, and the aristocratic collector or connoisseur. As with Vuitton ads, the idealization of colonial authority seems a particularly effective marketing tool, but here it is packaged in the guise of the aristocratic collector.

Because this process takes place on a large scale, it is really about the construction of a potentially enormous market through the manipulation—or, more properly, the construction—of mainstream taste. This is not to say that everyone will immediately rush out and purchase Toltec lamps but that both the aesthetic codes of pre-Columbian art and the significance and connotation of this art within Western culture will be understood more widely

Breaking the Maya Code
Michael D. Coe
The AZTECS
The MAYA
THE INCAS
Rediscover
Ancient America
Again and Again...
BREAKING THE MAYA CODE
By Michael D. Coe 112 illus. $14.95 paper
THE AZTECS
By Richard Townsend
THE MAYA
Fifth Edition Revised
By Michael D. Coe
THE INCAS AND THEIR ANCESTORS
The Archaeology of Peru
TEOTIHUACAN
Art from the City of the Gods
CHAVIN AND THE ORIGINS OF
ANDEAN CIVILIZATION
By Richard L. Burger
THE GODS AND SYMBOLS OF
ANCIENT MEXICO AND THE MAYA
An Illustrated Dictionary of Mesoamerican Religion
By Mary Ellen Miller and Karl Taube
260 illus. $34.95
MEXICO
From the Olmecs to the Aztecs
By Michael D. Coe 128 illus. $14.95 paper
KINGDOMS OF GOLD, KINGDOMS OF JADE
The Americas Before Columbus
By Brian M. Fagan 180 illus. $24.95
SCRIBES, WARRIORS AND KINGS
The City of Copan and the Ancient Maya
By William L. Fash 120 illus. $19.95 paper
CITIES OF ANCIENT MEXICO
By Jeremy A. Sabloff 152 illus. $11.95 paper
Available at bookstores or order directly
THAMES AND HUDSON INC.

FIGURE 4.3 Rediscover America, *book advertisement*

than before. The construction of a mass market that draws on the ideals embodied by the museum ultimately means the consumer is presumed to be more or less white, more or less middle class, and often but not always female (the assumption being that women tend to spend more time looking at catalogs and buying things than men). And despite the claims that elite culture is more accessible than ever before, the valorization of the colonial era ends up universalizing dominant Western values rather than enabling the consumer to rethink questions of culture and aesthetic value.

The fascination with archaeology and its association with colonial adventures can be seen in a range of venues and long predates the Indiana Jones movies. The desire for precious antiquities starts young and is identified with boisterous exploits not normally associated with academic pursuits: There is a children's game show currently being broadcast on the Nickelodeon channel called *Legends of the Hidden Temple* in which contestants get to live out the adventure of tomb robbing, here tactfully called "retrieving the treasure." Here the persistent appeal of the treasure hunt is explicitly linked to the activities of the heroic adventurer-archaeologist. A deep-voiced stone idol named "Olmec" recites the story of the particular treasure that is the topic of each episode, after which the children race through a pre-Columbian–type temple complex, fighting off guards dressed in Aztec-Mayan pastiche, with black painted faces obviously meant to be frightening. I am not making this up.

Legends of the Hidden Temple also reinforces another important point: There is always an object that explains and justifies the adventure. This becomes clear when we look at museum shops and see what gets reproduced and turned into salable commodities and what does not. Because of the continuing obsession with gold and treasure, jewelry has been one of the most important and popular categories for reproduction, both in museum shops and in the mail order catalogs of companies that reproduce ancient jewelry and ornaments depicted in European oil paintings, such as San Francisco's Jewelry Museum. The 1993 catalog of the Metropolitan Museum of Art is a treasure trove of gold jewelry in a range of styles that spans vast chasms of time and space: Greece and Rome, ancient Egypt, the aristocratic jewels of baroque Europe and czarist Russia, the museum makes all available to the consumer. Museum reproductions of ancient jewelry exemplify the complex and paradoxical nature of marketing codes because many of the items are extremely inviting aesthetically as a result of and in spite of their other associations. Although this jewelry is intrinsically attractive, it also appeals to the consumer because it refers to the gold of the conquistadors and fantasies of empire and at the same time embodies the fascination with archaeology and the "discovery" of ancient mysteries: The latter sanitizes the former. The buyer brings home the treasure, rather like Heinrich Schliemann, who retrieved the gold of Troy in the nineteenth century.

The Commodification of the Proper Name

The marketability of a museum reproduction piece has to do with an exchangeability of value, which is coded through the proper name of the artist or the culture that created the aesthetic style. (This is very similar to the way cosmetics and other luxury commodities have traditionally been sold.) Classical Greece, Renaissance Italy, and Tang dynasty China are names imbued with elegance and beauty; similarly, names such as Pierre-Auguste Renoir and Edgar Degas exceed the identity of the artists to which they refer. There is also a link between appropriations of exotic or historical styles in the decorative arts and the aesthetic appropriations that occur in high art. For example, designers of household objects such as dinner plates and bedsheets make use of African-style designs, as did the European artists who incorporated African aesthetics into their work. Both designers and artists code (or partially code) their work through the proper name *Africa* or, more precisely, the image of Africa available in the West. How do marketing strategies for each set of commodities interact and run these through a recognizable name?

The proper name in question can be that of a famous artist, culture, or place that evokes certain sensibilities. The British Museum's advertisement for David's nose explicitly refers not only to Michelangelo but also to the collector from whom the object was acquired and to the "fame" that surrounds the sculpture. The Smithsonian Incan robe names the culture that "inspired" the design and the geographical site associated with this culture: Cuzco, Peru (and to make sure everyone understands the images on the robe, the ad speaks of "exotic animals"). The design for a picture frame is taken from a Beardsley drawing; the frame becomes the "Aubrey Beardsley Frame." The more exalted the artist is, the more hyperbolic the ad copy is. Michelangelo is clearly valorized above all others and treated in ad copy as the greatest artist of all time. The Metropolitan Museum offers a "cast marble" plaque molded from the artist's *Pietà* sculpture for $165 (see Figure 4.4), and the catalog ad is a cacophony of capitalized names, all of which contribute to the allure of the object and to its putative good taste: the Virgin, Michelangelo, The Metropolitan Museum of Art (not "The Met," as elsewhere), The Department of Scientific Research at the Vatican Museum, Saint Peter's Basilica, Rome, Carrara (the source of the marble dust, which is mixed with resin and fashioned into the plaque and happily described as the very source of the marble used by Michelangelo for the original sculpture).

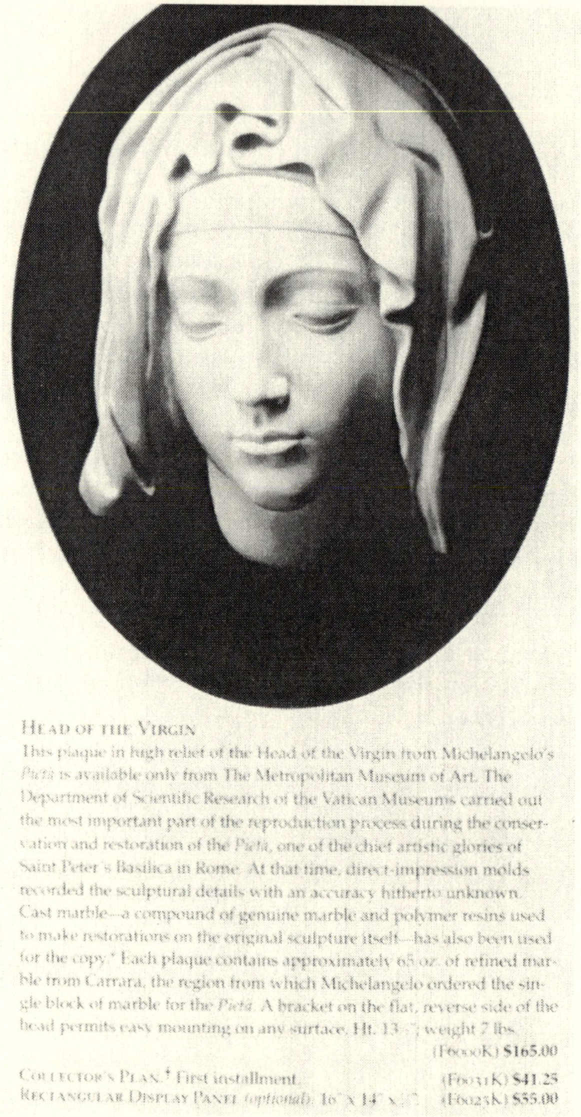
Head of the Virgin
This plaque in high relief of the Head of the Virgin from Michelangelo's *Pietà* is available only from The Metropolitan Museum of Art. The Department of Scientific Research of the Vatican Museums carried out the most important part of the reproduction process during the conservation and restoration of the *Pietà*, one of the chief artistic glories of Saint Peter's Basilica in Rome. At that time, direct-impression molds recorded the sculptural details with an accuracy hitherto unknown. Cast marble—a compound of genuine marble and polymer resins used to make restorations on the original sculpture itself—has also been used for the copy.* Each plaque contains approximately 65 oz. of refined marble from Carrara, the region from which Michelangelo ordered the single block of marble for the *Pietà*. A bracket on the flat, reverse side of the head permits easy mounting on any surface. Ht. 13; weight 7 lbs.
(F6000K) $165.00
Collector's Plan.† First installment. (F6031K) $41.25
Rectangular Display Panel (optional): 16" x 14" (F6023K) $55.00

FIGURE 4.4 "Head of the virgin," Metropolitan Museum of Art reproduction

The fashion industry's commodification of the designer's name is extremely similar to what occurs in the marketing of museum reproductions; techniques of marketing are more obvious in the former because fashion falls somewhere between art and commerce. The ability to purchase a bottle of Chanel perfume for $40 is meant to refer to the $3,000 suit that very few are able to afford. Chanel explicitly markets accessories this way because these cheaper, more accessible products constitute the bulk of its business. What is important are the link between the two classes of products and the way the name is enough to sell an idea of French luxury and sophistication. Thus, a tube of lipstick or a bottle of perfume plays with notions of the timelessness of true style, of valorized locales such as Paris, and of class and the attendant qualities of glamor and elegance.

Museum catalogs closely resemble fashion magazines in the way they construct chains of references.[20] A 1991 Metropolitan Museum catalog offered Diego Rivera plates, a 1993 catalog sold a Rivera-based scarf (see Figure 4.5), but both refer to mural works and the recent interest in

Mexican painting in North America. As with perfume, a consumer's ability to purchase a dinner plate based on the famous artist's design supposedly indicates "taste" because it refers to the far more expensive easel work. Rivera's work also appears exotic to some, but this exoticism is mediated through the European high art tradition that has legitimized Rivera and through the now-recognizable name of the artist. The types of objects being reproduced and ennobled with the artist's name seem increasingly to involve articles of clothing and household goods rather than prints or other straightforward reproductions of artists work. (I rarely see prints anymore except in students' apartments.) The shift to more utilitarian objects is no accident; it indicates the extent to which aesthetic value has become exchangeable in the marketplace. This shift helps break down the (false) distinction between high and low culture, but at the same time it transforms anything and everything into a potential commodity.

Class and Gender Anxieties

In North America the narratives of mass culture constantly assure citizens that they can change their class, provided they manage to move up. A large portion of the retail economy is dependent on the fiction that class position is fluid and indeed up to the consumer. At the same time, class continues to be a touchy issue as systemic inequalities become more entrenched. After living in Western Europe for a couple of years, I began to realize that in those older and somewhat more cohesive societies, even if people seek to accumulate money, there is less desire to transform class and even less of a belief that a person can successfully do so than in North America. (Although, having said that, I should point out that explicitly class-based codes of taste and deportment are utilized in advertising in Britain to an even greater extent than in North America.) In North America the fiction persists that (despite all evidence to the contrary) class does not really exist except as a kind of personal choice, and if it does by some chance persist in certain contexts, questions of class are reducible to taste and money. Again, the story insists that, much like poverty, a person's class is up to her or him.

Obviously class and taste are closely linked, as Pierre Bourdieu has shown in some detail in the French context,[21] but just because someone suddenly prefers a certain style of home decorating does not mean that she just as suddenly occupies a different class or is recognized as doing so by others. But advertisers want the consumer to think that class is reducible to choice, and they construct a market in which class markers are exchangeable as commodities. Everyone knows that putting someone in evening dress next to a product is a way of trying to convince people that the product is associated with the rich, with luxury, leisure, good taste, and sex.

Bourdieu suggests that taste is the result of education in certain sets of codes that fall along class lines. For instance, people from the upper class like the work of Wassily Kandinsky, and working-class people prefer sentimental paintings of animals. Again, this is true to some extent, but the very obviousness of such preferences quickly becomes uninteresting. The codes of class and taste are much more fragmented in contemporary North America than in France because they function as commodities and because a mass market in what used to be upper-class codes has been constructed. The signs of good taste are not completely exchangeable across any or all class lines, but a middle-class person can upgrade his or her status (or imagine it is possible to do so) through the purchase of certain commodities that refer to the old-school art collector and to the elite sensibilities that informed the collector. At the same time, the display of the object refers to the newer, North American ideology of individuality and the personal taste of the consumer.

Museum catalogs work so well because they evoke upper-class aesthetic codes, which attract the interest of the consumer, in part, because in North America the mainstream has been constructed as upper middle class. People do worry about the quality of their taste. Look at how the characters with whom viewers are supposed to identify are presented in the movies and on television, and closely examine the kind of clothes they wear. With the exception of shows like *Roseanne* that explicitly claim to construct a working-class milieu, upper-middle-class taste has been recoded as both ordinary and accessible and normalized to the extent that it is often invisible, as in the *Cosby* show. In films such as *Moonstruck* the story begins with the characters engaged in nonglamorous occupations—plumbing, bookkeeping, baking—but at a certain point everyone suddenly becomes extremely glamorous, with big houses, fancy restaurants, and operatic elegance. For me, this normalization of upper-middle-class taste is particularly apparent in the recent flurry of movies set in Seattle, where I grew up. Everyone seems to live in elegant, architecturally designed modern houses with sweeping views of Puget Sound. Everyone dresses stylishly and sports flattering haircuts. This smartness is not treated as something remarkable, but it is certainly not the Seattle most people experience.

The movement of taste occurs via objects but is reinforced by the narratives surrounding these objects, such as the Pietà plaque's desirability being dependent on the valorization of Michelangelo. Class anxieties can be discharged and occluded by the purchase of such objects, the availability of which democratizes taste and underlines the buyer's affiliation with the elite culture of fine art. The older discourse surrounding these objects concerned the popularization of patrician, upper-class taste and the movement of class signifiers to the middle class and hence was a discourse of accessibility. An associated idea was the supposed deterioration of upper-class codes. This notion of debased taste remains true of certain kinds of luxury commodities such as couture clothing, despite the talk in fashion magazines about how contemporary couture designers pirate their ideas from the street (the deterioration of standards is often the subtext here as well).

Although elite taste, and its accompanying colonial sensibility, is evoked in museum catalogs, class remains an ambiguous category. Although museum reproductions seem more explicitly tasteful than, say, the items offered in Franklin Mint ads, museum shops nevertheless market kitsch. The kitschlike qualities of the product must be concealed and glamorized so as to not lose the reproduction's association with high culture. The line between what does and does not constitute kitsch is very thin. Is a silk scarf based on a famous painting an example of bad taste? Is a key chain? Any museum reproduction could potentially sink into the obvious bad taste of the items marketed by the Franklin Mint, and indeed many items found in the Smithsonian catalog really do cross over. (Bad taste seems to be present when an object is used as another object, with lamps being especially suspect; for instance, the Metropolitan Museum sells a Buddha head mounted on a stand, whereas a similar head forms a lamp base in the Smithsonian catalog. And there is always the Inca bathrobe.) The British Museum operates on a slightly different symbolic economy, and the items offered in its catalog are not quite as immediately appealing as aesthetic objects as the Met's because they tend to be less upmarket and hence fall into the category of souvenirs. These objects make no claims to taste and high culture, and the buyer can cheerfully purchase Rosetta Stone tea towels and museum coasters. (But then, why not purchase tea towels decorated with the Rosetta Stone and contemplate the achievements of the ancient world while drying the dishes? Certainly the question of good and bad taste collapses with tea towels.)

One of the most persistent venues for colonialist imagery are advertisements for clothing and perfume. Women are special targets of a particular version of aestheticized exoticism that can easily slip into an explicitly colonial aesthetic. Commodified forms of cultural and ethnic difference appear on the bodies of women—generally but not exclusively white women—and on the objects women are assumed to buy, for instance, sheets and other household items. A great deal of thought has gone into the construction of the images used to advertise these products; the cosmetic and perfume industry takes in billions of dollars every year and spends vast sums on advertising.

White women occupy a particularly ambivalent role in the commodification of cultural difference because so much of the advertising seems to be directed at them (or to put the matter slightly differently, in mainstream media the women to whom the colonial images are directed are assumed to be white). White women have a double relation to the consumption of images of difference, on the one hand, occupying the role of object of desire much like the people and objects being exoticized and on the other, becoming the consumer-colonizer who objectifies others and commandeers whatever happens to please her eye.

Training for this double role begins at a tender age. I remember reading magazines as a young adolescent in which we were encouraged to wear exotic clothes or cosmetics, with exoticism being presented as something that made us more interesting and attractive (at the time to men and boys. Now the entire process has far more to do with extracting money from teenage girls). Exotic style also appeared as an assemblage of fragmented, disparate commodities and accordingly something we could take on and off at will. For young girls, difference was a role we could slip on when we imagined that our ordinary selves had become boring (something not available to those girls read by white people as different and not necessarily able to take the exotic gloss off when it became inconvenient). The main point of the magazine articles was instruction in the arts of consumption, and these oversaw our ability to acquire the skills to master the complex visual codes of girlish respectability but were spiced with the rather less respectable frisson of difference. This affirmation of something supposedly daring became a moment of liberation for us, but one that could occur only via the appropriation of images of women of color, most of which had extremely unsavory subtexts. As we layered on the black eyeliner, why did it not occur to us to pay attention to what happened again and again to Butterfly?

The colonial adventure—and the white privilege on which this adventure depends—is explicitly marketed in advertisements for products such as Ralph Lauren's Safari perfume (see Figure 4.6). Here a colonial version of women's liberation is evoked by the images in the ad, which refer to such independent, wealthy white women of colonial East Africa as Isak Dinesen and Beryl Markham. We see a mélange of romanticized images designed to appeal: the airplane, the luxury hotel, the blond woman dressed in a slip and riding a horse, and the product—perfume in an old-fashioned bottle. The images are visually fragmented but add up to a recognizable whole, bringing to mind a luxurious bygone past (suitably sanitized of colonial oppression) and making this seem appealing. Benetton's ad for Tribù perfume (see Figure 4.7) also utilizes fragmented images of exoticism but appeals to a younger and less exclusively white audience by constructing an equivalence between the European high culture of classical ballet and traditionally dressed people of color. In the Safari ad the colonial past is evoked and romanticized, and in the Tribù ad neocolonialism is erased, with the contemporary activities of, say, cotton multinationals concealed by Benetton's supposed celebration of difference. Africa continues to function as a backdrop to Western concerns but does so here through a rhetoric of inclusion. Multicultural advertisements for perfume and cotton clothing draw atten-

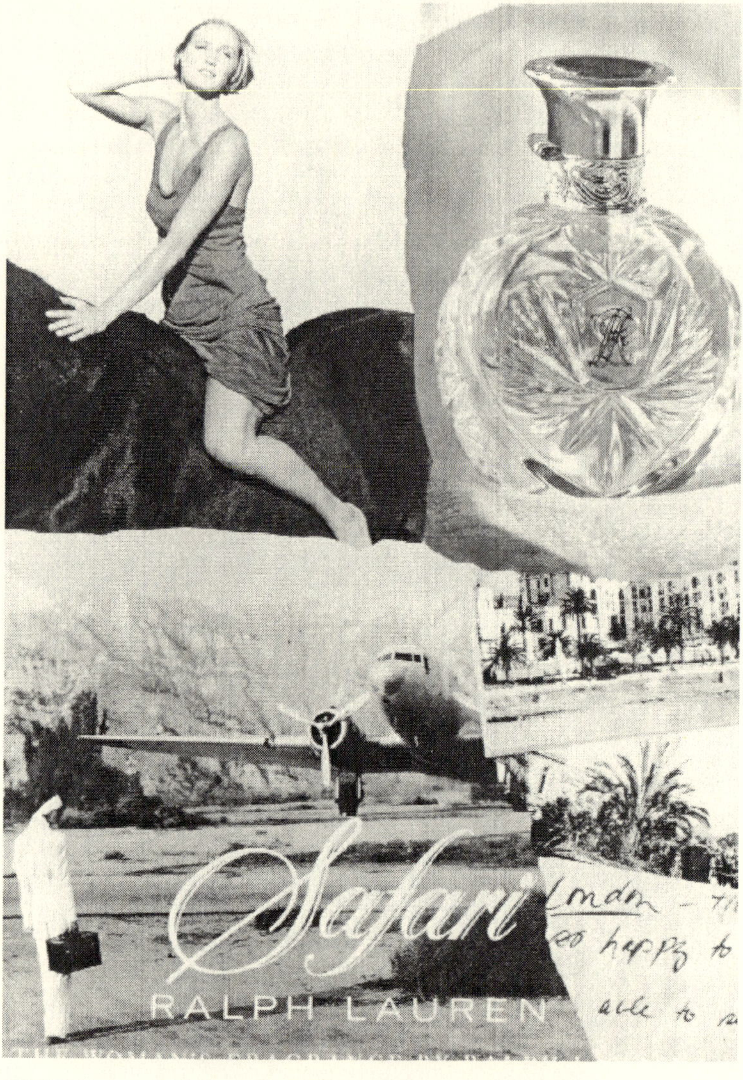

FIGURE 4.6 Ralph Lauren Safari perfume advertisement

FIGURE 4.7 *Benetton Tribù perfume advertisement*

tion away from the extent to which fragmented images of difference continue to function as a commodity in the West. Advertising seems infinitely able to recode and neutralize long-standing tropes while simultaneously intensifying them.

Dead Art

In the Vatican Museum tourists stump through gallery after gallery, up stairs, down corridors, until suddenly a hushed, insinuating voice announces, "You are about to enter the Sistine Chapel" and asks them to be quiet. Everybody obeys, perhaps fearing the voice of God. The soft female voice prepares and regulates the visitor's experience of Michelangelo's ceiling, marking it as a momentous event more important than the Raphaels or Berninis located elsewhere in the museum. The voice reminds tourists to pay attention and advises that their experience of the chapel will be both moving and sublime, unless they happen to be ignorant philistines. Remember, this is all taking place at the Vatican, and the people who administer the museum are Roman Catholic. What, then, precisely is being marked by deploying the hushed tone for an assemblage of paintings, and what might this have to do with the religious subject matter of the work? Is it designed to commemorate the presence of the artistic masterpiece? In other words, has the encounter with the high art of Western culture itself become a religious experience (with the stubborn atheist replaced by the stupid philistine)? Or does it constitute a faint trace of an archaic, sacred system of meaning because the Sistine Chapel is (or was), after all, a chapel, a place for worship?

The disembodied voice lets spectators make up their own mind about whether the essential event concerns God or Michelangelo but also lets them know that something extremely significant is supposed to happen as they contemplate these paintings. But the odor of sanctity around these paintings can, for some spectators, be off-putting. The helpful preparation for the sublime art experience can ultimately have a deadening effect on visitors because it leaves little room for miscalculation, for unexpected responses, or even for indifference to the ceiling.

Large Western art galleries such as the Vatican Museum share many key characteristics with ethnographic museums. They have similar agendas: One instructs the viewer about culture by displaying what is presumed to lie outside the West; the other guides the spectator to parallel conclusions by exhibiting the greatness that supposedly resides at the heart of Western culture. Although the discourse of cultural superiority is much more sublimated in exhibitions of Western painting than in displays of formerly colonized people and ancient empires, it can be seen in the way the canon of great Western art both constructs and is dependent on a notion of an aesthetic heritage, which is to say, a single stream of great art leading up to the present day. Like the displays in the old ethnographic museums, the art history canon is evolutionist. Some work gets in, other work does not, some art is considered influential on later artists, and other art is presented as little more than examples of an aesthetic dead end. In the art museum the spectator is presumed in some profound way to exist within this Western cultural heritage, with access to the internal codes of this heritage, so that she may experience a personal connection to the work. The story of art is told so that influences considered foreign to the European aesthetic tradition are kept to a minimum, unless they occur in a properly colonized context, such as the influence of Islamic design on Henri Matisse or reclining Mesoamerican *chacmool* figures on Henry Moore. With the help of the experts who decide what will and will not be seen, the spectator learns how to recognize work that deviates from the canon.[22]

Theodor Adorno writes in "Valéry Proust Museum":

> The German word, "*museal*" ["*museumlike*"], has unpleasant overtones. It describes objects to which the observer no longer has a vital relationship and which are in the process of dying. ... Museum and mausoleum are connected by more than phonetic association. Museums are like family sepulchres of works of art. ... Art treasures are hoarded in them, and their market value leaves no room for the pleasure of looking at them.[23]

The characterization of *museal* as a quality that describes objects in the process of dying suggests that the deadening of the art object as an event is always happening and is more likely to happen in the trophylike context of art museum displays. The lifelessness of museum art derives from the relation between objects and the people who come to look at them: Art objects, by their presence in a museum, are unable to engage the viewer in any dynamic way. Museums by their very nature have this effect because they are designed to demonstrate systems of genealogy and lineage rather than individual pieces. In other words, they are concerned with the dead and how they connect to us. ("And then Cezanne begat Picasso," but the corpses are exhibited for all to see in the gallery.) There is a peculiar quality about the museum building that blunts its contents, an airlessness and silence that hover just above the images on display.[24] The museum's ability to deaden its contents is obvious when the museum contains stuffed animals or the artifacts of extinct societies, but when it contains the high art of Western culture, a slightly different process is at work. The manipulation of life and death is as apparent in an art museum as in a natural history exhibition.

What interests me is how Western art is presented to a mainstream audience, to people who grew up more or less as I did, watching the occasional art program on public television and reading about New York artists in magazines. (In provincial Seattle there were a few of us who imagined that our lives would be considerably more fascinating and complete if only we could contemplate original masterpieces in the capitals of Europe.) I mean an audience with a superficial education in Western art combined with a belief that it is important. High art is subject to many expectations, none of which concerns death and anaesthetization; indeed, rather than deadening the viewer, art is supposed to have the opposite effect because (in theory at least) it can provide a transcendental experience and evoke a range of lofty sentiments. The nature of these sentiments has shifted since the nineteenth century, as have the aesthetic tools used to elicit noble thoughts, but the idea that art can lead to religious, patriotic, critical, or political awareness continues to obtain. High art in its mainstream incarnation is generally believed to manifest a special visual language that will permit the suitable viewer to uncover truths about the world that are otherwise hidden. (Although this language may be imagined as universal, it always seems to be a dialect of Greek.) This is certainly one explanation for the high prices these works command and the way they have been culturally reified. The ability of high art to raise the spectator's consciousness is a noble ideal, and sometimes it actually happens. But more often the experience of the museum-goer is rather different: Among people who enjoy art (but are not specialists), and who make a point of visiting museums as part of cultural holidays, the exalted response is actually a rarity. The transcendental experience usually does not take place for reasons of exhaustion, which has to do with how and where great art is housed.

At the National Gallery in London, a huge edifice full of centuries of paintings, it is very easy to come away with a blinding headache. There is simply too much to absorb: Image after image collapses time and space; it becomes impossible to look at any image without being affected by everything else. Art appears as a vast aggregate rather than as many discrete images or sets of images tied to particular contexts, and it is the aggregate that overwhelms the spectator. This has to do in part with the concept of a national collection, which must be large and comprehensive enough to impress the rubes with its status as state institution.

I remember moving as briskly as I possibly could through the National Gallery, deliberately averting my eyes from the Dutch landscapes so I would have something left for French romanticism. It is not that Dutch landscape painting is unsatisfactory in itself or even uninteresting to me personally; it was just that I felt bombarded by pictures and imagined that any superfluous image would burn a hole through my eyes and make it impossible for me to see anything else. I understood clearly that museum collections of art sap energy, that they can in fact have a deadening effect on the spectator, one that is often combined with something more malign.

Adorno is right again. Sometimes this effect can be quite frightful: On the same art holiday I passed out in Saint Peter's Basilica from all the bad taste, all the Berninis, the weirdness of the images, like the skeletal arm reaching out with an hourglass as a memento mori to all passersby. I swooned under Saint Theresa, and a woman from California whom I had never seen before had to revive me with grapes. Was this transcendence or fear? Was I dead?

To describe the effect of art on the spectator is still not to answer the question of why is it all too much. Is it because of the idea of a collection, especially a national collection? Is the viewer constantly overwhelmed by the monetary value of the works or indeed by the concept of pricelessness? Or are so many little transcendent experiences occurring that the brain has no choice but to explode? The failure of the museum art piece each and every time to properly awe the viewer is not a question of the rarity or sublimity of the images because, if truth be told, a lot of the work is boring or bad, even if it has been accepted into the canon of Great Western Art. There are simply too many images all in the same place, and the effect becomes a version of the nightmare shopping exhaustion a shopper experiences after closely examining too many similar jackets: The art objects seem to have been transformed into commodities.

I do not want to suggest that it is possible—or even desirable—to imagine a pure art object somehow free of the weight of the canon, the market, the dealers and critics, and all the conferences and university courses. Despite all the fine talk about superior values, an elaborate art industry mediates the way the spectator comes into contact with art in the West. There is no point in pretending that art is untouched by these constraints. Art is subject to market forces like any other product, which is not to argue that it is merely a commodity, sadly and irrevocably tainted by filthy lucre. Rather than seeking the airless space of hushed tones and predetermined greatness, we must recognize that a certain energy returns to the art object when it is seen as part of the society in which it exists, which includes the noise and vigor of the marketplace. A certain luster surrounds the art object and those who create, market, and collect high art, and this luster draws attention away from the extent to which art must conform to market forces. Similarly, the ethical luster of high art depends on a high level of dissimulation with respect to how art is produced and how it links up to and alibis other, often disagreeable aspects of the social order. The questions then arise, What makes one work valorized and admitted into the canon and another rejected? To what extent have politics and criticality become aesthetic commodities that can be exchanged in the art market?

The art market works according to a double process: When nineteenth-century academic art began to command higher prices in the market several years ago (because these works were in the price range of would-be collectors who could not afford more fashionable work), critics began to reassess this work, which meant more interest in it and even higher prices, which meant more critical articles. The museum is the end result of this process: Work that has been determined by the industry to be good is acquired and displayed by the museum.

It is a fact that a work's market value structures how it is seen. The Italian Renaissance and French impressionism have probably been the most successfully promoted periods of Western art, and hence the most valorized, as becomes immediately clear after a cursory glance at the art shows on PBS, curricula in art colleges, and the high end of the art section at bookstores. A great deal of this art *is* aesthetically interesting, but this changes nothing about the way it has been positioned and reified within the art industry. The more esoteric tastes are also subject to commodification, and the shifts in the status of particular genres are apparent in the turf battles in art history departments over what should be considered art and hence appropriate objects of study (for instance, is embroidery and other crafts traditionally done by women art? What about objects made for the tourist trade?).[25] Occasionally a moment of tension emerges between a work's market value and its cultural value: I recall the flurry of excitement when Japanese investors started buying impressionist paintings during the 1980s, not the least of which was the feeling among many in the Western art scene that something was not quite right when Asians "took" the work of the European masters to a country considered to be non-Western (although the dealers handling the sales probably had no problem with this).

In a short piece titled "Price and Meaning," Mexican essayist Octavio Paz wrote in 1963:

> It is no longer necessary for artists to die: they are embalmed while they are still alive. This danger goes by the name of success. The work must be "novel" and "rebellious." It is a matter of novelty that is mass-produced and of a rebellion that doesn't scare anyone. Artists have become sideshow monsters, scarecrows. And the works: plastic monsters neatly cut out, packaged, labelled, and provided with all sorts of stamped documents to get them through moral and aesthetic customs. Harmless monsters.[26]

Like any other commodity, art is subject to the economy of the marketplace, and artists have to take the market into account if they wish to survive as artists. Nearly anything can operate as currency in the system of exchange: Nationalism, ugliness, and, as Paz points out, criticality and rebellion can increase a work's market value and prestige. Paz may have had his own agenda with respect to his assessment of political art, but his remarks are to the point. Artists are expected to play a certain role in the social order and their art to have a certain rebellious function, which makes grand claims but is often unable to follow through. Paz is suggesting that art work is deadened when it is inserted into a system of exchange that determines value according to price and a predetermined criterion of criticality. The demand that work express a socially or politically critical sensibility becomes a way of circumscribing this criticality and of anticipating in advance what it would look like. This demand further circumscribes the sensibilities of the creator of the work, who is permitted to play the game of épater les bourgeois but not much else.

Despite the fact that fine art is subject to market forces, it continues to hold the high moral ground and to be talked about in quasi-religious terms. How did all the expectations of what art is able to do get attached to it? The expectations of the twentieth century are familiar: Art is supposed to promote some political agenda, to be critical or rebellious, to expose the hypocrisies of the social order, with artists functioning as Paz's "harmless monsters." Part of the problem involves confusion about what art is expected to achieve, but in general it is expected to do quite a lot. Some people say it reflects the realities of the world—in other words, politics; some say it is able to transcend the social and political context in which it is made; and some say it is supposed to save people by providing them with the experience of beauty or new insights into reality. Many people subscribe to one (if not all) of these views.

In the past the association of art with religion gave it a certain luster. This luster shone not only on paintings that expressed explicitly Christian subject matter but also on those that made use of classical and pagan allegorical themes, which were also supposed to uplift the morals of the viewer and aggrandize the power structure of the day.[27] (Artists slyly played with this expectation of piety, of course.) Today it seems that this anticipation of an aesthetic moral ground continues to function but now derives from the artist's putative role as social critic. (Contemporary artist Jeff Koons's appropriation of "bad taste" and kitschy images of sex with his wife have been read as critical of moral and aesthetic pretensions, and there were certainly factions that understood Andy Warhol's repetitive images of mass culture this way.)

Despite the realities of the market and the questions of commodification, Western art seems well able to maintain the noble agendas of the past. High art has historically been believed to express elevated ideals, and at least since the nineteenth century these ideals have not been concerned with religious experience or allegorical lessons but with the vacancy and corruption of the bourgeois, everyday world. Art has criticized mass society, consumption, bad taste, various kinds of oppression (although rarely the obvious kinds). Sometimes this critique actually works, and certain art pieces succeed in bringing contradictions and hypocrisies to the viewer's attention or in showing these in an unexpected and interesting way. However, criticality can be little more than snobbery or snobbery marking itself as nonsnobbery. If a contemporary artist paints a picture of Elvis Presley on velvet and exhibits it in a fashionable New York gallery, is it still a mark of bad, which is to say, working-class, taste? At times the disdain for mass culture seems to spring from an aristocratic nostalgia for the ancien régime (when the peasants knew their place) rather than from a critique of entrenched systems of power.

Critical Styles and Death

So much of the art of the last fifty years or so has made claims to criticality, which in part is the legacy of the Parisian ideas of bohemianism that have informed the art world since the nineteenth century. Again, critic Théophile Gautier exemplified a new attitude, which is still with us: Gautier's bohemian style gave him the air of someone who was able to see through the conventions of society, but at the same time these stylistic idiosyncrasies masked and excused his links to the French state and the extent to which he supported the status quo. Today it is taken for granted that if artists wish to be considered serious, they must find ways to express their distaste of contemporary culture (even if it is by engaging with the icons of mass culture) and of the existential issues of the day. Minimally, they ought to appear to do so. The drill is familiar: Bourgeois culture is boring and stultifying, we are all ordered about by machines, and the death instinct has been the organizing principle of society since Auschwitz and Hiroshima. This is all very true, but the issue here is the way artists have been talked about as if they have a special grasp of the gravity of these problems via the uplifting luster bestowed by high culture. Critiques of the status quo tend to be partial and easy to forget because the myth of the rebellious artist has been so effective. It is also easy to forget that because most contemporary art makes claims to criticality, it has become the commodity of choice for many collectors. I often (to my continuing embarrassment) experience a moment of surprise when I learn that an artist whose work I find interesting is politically conservative or worse. Surely if she dislikes the bourgeoisie's hideous, boring style, she will also dislike its politics, but apparently not. These are imagined as separate issues.

Outsiders have always had their roles to play in the social order, even if the outside ends up as a fictional space or is far less transgressive than everyone claims. The artist has been designated as the outsider in Western culture, and here I am thinking of Joseph Beuys and the animal he claimed was a coyote and his strange, constructed history—the artist becomes a prophet-shaman, and the work is given a transformative function. Even those with only a vague grasp of the contemporary art scene know enough to expect unhappy artist-geniuses to disparage mainstream-style commodity culture and to live in a marginal, yet interesting way. Cherokee artist Jimmie Durham points out that the notion of the artist as outsider abstracts artists from the ground on which they work and artificially separates aesthetics, politics, and spirituality. Contrasting a Native approach to aesthetics with that usually taken for granted in the West, Durham writes, "We do not feel that artists are the exclusive keepers of conscience for society: that is a responsibility shared by all members of society. The idea of artist-asconscience seems romantically, and falsely, shamanistic."[28] Is the artist supposed to criticize society so that the rest of us do not have to?

The notion that the artist is by definition a cultural critic overcodes other ways that the artist's position in both the art market and the larger society could be read. Vast amounts of money flow through the art industry, with some of this money being siphoned off by artists shrewd enough to grasp artistic trends and skilled enough to put this knowledge to work. The question of an artist's success can be tricky, and we are wise not to decide too much in advance about what success or failure might mean in terms of the quality of the work. Certainly success in the art world is not read in quite the same way as, say, success in law or real estate but instead can appear as something that naturally accrues to an artist who is good, with a veil drawn over the question of market forces. Of course, very few artists are actually marked as good—hence the cutthroat social relations and strictly enforced pecking orders in the contemporary art world. If the way successful artists get written up in both art and mainstream journals is any indication, success and accumulation of wealth are naturalized and not presented as particularly contradictory to the artist's function as critic. Criticality has come to be very narrowly defined, at least in part because of its status as a currency that can be exchanged for success in the marketplace. A critique of mass production does not necessarily constitute a critique of capitalism in general but can refer to an aristocratic disdain for the ordinary, something like Andy Warhol and his soup cans. Yes, we know mass production is ugly and oppressive, but it is certainly possible to recognize this and still maintain reactionary ideas, which can be concealed by the ambivalence of the message.

Expectations of criticality influence how an artist's success is read. That a very few artists have become rich does not necessarily mean that they have renounced their critical function because in the art world selling out tends to be viewed more as a question of taste and sensibility than of accumulation of money and power. Part of this problem with assessing an artist's success has to do with the difficult concept of selling out, a vague, yet insulting term that can be hurled at anyone for nearly any reason, but part of it concerns the dissembling of the artist's relation to the market in which she shows and sells work. An artist can work hard to amass wealth and praise from the powerful and still be seen as critical of the system that makes this possible, as long as she does not begin to look or act like the bourgeois-style rich in any obvious way.

Many people seem to cling to a mystified understanding of artistic genius and to the idea that talent wells up unbidden in artists, writers, and musicians, horrible and painful and Pythia-like (an artist's years of training are elided by this notion). This understanding goes along with the profoundly evolutionist notion that certain geniuses are so far ahead of their time that they can be appreciated only after their death: discovered, as it were, by a more advanced sensibility. There *is* something mysterious about creativity, but this does not necessarily have anything to do with an artist's success or failure. An oeuvre's reception is another issue entirely but tends to be treated as if it were coextensive with intrinsic merit. The artist is one of the few twentieth-century figures for whom talent is seen as a guarantee of success because this "gift" will be able to transcend all other considerations, including dealers, indifferent critics, philistine collectors, and more. Thus, the acknowledgment of aesthetic merit by the marketplace becomes identical to that merit itself, and being marked as good by the art system is generally taken to mean that an artist is in fact good, that her message is strong, that she is in some profound way critical and provoking.

I am not convinced that, as Pierre Bourdieu suggests,[29] the artists or writer loses symbolic authority or cultural capital with economic success. This may have been true at one time, but the cachet of the impoverished artist is no longer quite convincing, and today the successful artist's cultural capital simply migrates to style. Because rich artists prefer to live in expensive, yet cool lofts in Manhattan rather than in big, ugly, tasteless houses in New Jersey, and to wear Comme des Garçons rather than Valentino, their personal taste becomes a mark of their critical stance. (This is a version of an old, old story: As the Greeks keep telling us, beauty equals the good.) Taste acts as a visual substitute for a more substantially political critique of culture. Not all that much has changed since the days of Théophile Gautier. But the intellectual and artistic avant-gardes have always had a tendency to refer to matters of style rather than to theories of alienated labor and commodity fetishism. This emphasis on style seems very cynical, given the transformative claims of much of this work. But perhaps the level of cynicism is the inevitable result, not of the failure of art to live up to rigorous (and hypocritical) expectations of criticality, but of these expectations becoming so entrenched.

The artist is expected by the public to maintain a bohemian mode of life despite her successes, which becomes a mark of authenticity that supposedly goes beyond personal taste. A collector is usually far less anxious about his or her class position than an artist or critic, and by purchasing critical art, the collector inherits the mana of the sharp-eyed cultural critic. Like anyone else, wealthy collectors want to imagine that they are smart and wary (and indeed some are), and they want to inform people that, although they may be bourgeois, they are not *really* bourgeois because they know enough to buy interesting, antiestablishment paintings. The status of the work of art as a commodity means that it functions accordingly in the market, but this issue is more complex when the content of the work severely challenges the position of those who treat it as such. For instance, Leon Golub's images of mercenaries and political executions are very creepy and strong, and his work is purchased by corporations. Given the content of his work, this seems a paradox: Although the work is good and addresses difficult issues, given the unsavory political activities of many multinationals, why would a corporation want to own a Golub, a work that could remind people of the human cost of political intervention? As an investment? The work is transformed into a pure commodity by the art market, and consequently the actual image is unimportant, a move that is breathtaking in its cynicism but probably an accurate description of the way things actually work. Nevertheless, those who recall what happened to Salvador Allende might ask if any Golub images of political torture are by chance in the art collection of the corporation that owns Anaconda Copper.

The Marketing of Marginality

The marketing of 1980s New York artist Jean-Michel Basquiat is exemplary of how false demands and expectations can turn a body of art work and the artist himself into something dead, into commodities. In this case the artist actually died, a fact quickly incorporated into the myth being flogged in the marketplace. It does not really matter if this particular artist was complicit in the way he was being sold (when he was alive) because the terms had been set up long before he came on the scene. Basquiat's work can be disingenuous, and his relation to the art world was somewhat ambivalent, but his paintings are about something in the world (a quality that becomes apparent when Basquiat's work is compared to that of some of the other names of the 1980s, for instance, Julian Schnabel).

Basquiat was marketed as a child of the ghetto, as a "natural" artist, as a drug-obsessed idiot savant who was unable to handle success (unlike presumably more knowledgeable white people, went the silent subtext). He came from middle-class Brooklyn and had an accountant father, a fact a bit difficult to romanticize and equally difficult to sell, especially in the case of a young African-American artist. Basquiat was constructed (and constructed himself) as a commodified entity and inserted into a narrative that links up to other, more explicitly racist narratives. I recall people in the mid-1980s talking about Basquiat's work as if he were the true voice of urban authenticity and as if his work were a way for white spectators to access a cultural truth usually denied them. (This whiff of cultural voyeurism is also apparent in the way some white people talk about rap music, which also becomes a way of aggrandizing their claim to hipness.) Such characterizations are always ambivalent: Should the artist affirm or reject narratives of authenticity and genius or even pay attention to the rather problematic subtexts of these? Does thinking about questions of genius at all induce paralysis in the artist? Basquiat's supposed authenticity was rarely talked about (at least in white circles) as a particularly African-American issue, except that his blackness made this authenticity appear particularly gritty and genuine, to some at least. Race became something for sale, a phenomenon that certainly did not begin with Basquiat. His work was rarely addressed as something that might derive from a particular experience or community, and the extent to which his work addressed issues of racism was generally elided.

Rather, the Basquiat persona that circulated in the art world referred to the old story that insists that people designated as outsiders have more immediate access to pure, unconscious experience, which means that their work is seen as less intellectually based than that of artists designated as insiders. Basquiat was, after all, a graffiti artist and exuded the aura of the street rather than the art college (certainly the extent of his training was passed over in the mythologizing). His public image manifested multiple identities: part bohemian, part African American, part heroin addict, all of which were read as outsider by moneyed average art collectors and as romantic by others. Basquiat walked a particular edge and took risks that others could or would not, which seemed to delight the people who surrounded him and sought to make money off his work. His stance enabled them to imagine they were calling their own existence and certainties into question without actually having to do so. The artist does shock the bourgeoisie, but the bourgeoisie loves it and is prepared to pay good money for the experience.

There is still something of a mystery in the art world's reception of Basquiat (and one that ultimately reinforces the belief in the triumph of genius): There is no question that much of his work is very good and very critical of some of the most cherished notions of Western culture. I think bell hooks is right when she says that Basquiat called the European aesthetic tradition into question and "takes the Eurocentric valuation of the great and beautiful and demands that we acknowledge the brutal reality it masks."[30] See, for instance, *Native Carrying Some Guns, Bibles, Amorites on Safari* (1982), which depicts a very shocked but human-looking black man standing next to a cartoonlike, empty-eyed white man wearing a pith helmet. This work undoes the racial and historical certainties presumably maintained by many patrons of the arts, and I expect that such images would make rich white collectors a little uneasy. At the same time, Basquiat did work within the Western high art tradition, but this does not fully explain why he was taken up by such collectors. Given the nature of his work, how do we account for his success?

Could it be that collecting political art—by museums or private collectors—is a way of discharging the message of the work, in other words, of transforming the critical potential of such work into something dead and decided and imbuing it with the *museal* quality described by Adorno? Because political space is subject to commodification, a certain type of exhibition can only reiterate this commodification and thus constitute a display of the dead. Collecting art such as Basquiat's may become a way for the bourgeoisie to discharge any residual guilt (if it feels any—an unlikely story, I am told), but also, and more accurately, to discharge anxiety about lack of taste and the notion that money means no taste. (This interpretation may be entirely too complicated: Artist friends assure me that most collectors lack the apparatus to see the critical subtext of the work, although in Basquiat's case it is hard to see how they could have avoided it.) Again, the underlying machine refers to an aristocratic ideal in which criticality is coded as an aristocratic prerogative rather than something that might actually call the social and political order into question. But no, the elegant *wétiko* aesthete prefers to stand above the fray surveying the world below. Condemnation of mainstream culture, including racism, can derive from an aristocratic disdain of the masses.

Art and Commerce

Despite the exalted ideals of high culture and the claims of aesthetic purity, public productions of high culture events are supported by corporate money. Advertisements for the ballet, PBS presentations of English novels, and important art exhibitions all tend to be accompanied by the now-ubiquitous corporate logo. The usual argument is that, despite the unsavory motives of business, at least the work gets mounted, the actors get jobs, the artists get shown, and so on. This is true, and in any case there really is no pure space of high art (if indeed there ever was). After all, corporate advertising supports prime-time cop shows as well, so why not take the money for something that might prove more interesting? But we need to pay attention to how corporate values have allied with and ultimately usurped the lofty pretensions of high culture. In the introduction to *Museums and the Shaping of Knowledge* Eilean Hooper-Greenhill describes a fairly typical advertisement for an exhibition on Claude Monet that appeared in the London *Independent* in 1990:

> Discover how one man's vision can change the way you look at the world.
>
> In every series, no two pictures are exactly alike. A single theme. The same object. But enveloped in varying light, changing seasons and atmosphere. This is Monet in the '90s.
>
> Digital Equipment Corporation and its employees are proud to sponsor the exhibition that brings together, for the first time, the series paintings of Claude Monet.[31]

This advertisement has several curious features. The first word, *discover,* links the reader to a grand tradition of Western exploration, which resonates most emphatically with the colonial project. This reminder that the show concerns the high aesthetic tradition is reiterated by the claim that contemplating this work will provide the viewer with a transformative experience. Conquest and transcendence are all in the first sentence. The second section plays with temporality: The 1890s of Monet and the 1990s of the exhibition are collapsed in a deliberately ambiguous way. This temporal collapse is linked to the idea of change and the way these paintings are simultaneously the same and different, possibly like the nineteenth and the twentieth centuries (which are turning out to be a lot more alike than I would have predicted if the Dickensian conditions in the cities are any indication). The final section of the ad stresses the proactive role of the corporation, which has brought these works together for the first time in one hundred years. Thus, the corporation not only makes a new vision possible but also understands the need to change and stay the same. The message is designed to be very reassuring indeed.

The reader of this advertisement is supposed to feel indebted to corporate largesse for the opportunity to experience the magic moment of transcendence that Monet's work will generate. Formerly those of us who benefited from philanthropic gestures were supposed to thank the lords and lordlike individuals who made such events and venues possible, bringing art and libraries to the people. Today noblesse oblige is much more insidious: The (mythical) average spectator is supposed to identify with the corporate agenda, or, rather, the corporation's agenda has become identified with everyone else's. This is in many respects the point of the exhibition. It is the advertisement's evocation of corporate "pride" and the inclusion of the reference to its "employees" that are the key to the spectator's experience of Monet's work. The advertisement presents the corporation as a large family that the viewer can be part of by attending the Monet show. In the past most people probably did not imagine a personal connection with the philanthropic gesture or Peggy Guggenheim's world, and indeed the circulation of the philanthropic proper name ran on a different economy than corporate sponsorship. The old way ultimately referred to feudalism; the new way insists that everyone is equal (as long as we ignore all the nasty underlying power issues).

At this stage of the New World Order I can scarcely imagine an alternative to the marketplace of images and ideas or an answer to the old question "What is art?" I feel rather sad as I reread Walter Benjamin's high hopes for a politically engaged art in "The Work of Art in the Age of Mechanical Reproduction,"[32] hopes that turn out to have been overly optimistic. Capital moves very, very quickly and seems able to transform anything into a commodity. Benjamin thought that art could be liberated from its dependence on ritual, but perhaps ritual is not such a bad idea after all or is not something that needs to be imagined as separate from aesthetics. One possible way to circumvent the problem of the marketplace (if artists want to do so) might be to think of art as a ceremony because ceremony grounds art to society differently than commodification does—value runs through land rather than money. This is not an easy task: Ana Mendieta and other performance artists in the 1960s and 1970s sought to tie the work to an event rather than a product that could be bought and sold, and it turned out that art was unable to continue without the market (but artists in those days did seem to have more fun, which is something at least). Ceremony seems to work only if it is based on common sense and is understood as part of a larger system of meaning, one that helps people see the point of this system and how it is connected to the things they do (this is why the ceremony needs to be real rather than another commodity, as so often happens in the New Age). Without ceremony, everything floats through time and space; in the end there are only corporations. This is not how things were supposed to turn out.

5

Dreams and Landscapes: The Delineation of Wild Spaces

> A heaven with gold-paved streets lived inside the minds of [fifteenth century] Europeans, and a far God who didn't live on land but in a distant place with mansions, gold, and winged people, those who had lived well enough to escape the earth. The dominant belief system looked away from land. ... It did not value the plants or animals that fed the people. The living world was not a sacred, alive thing. ... From a contemporary perspective these men's ignorance about the world was a not-knowing that had devastating consequences for people and for the land, as much as it had in their own land, with their own people.[1]

The dominant European mentality of the fifteenth and sixteenth centuries described by Chickasaw writer Linda Hogan would have profound effects on how land was represented in the West, as well as on the representation of people who sought to inhabit the land in an ancient way. Once human beings began to imagine that they could usurp the godlike function of the earth to give and withhold life, the sacred contract between the human and nonhuman worlds was broken, and there was no longer any effective mechanism that could check the emergence of *wétiko* sickness and commodity fetishism. In an earlier chapter I raised the question of what people in Western culture seem so desperate about, desperate to the point that they must cannibalize cultures deemed more interesting or authentic in order to locate meaning. Here I attempt to map out the source of this anxiety, which I believe is alienation from land.

problem

crux

This is not a new problem. The subordination of the earth to a hierarchical system that considered land inherently in need of discipline (by those humans deemed best to judge, who were rarely farmers) was carried out in policies and decisions designed to bring land under human purview. These had profound effects on how human activities were conceived and regulated in the everyday world both in Europe and in the colonial societies of the Americas. For hundreds of years prior to the invasions of North and South America, Christian law concerned itself with adjudicating land use, making rulings about jurisdiction over land, the rights of non-Christians to property, and the legal conditions constituting just war over territory. Christian doctrine asserted (although put in different terms today) that Christians had a duty to make the land productive; what constituted productivity was carefully laid out by the lawyers of the church. Canon law developed the legal category of *terra nullius,* or "empty land," which in the colonial period was first used to justify Portuguese incursions into West Africa in the fifteenth century (this category originated much earlier during the Christianization of Eastern Europe). The French utilized the concept of *terra nullius* in what is now Canada when Jacques Cartier claimed rights of discovery for the French crown on the lands over which he traveled. Neither West Africa nor Canada was uninhabited, but the people who lived in these territories were not considered inhabitants according to European law. This idea derived from notions of proper use of land and the universalization of Greek and Roman concepts of land use. All people, Christian or not, were considered subject to natural law, which was thought to be based on the faculty of human reason. Living according to reason meant living in fixed settlements with an established political hierarchy—in other words, in some version of the Greek polis.

Egalitarian systems of land use were seen as inherently nonproductive, static, incapable of assimilating notions of progress, political freedom, and, in some instances, free trade (for instance, the fur trade in North America). Thus, at the most basic level of survival—how people produced the food that kept them alive—Europeans were confident that they knew best and were prepared to universalize and impose their own system on others.

According to *terra nullius,* nomadic and migratory peoples did not demonstrate reason in their way of life and were therefore not considered to truly occupy or inhabit the land. The fear of unsettled people runs deep in European thinking and has periodically flared up in continuing attempts to exterminate Gypsies. This fear is also apparent in all the wandering Jew stories of the nineteenth century. The reasons someone might have to move across land—for instance, trade or animal husbandry—were not quite good enough, and such people tended to be objects of suspicion. Because indigenous people in nearly every part of the world supposedly misused the land (which happened to lie in territories coveted by the European powers), they were not considered worthy of the territories in which they lived. This legal principle led to the bizarre conceits of the civilizing mission, in which colonists claimed that they were doing indigenous people a favor by permitting them to observe what productive use of land was all about (on expropriated land, of course).

Terra nullius is not simply an idea in dusty lawbooks of the distant past. Just one hundred years ago in British Columbia British colonists argued that Native fishing and hunting did not constitute proper land use because these activities were, according to a universalized British definition, sports. And very recently some of the talk from Hydro Quebec spokespeople about the James Bay II hydroelectric project has suggested that because Cree people are hunters, they do not make adequate, productive use of the land the provincial government wishes to flood. And the *terra nullius* argument used in the law courts to expropriate aboriginal land was not overturned by the Australian Supreme Court until 1991. During the 1990 standoff between the Mohawk nation and the governments of Quebec and Canada, the mayor of the town of Oka asserted that the lands under dispute—a Mohawk burial ground bordering the town—would be put to properly productive use as a golf course. The current conflict between indigenous people and the Mexican government turns on questions of land use and free trade, with the authorities subscribing to the notion that land is really productive only if it is subject to high-yield agribusiness techniques. We can see that to a rather stunning extent questions of land and of proper land use continue to rely on notions of natural law ultimately derived from Christian doctrine.

If Western concepts of productive land use are based on reason, then rationality has proved to be a false friend where the earth is concerned (as it has in so many other areas). The profound alienation of human beings from what sustains life has had severe effects, some of which are only beginning to bear their disagreeable fruit. If land is the basis of life, then paying attention to how it has been conceived in the West, and how it is assumed to be subject to a purely pragmatic system of calculation, can start to answer the question of what precisely has been the great flaw of Western culture and of the Western project in general.

Western Culture and How It Got That Way

I have been talking about Western culture in a way that assumes the reader knows what I mean by this appellation. In one sense any concept of a single, unified Western culture is a construction based on a multitude of transcultural and transhistorical fictions that do not hold up under close inspection—too many margins, too many subcultures. Nevertheless, when the term comes up in conversation, it rarely has to be defined, even though it refers to an extremely complex cluster of ideas and events that have shifted enormously in the past two millennia. Especially if the discussion is running at a fairly general level, the idea of Western culture tends to be casually thrown about as a kind of conceptual shorthand. People recognize the existence of a constantly fluctuating, yet strangely cohesive entity named

Western culture and tend to have no problem describing what this phrase means, both in terms of exemplary texts (many people's minds immediately turn to Aristotle and Hegel) and, for the less confident, exemplary attitudes about hierarchy and power.

When I asked university students in an upper-levels seminar to define Western culture, this not-so-random sample came up with capitalism, Christianity, automobiles, television, and the atom bomb. This list is really remarkably comprehensive insofar as it encompasses a system of exchange, the sacred and technological orders, the organization of space and representation, and technologies of destruction. Other definitions focused on patriarchy or environmental degradation, but everyone seemed to agree that hierarchical beliefs have permeated the hoary (and frightful) triumvirate of church, state, and family. For these students, then, the term *Western culture* ultimately has to do with notions of cultural superiority and science, of high culture and consumption, and of a flattening and dismissal of other cultural traditions. Although such descriptions refer to and attempt to account for real phenomena—and to that extent are true—they do tend to describe some of the effects, rather than the causes, that the complex of practices called Western culture has had in the world. These descriptions also focus on more recent manifestations of the Western project, such as the movements of colonialism and neocolonialism in the past five hundred years.

The fundamental causes of what I am loosely identifying as Western culture are sometimes more difficult to calculate. Like any cultural tradition, Western culture comprises layers of older and related cultures, including Roman, old European, Christian, and pagan (both classical and other) elements, as well as the somewhat less proximate but important influences of Africa and Asia and, more recently, the Americas. Communities designated as subcultural have had effects, although these tend to be vigorously denied by those who consider themselves guardians of the mainstream. The play between dominant and subordinate cultures and subcultures is complex, but the relation between the two does not easily shift. Despite the instability of the border separating mainline European cultures from those designated as other, both internal and external, a dominant ethos has had the upper hand in the West since, say, the twelfth century. This stream continues to be dominant in a range of economic, political, and cultural institutions (what Louis Althusser would call ideological state apparatuses), although it is increasingly subject to challenge. The negative effects of the Western project, such as those identified by my students, have been the result of certain traits that are and have for some time been dominant in the assortment of related cultures we recognize as Western. At base, these traits organize people's relations to power and to land and were imposed on

European people over several centuries before being exported to the colonies.

Hierarchical social and political systems have consistently been valorized in the most orthodox forms of Western thinking, although they do appear in other parts of the world. (Jack Forbes writes: "It is very sad, but the 'heroes' of European historiography, the heroes of the history textbooks, are usually imperialists, butchers, founders of authoritarian regimes, exploiters of the poor, liars, cheats, and torturers."[2]) Although hierarchy is a critical factor, the Western disease is not solely one of power, violence, or imperial aspirations. Certainly many other societies have established repressive regimes in which violence is directed toward people living within them and those identified as enemies, but these regimes have maintained ceremonial apparatuses in which a sacred view of the earth is central. The existence of earth-based belief systems did not prevent either hierarchical social orders or environmental problems—Sumer, one of the earliest city-states, had a problem with the salination of farmland as a result of immoderate irrigation practices—but these beliefs did help prevent a transformation of a system in which some humans dominate other humans into one in which humans dominate nature and life itself. Pharaoh was a megalomaniac, but he maintained a healthy respect for the earth.

In the Christian West the hierarchical social order has been ontologized and has become a lens through which the entire world may be examined, ranked, and assigned a position within a preexisting scale of values. The person doing the assessing in effect takes on a godlike function, which assumes that he (or very rarely, she) is made in the image of God. The great chain of being further links up to scientistic ideologies and to both the older Judeo-Christian notions of the role of human beings on the earth and Hellenic-Roman ideas of authority, on which many contemporary scientific preoccupations are secretly based.

Western culture separates itself from all others by its peculiar attitudes toward the relation between human beings and land in terms of the nature of land (i.e., what the land inherently is) and the uses to which land ought to be put (i.e., what land is good for). People in most parts of the world experience land as something alive that gives of itself to sustain our lives. This is what people mean by the term *mother earth,* the giver of life.

The notion that the world is a dead and machinelike place best understood by mathematics Ph.D.s has eclipsed the older sacred systems in which the paramount concern of society was maintaining the careful balance between human beings and plants, animals, rocks, and rivers. Such systems obtained in Europe before the church imposed its version of the sacred order and initiated projects to standardize doctrine and belief. The declaration of Christianity as the state religion of Rome was followed very quickly by the demise of the old pagan order (or at least those aspects of the old religion visible to authorities); seasonal ceremonies were banned and temple treasuries emptied. (This rapid overturning of ancient meaning structures was rather like what happened in Mexico after the arrival of the Spaniards and must have been nearly as painful.) The combination of Christianity and the old Roman bureaucracies was a perfect recipe for a repressive system, and as this new system expanded across the barbarian universe, hierarchy increasingly came to be privileged over balance in terms of the church's internal structure and the faithful's relationship to the outside world and to the earth. Thou shalt have dominion over the earth, people were told, but at the same time they were conceived (in a rather odd metaphoric turn) as an ignorant, bleating flock of sheep subject to the authority of the priests. The Christian church remains a paradox, or what would be a paradox in an earth-based cosmological order: On the one hand, the church does maintain a sacred worldview and casts a suspicious eye on some high technology; on the other, it identifies untamed land (and people) with the devil.

But deep in the heart of Western culture many communities of people who actually lived on the land rejected the idea that the earth was a dead thing. Both pagans (the word *pagan* is derived from the Latin for "peasant" or "country person") and later certain kinds of Christians, such as Anabaptists and others designated as heretics, opposed the new order. For centuries various millennial movements seeking some version of social equality periodically surfaced in different parts of Europe, a phenomenon that reflected a profound unhappiness with the way the sacred order was being organized by the religious bureaucracies. Some of these heretical groups sought to return to a view of land in which human dominance was not the end and combined this with explicitly nonhierarchical social agendas, sometimes using distinctly revolutionary language. But the rigid hierarchical structure imposed on the natural world also affected how people were conceived by the authorities: Anyone who put the existing social apparatus into question had to go. Because many of the ideas promulgated by the supposed heretics openly called for a return to a belief system to which many subscribed in secret, their ideas did actually threaten this apparatus. The church and most secular governments of the time sought to repress deviant social movements by any means necessary, and the history of Europe is punctuated with multitudinous instances of the bloody spectacle of heretic after heretic being put to death. (As in Tenochtitlán, human sacrifice ensured the continuation of the sacred and social orders.)

In a somewhat less spectacular rejection of hierarchical thinking, farmers living close to the land tended to recognize that dominance of the earth was an impossible fiction and that a collective approach to farming worked best. The old ways never entirely disappeared, and traces can be seen not only in farming practices but also in aesthetic representations of the world. An older view of land may have even crept into high culture in allegorical paintings and literature that utilized classical narratives as their subject, in which pagan figures formed the cast of characters.

Western culture as a unified, imperial force did not spring fully armed into the world; rather, small-scale societies warring and trading in the place called Europe had to learn how to act like an empire. These societies transformed themselves into expansionist regimes—or, from a slightly different perspective, they became cannibalized—over centuries of internal and external conflict. In one sense, it is not unreasonable to suggest that Europe constructed itself as an imperial system through its conflicts with Araby.[3] But imperial systems are as concerned with the regulation of internal peoples as with conquered peoples, so becoming an empire means establishing an imperial relationship with the former. The Crusades sought to free Palestine from the infidel but were also coextensive with the suppression of Christian heterodoxy and the persecution of Jews in Europe. The wars against Araby were closely linked to the invention of the Holy Inquisition and to what Pierre Clastres calls the first instance of ethnocide in European history: the Albigensian crusade against the Cathar heresy in the eleventh century.[4] Suppression of heterodoxy was the pretext, but this crusade was undertaken to acquire territory and to obliterate the culture of southern France, which included the doctrinal specificity of Catharism and the music and poetry of the troubadours.

The ideas of orthodox Christianity merged with a scientistic discourse after the eighteenth century, and the division of land into productive and nonproductive usages was augmented by a mechanistic view of nature. Unfortunately for those of us who worry about the relation between environmental deterioration and rising cancer rates, neither Christianity nor the new sciences seemed particularly interested in questioning the idea that the land was somehow separate from the human endeavors that occurred on it. This view has very recently begun to shift, but it may very well be too late. The machine is fixed pretty firmly in place.

When attitudes began to change in the eighteenth century and focus on new, secular systems of knowledge, orthodox Christianity was unable to fight against the new symbolic order (although it certainly attempted to do so). There are many reasons for this failure, but most probably the conceptual rigidity of the established churches ultimately brought the old system down. For a very long time orthodox Christianity had been based on a hierarchical chain of being that viewed any deviance from the party line with suspicion, and the burnings of supposedly heterodox deviant witches were well within memory. At first scientific thought and rationality must have seemed to offer the potential for emancipation from the constraints of the church and the divine right of kings, but scientism was to go hand in hand with increasing control and regulation of land, European women, and the everyday lives of colonized people.

Again, Deleuze and Guattari's idea of a process of deterritorialization and recoding helps explain what happened to (and what went wrong with) a potentially liberating discourse. We can imagine how science and individualism were able to seduce with promises of free and open inquiry. The assumptions that drove the scientific endeavor were naturalized and, like linear time, made to seem real or at least the only relevant way of looking at the world.[5] Although over the centuries many Europeans have been uneasy with the destructive potential of science and its technological applications (an unease apparent in phenomena as diverse as the Luddite movement of the early nineteenth century and the continuing fascination with Mary Shelley's *Frankenstein*), today the dominant discourse tells us again and again that because land is dead, its value can be calculated in dollars and cents. We are usually also informed in the same breath that everything is just fine.

At the bottom of this insistence that land is a commodity like any other is, I think, a real fear of the earth, particularly of the extent to which it exists outside of and beyond the dominion of humans. This fear, of course, reverses the idea that it is so-called primitive people who fear natural phenomena and reveals this idea as a projection of the anxiety caused by alienation from the earth. The source of the fear seems simple: What if the earth refuses to be dominated?

Freedom from churchly repression was interpreted by those seeking to fill the new, secular power vacuum as an opportunity to bring about more efficient control of both land and people. Ultimately the hierarchies of the church did not dissolve but were merely renamed, reformulated, and in many respects rendered even more stable and intense; the Christian idea that land in a wild state by definition requires domination and discipline mutated into the scientific dream of total control of nature.[6] Because of claims of pure, objective neutrality, the hyperrational approach concealed its affiliation with entrenched systems of power, which made it more difficult to criticize. Science has a tendency to present itself as somehow above human endeavors and claims. The fetishization of rationality is apparent even in approaches that were critical in other ways. If we think of the orthodox Left as the official opposition within Western culture, we see a conspiracy of silence around questions of land in the latter's propensity to embrace industrial progress (and, in some instances, its affirmation of the European colonialist agenda). Those who refused to accept rationality and progress as a universal model went from being called infidels to being considered just plain stupid. Expertise could be acquired by anyone—or at least that was how the story went—and for that reason appeared liberating and able to transcend class and the old feudal system. Cause and effect were defined much more narrowly, and the refusal to recognize certain effects of the scientific enterprise was presented as a breaking free from superstitions. The result was a system of calculation in which cynicism ruled.

There are still many people who think that science will save us because they believe that science is actually true. But this belief assumes that the alienation from land on which much (although to be excruciatingly fair, not quite all) Western science is based is irrelevant to its practice and therefore that the effects of this alienation on how people organize and represent themselves are negligible. But Christian and scientistic claims to truth do affect how people in this society live and how other cultures are represented.

How Ideas About Land Structure Ideas About People

The Western, Christian view of land and of the earth, although central to an understanding of the nature of European colonial expansion and by extension, the nature of European racism, has not always received as much attention in current critiques of colonialism as have religious or cultural matters. The colonial project clearly drew on and manifested the conception of land dominant within Europe. In general, people living outside of Europe were identified with the land they occupied, imagined as being part of the natural world and as existing in some profound way without culture, purely at the subsistence level. The notion that land exists to be exploited lies just below the surface of colonial representation. Certainly the colonial enterprise both expressed and produced complexes of ideas about colonized people that were used to explain and justify European domination. But a colonial mentality is in one sense less a question of negative stereotypes about people than of how land is conceived and treated both in discourse and in the world. Critiques of colonial ideologies have tended to focus on people, and the inattention to questions of land is itself symptomatic of a naturalization of the dominant Western view and of the extent to which a distorting lens continues to deflect attention away from our increasing distance from the earth.

Orthodox Western views of land and culture continue to be universalized, sometimes in bizarre ways. For instance, why has landscape painting become a sign of debased (in other words, working-class) taste? Naturalistic images of the natural world are mass produced and sold at discount warehouse stores and in the parking lot art shows so derided by the guardians of high culture. There are exceptions—impressionist work and some Old Masters come to mind—but in general representations of nature are coded on the great scale of aesthetic value as veering dangerously close to the hackneyed and sentimental.

How do ideas about land use play out in colonial notions of cultural superiority and in their aesthetic representation? Obviously, the fear, loathing, and desire that underlie Western conceptions of land move through a range of venues: art high and low, literature, politics. The perilous jungle, the enchanted forest, the mysterious ocean—dread and longing go hand in hand. The bottomless fear of wild land and unsettled people that comes from Judeo-Greek-Christian tradition is only part of the story. The will to dominate the earth is also based on plain old self-interest: The colonist wants the gold and the farmland; the Nazi wants those oil paintings hanging in Jewish houses. Racism depends on both fear and greed, and as with the unease that underlies the dream of domination of the earth, racism is based on the possibility that the other will resist.

Attempts to contain this ambivalence between desire and fear are apparent in aesthetic works and tend to operate in at least two ways. First, the wild land or foreign people can be represented in such a way that they provide a significant lesson to the viewer; this is the didactic solution. People from other cultures are made to appear violent and dangerous, and the narrative assures the Westerner that if she ventures outside of the conceptual certainties of the West, she is likely to die or go crazy or both. Similarly, if the urban white person undertakes to visit the wilderness, she is certainly very likely to starve or be eaten by marauding grizzly bears. Many movies use this type of didactic instruction as their primary storyline (think of *Deliverance* [1972]).

Second, difference is domesticated and thereby made manageable. This is the primary operation of the process of appropriation, which seeks to absorb difference and make it part of the so-called larger culture. Difference is transformed into something that is no longer all that different and hence ceases to be dangerous. There is no real contradiction between the two approaches, as they are really two sides of the same coin, like the virgin-whore dichotomy. (Everyone knows the evil dragon lady witches are more interesting than the nice girls, but they could not exist without the latter as a counterpoint and vice versa.) The image of a fearsome undressed angry person of color doing something violent fascinated the colonist, but this construction was dependent on the converse fiction of the meek and complacent servant who enjoyed being taught the virtues of civilized existence.

One of the paradoxes of difference is the way attempts to represent the so-called other so often ends up as little more than another depiction of the self. The mirror metaphor continues to be useful as a way of underlining the shifting, fragmentary character of images of cultural and other differences and the ways these reflect the preoccupations of those creating the images. These fragments move around in both space and time and continually recombine in new patterns, which is one reason that images of difference can be so ambiguous. This is especially true if the mirror can be imagined as a combination of Tezcatlipoca's smoking mirror and Louis Althusser's mirror of ideology, which reformulated the baby mirror of Jacques Lacan. The smoke parts from time to time to allow little more than momentary glimpses, and attempts to definitively characterize the other are bound to dissolve in the mist. There is no wholeness, no presence, and there never can be. This is the lesson.

For instance, the Arab world is an old, old adversary of Christian Europe, and the religion and culture of this adversary were repeatedly described (usually negatively) by artists and writers in Christian countries over the centuries. It can be said that in such descriptions Europeans sought to represent the other. But these representations had very little to do with Islam or with Muslim people, both because of errors of fact (which were sometimes deliberate) and because the agenda within which the representations occurred had been decided in advance. Islam was the enemy and that was that, even if this enemy turned out to be a source of erotic or aesthetic interest for some. The antagonistic scenario did not shift even after the Ottoman Turks ceased to compete with the European countries for territory in the early eighteenth century. Any new information about this part of the world was arranged within a preexisting conceptual framework in which everyone took her or his assigned place and played assigned roles in the great *Cristiano y Moro* spectacle. As a result, European representations of Islam were really about the inevitable triumph of Christianity or, in later years, the triumph of Western science, economics, or politics. This is apparent in the way such explicitly colonialist work as French Orientalist painting and literature was able to generate ambivalence. Fear and desire, fascination and revulsion are simultaneously evoked in so many nineteenth-century Orientalist works as a way of raising these sensations and then quickly discharging or transforming them into something nonthreatening.

Contemporary representations of Araby draw on a long tradition of anti-Islamic feeling in the West and utilize extremely archaic and persistent imagery (such as Crusader tropes). Islamic people continue to be characterized as violent, fanatical, and anarchic and somehow inherently in need of Western discipline and domination. This story is far from over, as we saw most recently in Gulf War rhetoric.

Orientalist Dreams

The discursive techniques that characterize Orientalism are well known as a result of the work of Edward Said and others.[7] European powers deployed a combination of military, political, and scholarly practices to circumscribe and dominate the part of the world they called the Orient. The practices that explained cultural difference simultaneously constructed European identity, as Europeans and Muslims were always conceived in relation to each other, generally in antagonistic relation. This relationality is equally true of similar practices brought to bear on other parts of the world. What this means is that ideologies of difference, as well as narratives that purport to be about different cultures (such as *Madame Butterfly* or *Hiawatha*), end up being about Western self-identity. The story remains a Western story; the Westerner is always in the frame, regardless of whether we can see him in the picture.

I first raised the bizarre levels of ambivalence apparent in the European conception of Araby with Gautier's effusive and ironic remarks on the Orientalizing of Paris after the conquest of Algeria in 1830–1845. Araby is the oldest enemy of the West and one of the first areas where Western artists and writers sought to represent cultural difference as such and to derive excitement from it. Napoleon's Egyptian campaign had ushered in a new interest in this part of the world on the part of European, particularly French, artists and set the stage for the extremely aestheticized treatment of later colonial adventures in Araby. But aestheticized and highly charged forms of ambivalence really took on a life of their own after Algeria became a French colony.

France invaded Algeria in 1830. The immediate pretext for the invasion was a diplomatic incident in which the enraged Ottoman Dey of Algiers struck the French consul in the face with a flyswatter. The French Army occupied the city of Algiers fairly quickly but spent fifteen years attempting to conquer the hinterland before finally subduing the resistance led by Abd al-Qadr. The war for Algeria was one of the bloodiest colonial wars of all time because of the scorched-earth tactics of the French and their use of starvation and massacre as a means of military pacification. (Such tactics were of considerable interest to other colonial powers. For instance, the U.S. Army used similar techniques during the Plains Indian wars of the 1870s and 1880s.) The invasion was accompanied by a great deal of propaganda in France: Would-be soldiers and their families were assured that they would be hailed as liberators in Algiers, particularly by Muslim women (the curious fiction that Muslim women are waiting to be freed by Westerners from oppression is nothing new), and Saint Louis, the crusader king who died attempting to conquer Tunis in 1270, was evoked as a worthy predecessor. A pamphlet distributed by the French Ministry of War exemplified the hyperbolic language of colonial war: "For a long time philosophy, humanity, and religion have been demanding the annihilation of a power whose every maxim is a constant insult to all morality, all civilization. There can never have been a valid excuse for tolerating Algiers."[8]

The evocation of the Crusades (and of civilization) was not merely a device to fan anti-Muslim feeling. It also reinforced rulings in Christian canon law about land use and jurisdiction. Many of the legal principles utilized during the colonial period derived from judgments made during the Crusades and particularly referred to the question of whether infidels had a right to their land, or *dominium* over territory. The problem of just war was a subject of some debate in church circles, as they wanted to conquer people but at the same time feel good about it.

By 1830 the language was less explicitly religious, but the old arguments were repeated: The Algerians did not properly use the land, their political system was anarchic and hence unable to promote a society in which its members could live according to reason, and there were too many nomads wandering throughout the country. In short, the French knew best how to run the place. Moreover, and also according to canon law, the French argued that they had a legitimate claim to the country because Algeria had once been Roman and Christian and indeed the home of Saint Augustine. The agenda of the French colonial government was absolutely clear, as were the agendas of other European powers in their colonies. The following words of the Commission d'Agrique in 1833 are not atypical and show how medieval notions of Western cultural superiority, which were based on particular forms of social order, land use, and work, continued to obtain in the colonial period: "To bring [the Algerian] . . . peoples under the subjection of our social order, to force them to labour the soil, to make of them industrial machines, and at last taxable, would be a very fine thing."[9]

These notions of land and society structured the images of harems, battles, religion, and desert landscapes that were conventionalized in French Orientalist painting. At the same time, colonial identities were constructed through representations of colonized people and representations of the land, which occurred even when Europeans were technically absent from the image or narrative. Islamic violence and disorder; a malign, abused landscape; and exotic objects of lust had as their antithesis European order and democracy, organized farming techniques, and pious, industrious people.

Orientalist themes enjoyed considerable official favor in French painting throughout the nineteenth century and were actively promoted within the government-sponsored Salon system, through which painters exhibited and sold their work. Most Orientalist images aggrandized the French project in Algeria presumably because, then as now, painters knew who paid the bills, despite all the fine talk about aesthetic independence. Artists could do very well from lucrative government commissions, and official battle painters accompanied the French Army in its pacification of Algeria. Orientalist painting was extraordinarily popular and became so fashionable after 1830 that it often merited a special section in Salon catalogs. The genre became a favorite of the buying bourgeoisie, and various French governments, enthusiastic about Orientalism, commissioned and purchased numerous paintings of this type to be exhibited in museums, palaces, and public institutions.

Orientalist themes captured the attention of artists working in the entire range of stylistic approaches, from neoclassicism to impressionism. The subject matter of these works ranged from battle pieces, nudes, landscapes, and portraiture to scenes drawn from fantasy, and in general the images in French Orientalism emphasized violence, sexuality, and religion, although to a lesser extent idyllic or pastoral scenes were common. A fascination with Muslim violence and sexuality repeated the preoccupations of medieval polemicists, and a fixation on harems and barbaric execution still seems to be with us. Linda Nochlin has written of the bizarre and complex psychosexual preoccupations of painters such as Eugène Delacroix, whose *Death of Sardanapalus* (1828) depicted an indifferent Oriental potentate having his women and horses put to death.[10] Grotesque displays of power, especially over women, were a constant topic. Inventive tortures both titillated Salon audiences and fanned patriotic sentiments, and meticulous, descriptive detail reinforced the veracity of these images. New techniques allowed these images to be mass produced and circulated throughout the country. The reiteration of these themes in high art accentuated the status of the colony as a bizarre spectacle existing to delight or horrify the European viewer. The quality of timelessness and the presentation of Araby as a static, decadent entity well past its prime helped create an imaginary Orient undifferentiated by place, time, and national or cultural specificity.

It can be rather difficult at this distance to account for the popularity of this genre, which in effect reflected the somewhat mysterious desire of the French to see highly aestheticized images of Arabs, including those recently subjugated by the French Army. The closest parallel in North America is the images of Native people found in some popular art, but a fictive temporal distance is enforced in these works and indeed is part of the reason for the attraction: The buyer can imagine a pristine, yet distant past untouched by unpleasant conflicts over territory. A similar process is apparent in some streams of Orientalist work. Orientalism was most popular in France during and immediately after the fifteen-year colonial war in Algeria, which in effect becomes something like, say, large numbers of Americans flocking to buy idealized and arousing pictures of Iraqis during the Gulf War, a quite unimaginable phenomenon. To my eye, most of the images in Orientalist works are intensely hackneyed and sentimental, and their attempts to titillate translate as clumsy and inane, like so much academic art of the nineteenth century. But the aesthetic conventions in such works reflected the taste of the times; these were the kinds of images people expected to encounter.

There are other reasons for the popularity of Orientalist painting. Interest in such work was a version of the desire to display trophies of war, here narrativized images rather than enemy rifles, body parts, or actual artifacts. John Berger makes this point about voyeurism and possession in his reading of Jean Ingres's harem scene *La Grande Odalisque* (1814), which predated the invasion of Algeria and which helped provoke an interest in Araby by feeding scopophilic fantasies.[11]

A new threshold was crossed in the way colonial possession of territory and of the image of this territory was collapsed together in Orientalist art: Whereas dying Gauls and other defeated enemies had always been part of the repertoire of images available to Western artists, now a wholesale explosion of images of the enemy occurred and took on a life of its own, with the system of representation itself being the point of the endeavor. The work referred to abstract notions such as patriotism or civilization rather than to the things being portrayed, and although allegorical works have always referred to abstract ideas, here the paintings ostensibly referred to actual people subjugated by the French in an actual place. Whereas the dying Gaul was an aestheticized, heroicized version of something that purported to be real, with Orientalism artists and consumers of art did not seem to care whether the image had anything to do with the reality (again, this is like much contemporary representation of Native people). It is a question, not of expecting artists to paint as if they were documentary journalists, but of seeing how Algeria and other parts of Araby functioned as a pretext for some extremely unpleasant concerns, which were themselves the raison d'être of the endeavor.

The spectator contemplated Paul-Leon Bouchard's *Les Muets de Serail* (1882), where African men are about to garrote exquisitely terrified blond harem beauties; Jean-Joseph Benjamin-Constant's *The Sharif's Justice* (1884), where dead naked women (with erect nipples) lie amid overturned furniture in an aftermath of violence; Alexandre Decamps's *The Punishment of the Hooks* (1837), where bound prisoners are impaled on hideous hooks for unspecified crimes, making possible a horrifying festival of death. The point of these works was to evoke and discharge certain ambivalent and uncomfortable sensations and to make the viewer experience delight and horror at the same time, all the while feeling superior. The point was to generate ambivalence and then neutralize it. Because of this ability to do so, Araby was continually mined for images that could assuage Western anxieties about the cultural superiority on which the West constantly insisted.

Colonial Representation and Landscape

There are many different ways to objectify Araby. Landscape paintings of the Algerian colony tended not to depict French colonials as part of the scene, and indeed many Orientalist works did not show people occupying the land at all. People were shown living in houses in paintings of cities such as Algiers or Constantine, but in scenes of the countryside the construction of the images illustrated the applicability of *terra nullius* to colonial Algeria. People moved through the land, but there was no evidence of its being put to the productive use demanded by the legal code. Given all the propaganda about how the French would make the desert bloom (and for this reason deserved to possess and administer the colony), these works were evidently not painted in a political vacuum. Battle paintings, in contrast, narrativized the colonial project and accordingly constructed the European and Arab characters in terms of extreme difference. The action of the battle became a way of illustrating these differences, even in works executed prior to the conquest of Algeria, such as Antoine-Jean Gros's *Battle of Aboukir* (1806), which heroicized the French general Murat during Napoleon Bonaparte's Egyptian expedition.

Both battle paintings and less explicitly patriotic works offered important lessons to the European viewer. One concerned the possible effects of the alien landscape on the colonist: The land itself could be deadly, and Algeria elicited all the fear and ambivalence about the wild earth's potential to harm the European Christian. Charles Baudelaire wrote in 1851 of French landscape painter Eugene Fromentin, who was awarded the Legion d'Honneur for his images of Algeria: "There are travellers with neither poetry nor soul, and his soul is one of the rarest and most poetic that I know. But light and heat, which cast a kind of tropical madness into certain brains, shaking them with an unappeasable frenzy and driving them to unknown dances, only pour the sweetness and repose of contemplation into his soul. It is ecstasy rather than fanaticism."[12]

Baudelaire exemplified the view that any encounter with difference could go either way. A confrontation between the artist qua colonialist and foreign lands and people could cure the diseases of Western culture, yet it could kill or maim those who were unprepared, or perhaps too weak, to do battle with the landscape and survive. Sometimes difference could do both, which was one reason it provoked ambivalence, a sensation that remained pleasurable as long as the colonist was in control.

Baudelaire's remarks on fanaticism and frenzy seem to reflect the fear of going native that we see in so much colonial literature. Baudelaire suggests that the desert light itself affects European perceptions, having the potential to render the traveler insane and to transform the European into the (presumably Muslim) "fanatic." He further implies that it is possible to attain mystical, contemplative ecstasy in the desert landscape without losing colonial identity and slipping into the fanaticism of the native. Here Baudelaire is underlining the equivalence between Islam and madness found in so much Western writing in the past eight hundred years, from Crusader polemic to poetic Orientalism to twentieth-century political analyses. Everything has already been decided, and no movement is possible: If the desert produces Muslim fanaticism, and the Arabs have succumbed to this insanity, then Europeans will be unable to comprehend and respect either the landscape or the different relation Arabs might have to the land on which they live. That Arab people survive and even go about their everyday business on land supposed to drive people insane makes no difference to the colonists' conception of this land, and Arab activities become no more than an opaque spectacle for the colonist. Rather, the European in the desert may only guard against going native, as Fromentin was able to do in his repetitive, benign scenes of falconry and idealized landscapes. If difference can be domesticated, it will no longer be a dangerous source of madness.

Baudelaire's praise of Fromentin's picturesque art is somewhat surprising, given some of the poet's other preoccupations. Fromentin first went to paint Algeria in 1846, very soon after Abd al-Qadr's resistance movement had been suppressed. Paintings that portrayed the colony as a kind of living Bible, existing in pristine innocence and picturesque charm, are typical of his work. Both the war and the colonial presence in general are absent or occluded. Fromentin's scenes idealize the landscape, which in his work is not quite the Sahara Desert proper; rather, he depicts the area closer to the coast that was expropriated and turned into farmland for French settlers. At the time Fromentin was painting, there was a great deal of devastation of the landscape, which was still recovering from the French techniques of total war. Arab farmers were being thrown off their land, and it was being turned over to Europeans. Why, then, did Fromentin paint sweetly quaint scenes from which Europeans are completely absent? The total elision of political and economic reality in these works seems to deliberately conceal the effects of the colonial presence (obviously, this appealed to Parisian buyers). Fromentin's landscapes also point to the function of images of primitive innocence in colonial countries: Europeans were able to envisage a place, which fortunately *they already owned,* to escape to when the industrial world got to be too much.

History painters generally are not very subtle, and it is worth paying attention to these works for precisely this reason. The propagandistic agendas of such epic paintings are completely in the open and continue to obtain today, although now their mechanisms are at least partly concealed by more sophisticated narrativizing techniques. History painting, which includes patriotic battle pieces as well as idealized, didactic scenes from history (such as David's illustrations of important moments in the Roman republic), was designed to provide lessons about proper behavior and sacrifice to the state.

Antoine-Jean Gros was commissioned by Napoleon to paint scenes illustrating the Egyptian campaign, and Gros's most famous work, *Bonaparte Visits the Pesthouse at Jaffa* (1804), can almost be described as a religious painting in its Christlike glorification of the French general. The function of such work is obviously to aggrandize the Napoleonic project but also to create an image of a unified French nation. To this end these paintings were

FIGURE 5.1 Battle at Aboukir *(Murat defeating the Turkish Army at Aboukir),*

coextensive with the standardization of language and the educational system undertaken in the early nineteenth century. Gros's *Battle at Aboukir* (see Figure 5.1) is a good example of how history painting constructed a patriotic narrative through the depiction of the Egyptian enemy. In this work the French were everything the Egyptians were not; the reverse was equally true.

Battle at Aboukir illustrates General Murat's victory over Mustapha Pasha during Napoleon's Egyptian campaign. The uniformed Murat rides a white horse and wears a composed expression. To his right, the pasha's son offers a scimitar to the French general with one hand and grasps his father's arm with the other to keep the latter from falling off his horse. The pasha and his son are light-skinned and richly dressed, in contrast to most other Egyptian fighters, who are dark-skinned and naked. The Egyptian rulers were Turkish, and the painting can also be seen as a polemic against Ottoman rule in general (which at that time encompassed most of Araby—in other words, those territories on which the European powers had cast a covetous eye). According to an 1806 Salon catalog, the basket worn around the neck of the fallen Egyptian in the left foreground contains the severed head of a French general.[13] (Severed heads appear in similar works; for instance, in Girodet's *Revolt in Cairo* [1810] an enraged Arab in the foreground clutches the blond, typically Christlike head of a Frenchman in one hand and a giant knife in the other.) The background depicts a fort with a minaret, and dead bodies are strewn about the foreground. The focus of the scene is the heroic Murat, who (along with his horse) is the most clearly delineated figure in the work. He is calm in victory, for the offering of the scimitar suggests that he has won the battle despite the continuation of the action.

Murat's composure acts as a retrojection of the course of events: The French victory against the disordered Egyptians is and always was inevitable, the general knows it, we know it, and the Egyptians and other supposedly lesser races know it as well. The French appear absolutely certain of their destiny: The order and rationality of the Enlightenment will necessarily prevail against Oriental anarchy and decadence. After all, Napoleon was so sure of his universal purpose that he could not help announcing to the (presumably bemused) Egyptians: "*Nous sommes les vrais musulmans.*"

Murat is positioned higher than Mustapha Pasha and his son, with his horse also placed above the falling mount of the pasha. The latter's facial expression is desperate as he vainly reaches to avoid falling; clearly if he cannot stay on his horse, he certainly cannot rule a nation and must give way to the more efficient French conquerors. The son wears a pleading expression, and his white skin and pink clothing make him appear softened by a life of luxury. The feminization of the son also refers to the sexual decadence thought to characterize Muslims (by which Europeans meant both homosexuality and sexual excess) and to the idea that Muslim rulers were weak and hence like women. The catalog's emphasis on the barely visible head in the basket attests to the barbarous practices supposedly dear to Arabs and is designed to patriotically arouse and terrify the French viewer. The naked Africans are intended to evoke the tropes of both savagery and hierarchical Ottoman society, but in this scene both are easily cowed by French military superiority, which presumably derives strength from the republican virtues of the French Revolution (something Bonaparte would soon remedy). The lack of affect on the part of the French soldiers points to European rationality. This convention goes back to the earlier history paintings of David in which the only people expressing any emotion are the women at the edge of the action. Emotion is clearly not rational, nor should it have anything to do with government. A steady line of French soldiers appears to the left, and the tangle of Egyptians attempting to flee in what is meant to look like cowardly anarchy, depicted at the right, adds to the contrast between the two groups. The French line seems to stretch on endlessly.

Forty-five years later Theodore Chasseriau painted *Arab Horsemen Taking Away Their Dead After Battle* (1850) (see Figure 5.2). This painting also depicts an Arab defeat, but there are no French soldiers in this painting, even though it portrays a scene from the Algerian war. Here the story is

FIGURE 5.2 Arab Horsemen Carrying Away Their Dead, *Théodore Chassériau, 1850 (courtesy of the Fogg Art Museum, Harvard University Art Museums, be-*

told with more subtlety, although its propagandistic function is similar to that of *Aboukir.* This scene illustrates the aftermath of a battle between Algerian tribesmen and French soldiers, although elements in the presentation may have been influenced by Victor Hugo's *La bataille perdu* from *Les orientales* (Hugo, like Gautier, considerably influenced how Orientalist themes were treated aesthetically).[14] Weapons and dead Arabs sprawl in the foreground, and to the left other dead bodies are being loaded onto horses. At the center of the painting a mounted, robed man surveys the scene, and in the distance figures perform actions similar to those taking place in the foreground. The action that results from defeat goes on and on, like the endless and wholly inevitable French victory implied by the defeat of the Arab soldiers. The landscape is desolate, which becomes a way of referring to the war and, more likely, to the supposedly chronic mismanagement of the colony on the part of the Algerians. Certainly the landscape is not occupied in any permanent way. The melancholy of defeat is the primary theme of this painting: The Algerians have lost the battle, and the French remain an unseen presence in this scene.

The Arab defeat is idealized by the presentation of the dead, particularly the seminude corpse displayed in the foreground, which is beautifully delineated and rather noble in its pose. Again, we can see vaguely Christlike references in this image, here Algerian rather than French. Why is the dead enemy heroicized in this way? The French-Arab reversal is key: The quality of nobility attributed to the enemy is a way of affirming similar qualities in the victors. In this respect the mode of death is absolutely critical. The unknown French soldier killed the central figure with a clean thrust into the chest, without the necessity of messy severed body parts, almost, it seems, without violence. The reference to French honor and heroism in warfare is implicit, and certainly the viewer sees no scorched earth or massacred villagers. The mounted man watching the scene is the leader of the Algerians, and his presentation expresses a certain heroism as well, as if he is a truly noble enemy who has been honorably defeated in a fair fight between equals. Again, the inevitability of the outcome is the point of the story, here with respect to future battles, which have also been decided in advance.

The dead Arabs strewn across the canvases of these and other paintings have a distinct purpose. National identity is constructed through the consumption and display of dead bodies, and, as always, the dead bodies of choice are those designated as foreign and subordinate. These works exemplify the sacrificial moment that so fascinated Bataille, where the other is sacrificed to bind the community as one, in this instance the one being the colonial nation, which itself must be constructed as such. The landscape becomes the space where the great game can be played out and where heroic adventures can be undertaken. But ambivalences about difference and about wild landscapes continue to underlie representations of Western heroism and superiority.

The aesthetic conventions apparent in nineteenth-century French paintings continue to resonate in much contemporary Western work that has Araby as its subject or its backdrop. Contemporary material tends to focus on Western ambivalences about colonial roles to a greater extent than the less self-reflective works of earlier periods, and a certain self-referentiality about issues of difference and the role Western culture has assigned to itself is more a part of the work itself. Uncomplicated notions of cultural superiority do not quite wash after the insanity of World Wars I and II. Westerners knew something had gone wrong but were not always sure precisely what that was.

Colonial Nightmares

"The people of each country get more like the people of every other country. They have no character, no beauty, no ideals, no culture—nothing, nothing."

Her husband reached over and patted her hand. "You're right. You're right," he said smiling. "Everything's getting gray, and it'll be grayer. But some

> places'll withstand the malady longer than you think. You'll see, in the Sahara here. ..."[15]

> Several times they came upon groups of dark men mounted on mehara. These held the reins proudly, their kohl-farded eyes were fierce above the draped indigo veils that hid their faces.
>
> For the first time she felt a faint thrill of excitement. "It is rather wonderful," she thought, "to be riding past such people in the Atomic Age."[16]

In Paul Bowles's 1949 colonial tale *The Sheltering Sky* the Orientalist topos is refigured through the landscape of the Sahara Desert and through the experience of the postwar Western intellectual who seeks to escape Western culture yet is unable to survive the encounter with the alien landscape.[17] The Sahara Desert has long existed as a place of forgetting in Orientalist art and literature. The vastness of the landscape has exercised a pull on the sick at heart, and it appears as a site where no questions are asked, where time is in suspension, where it is possible to join the French Foreign Legion "to forget." (The obvious question arises, What is the Westerner seeking to forget?) Here the colonial adventure itself becomes the cure for heartbreak and loss and the alien landscape the potential, yet hazardous source of that cure. In a profound way the desert exists at the limit of possibilities of the encounter between people and landscape. For Baudelaire, the Algerian Sahara affects painter and tourist alike, both of whom must navigate the line he has drawn between frenzy and contemplation, ecstasy and fanaticism. For Bowles, the Algerian desert is indifferent, dangerous, a site of death and madness, yet a source of ambivalence and desire. But what precisely is the relation between the desire to experience difference and the possibilities for forgetting that can occur in the Sahara Desert of French colonial Algeria, in Bowles's 1949 as much as Baudelaire's 1851? In *The Sheltering Sky* the colonial violence turns inward, and Port and Kit Moresby, the American protagonists of Bowles's story, perish as a result of their confrontation with the Saharan landscape.

The story articulates the familiar theme of post–World War II alienation. Kit and Port, a pair of wealthy aesthetes from New York, with their friend Tunner decide to visit the Sahara Desert, setting out from Oran on the Algerian coast. *The Sheltering Sky* is a complex and in many ways quite compelling novel, and there are several approaches that could be taken to this text. It is the overall structure of the story that interests me here and the way the narrative is so emphatically constructed around disaster. The trajectory of events is wholly unidirectional: As the characters move south, the situation becomes increasingly grave, and there is a certain inevitability to the unhappy chain of events. But the catastrophe that Kit and Port's trip becomes also occurs in a specific place—the Sahara Desert—and I ask to what extent the disastrous outcome is a condition of a particular relation the characters have to this place, this landscape.

As the characters venture south into the desert, several things happen: Kit sleeps with Tunner, and, sensing this, Port decides that he and Kit must abandon their friend and set out alone. This proves to be a bad move: Port quickly falls ill and dies, and Tunner's arrival on the scene provokes Kit to run away and join a camel caravan traveling further south. Kit becomes the lover of the handsome Taureg Belqassim, who disguises her as a Taureg boy and takes her home to live in a room on his roof. Belqassim's wives react antagonistically to their discovery of Kit's gender (although the audience for Bernardo Bertolucci's film version never knows for sure, as Arabic speech is not translated), so Kit runs away, eventually to be brought back by colonial functionaries to Oran, where Tunner awaits. After these experiences Kit is quite mad and silent.

For Kit and Port, the forgetting they seek is of World War II and the encroaching sameness and monotony of Western culture, which they envisage as a sickness. They also hope to forget their alienation from each other. But they are the ones who become ill, and their ailment appears to be caused by the disjunction between the way they imagine their adventure and the reality of the external world, which has ideas of its own. In Bowles's story everything goes bad. Kit is literally struck dumb by her experience. The apparent wildness and indifference of the desert ultimately silence the European. In the film version of the story, as Port collapses with fever, he deliriously says, "I've bit my tongue. I've always wondered what it would be like to bite my tongue." The silence of the visitors reflects the silence of the Saharan landscape, which evokes a profound terror: Because Kit and Port are unable to hear, the land refuses to speak to them. A closer reading of the story, however, suggests that the disaster of their journey is less a question of the way reality imposes itself on the characters' imaginary adventure than of the extent to which their imaginary is itself structured within a colonial exemplar. Kit and Port dream of being free of culture, floating signifiers in charge of their experience in the desert; this is where their desire locates itself. But this desire is impossible to realize because their detachment from their social and cultural matrix only reinforces the alienated, Cartesian subjectivity that is at the root of their malaise.

Travel and Delirium

Bowles clearly maintains a link between travel and madness, as (at some level) have other Western novelists who write of the unfortunate experiences Europeans encounter in non-European countries. Indeed, this has become a trope of Western literature and film: White people always seem to be dying undignified deaths or going crazy in hot countries. In a similar vein, for the white protagonists of *The Sheltering Sky,* the farther into the desert they go, the worse things become for them (this situation of course, is reminiscent of *Heart of Darkness—Apocalypse Now* (1979): Away from the town, from civilization, all order drops away, and there are death, violence, and madness). Port is killed by an "alien" disease (typhoid, a disease associated with contamination), and Kit's madness is closely linked to her sexual encounters with native males; as Kit's personality unravels, her lovers become increasingly darker-skinned and, hence for Bowles, both more alien and more indicative of her disintegration. Although the characters are seeking to flee Western culture, in the narrative all difference becomes threatening and disturbing: the desert wilderness, the Arab dances, the obligatory sexual encounters. In the film this threat is underlined by the use of Arabic-style music at ominous points in the narrative.

This theme needs closer examination: Why does life so often turn out badly for such people in novels and films? In *The Sheltering Sky* this unraveling seems to derive from the characters' desire to seek a movement across colonized space whereby they are able to operate as free, sovereign subjects and to achieve a certain experience. The notion that it is possible to achieve a particular type of authentic, intense experience from contact with different, colonized people assumes a radical difference between the colonizers and the people they encounter, and it is precisely this presumed difference that provides the interest and stimulation for the characters.

Here I want to distinguish between the view that cultural and linguistic differences exist and may be recognized and respected as such and the colonial notion of the absolute incommensurability of the colonized or Orientalized other and the European. The intensity of experience sought by Kit and Port both assumes and is produced by this notion of radical difference, which itself must be produced and maintained through a range of colonialist constructs.[18] As the characters seek to escape the grayness and alienation of Western culture, they attempt to maintain the interest produced by the appearance of difference, of exotic peoples and landscapes. In Fanon's discussion of the colony as a Manichean world, the colonist maintains a notion of absolute difference with respect to the indigenous people. In the colony proper the native is often despised and seen as a unit of labor or as an inconvenience, but in *The Sheltering Sky* this Manicheanism is maintained but differentially valorized. The characters want to retain their authority with respect to the Algerians, and at the same time the appearance of difference excites them and reminds them that they are the masters. Rather than attempting to render difference safe and comprehensible, the Western intellectual in this instance affirms the ambivalence of cultural dislocation and the belief that difference constitutes a dangerous edge to be successfully negotiated.

In the beginning of the story Port walks the streets of Oran and thinks, "How friendly are they? Their faces are masks. They all look a thousand years old. What little energy they have is only the blind, mass desire to live, since no one of them eats enough to give him his own personal force. ...

They have no religion left. Are they Moslems or Christians? They don't know."[19] The apparent opacity of the Algerian is something that Port expects to encounter and indeed affirms; he has decided in advance that at some level the people and cultures he encounters will be incomprehensible, and indeed this is part of the experience he is looking for. This incomprehensibility both substitutes for and marks his escape from the gray sameness of Western culture. For Port, the people of Oran are barely animal, not even conscious of their own religious beliefs, and *he is there,* able to walk among them and consume the spectacle of difference and the apparent repetition of the alien face. At this point in the story Port believes he can control the experience provoked by his inspection of the Arabs of Oran, as he feels himself to be standing above an undifferentiated mass that exists to stimulate his interest.

For modernist writers such as Bowles, the problem of truth has long been called into question and has migrated to *experience,* that is, to the truth created out of personal experience and to the extent to which this experience can be designated as authentic. This issue is nothing particularly new but has become more urgent in the twentieth century as old certainties fall by the wayside. It is through the question of authentic experience that a particular relation to the exotic is articulated, in which authenticity is available only outside of Western, bourgeois society. During the colonial period many Westerners believed that intense, authentic experience had become impossible in European culture and so turned to the exotic to find liberation from bourgeois constraints. Within this notion, the complex of traits and attributes called "Sahara" is able to function as a source of this disturbing, yet intense experience, and its ability to produce energy and excitement is possible precisely because of the apparent strangeness of the landscape and the dangers of traveling through it.

The notion that cultural difference provides authentic experience means that different people and places will function again and again as a kind of *pharmakon* for the Western colonialist subject.[20] Experience is presented as something that can (appear to) cure the Western disease of alienation and ennui but can also kill and render insane. This was the message of the more violent end of Orientalist painting, of the more thrilling opera stories, and of the miscegenation melodrama films of the 1940s and 1950s. We recall here the double function of the *pharmakon,* the ambivalent nature of the medicine that cures and kills and carries the disease outside the gates of the city. For the colonist, the ambivalence seems to involve the way encounters with different people or places generate extreme anxiety about authority, that is, about her ability to remain in control of the experience and her position relative to the various things she encounters. The notion of giving up authority voluntarily is both elided and rendered intolerable to the Western subject, and in colonial tales such as *The Sheltering Sky,* when the structure of colonial authority that sustains the characters is seriously shaken or disappears, they become disoriented and ill. I believe this is the source of the equivalence between going native and madness; in such stories the encounter with difference produces a kind of poison, and in this sense we can say that Kit and Port suffer from difference poisoning.

For Bowles, any crossing of boundaries (cultural, class, gender, geographic) necessarily results in disaster, not because of the way questions of power and authority overdetermine the nature of the encounters, but because he maintains a notion of radical difference and this difference itself is dangerous. The reasons for this danger are never addressed explicitly in the story but seem to entail the way difference calls the (colonialist) identities of the characters into question and further marks their profound alienation from each other and from culture and land. This alienation is not situational for Bowles; it is an ontological state from which there is no escape. Although Kit and Port pursue and affirm difference as the antidote to the gray wasteland of postwar Europe, in the story any outside to Western culture becomes even more threatening and degraded.

Aristocratic Dreams

Why do Europeans so often affirm the notion of going to the desert (or another exotic locale) for an authentic experience? Part of the attraction lies in the way experience itself is commodified and made to seem available to the colonist. Within this construct, the notion of experience itself appears as an a priori category or, perhaps more accurately, as a template within which various experiences will be made to adapt and assimilate. The experiences sought by many hoping to escape Western culture are neatly wrapped up and presented as items to be consumed by properly sophisticated palates; the desire for the exotic remains superficial and dilettantish, with everything spelled out in advance and no room for nuances or, rather, a willful blindness to nuances. Again, this desire to consume culture refers to an aristocratic moment, where experience is something to be sampled like fine wine.

The characters articulate the dream of authenticity through the experience of difference, which becomes pure experience and pure spectacle. Kit and Port, as do many in such stories, also seek to exceed the limits of bourgeois culture. In the earliest part of both the book and film, Port carefully distinguishes between themselves and the bourgeois tourist:

> They had crossed the Atlantic for the first time since 1939, with a great deal of luggage and the intention of keeping as far as possible from the places which had been touched by the war. For, as he claimed, another important difference between tourist and traveller is that the former accepts his own civilization without question; not so the traveller, who compares it with the others, and rejects those elements he finds not to his liking.[21]

Desire, then, is structured in the text as the ability to stand above culture and freely choose among "elements" (including World War II), all of which appear available to Kit and Port. I immediately begin to wonder which elements of Western culture the characters are able or likely to reject and which they will continue to affirm. Kit and Port certainly do not reject their money, luggage, privilege, and authority. Rather, they attempt to attain the experience they seek by exhibiting more privilege and authority—that is, by doing their best to live out their desires in an aristocratic manner. Playing games from the ancien régime is one way of avoiding bourgeois conventions and has consistently appealed to a certain stream of intellectual bohemia.

The relation of exoticism to colonial authority is intricate and multilayered, although it tends to rest on morphological signs; for instance, in the case of Araby, on jewelry, tattoos, weapons, and animals such as the dromedary or gazelle. The colonist's relation to exoticism also refers to a European aristocratic ethos insofar as the bourgeois subject seems able to conceive of her own difference only as that which is not bourgeois, which means that any outside to Western culture tends to be thought of through, and limited by, a European aristocratic exemplar. The desire for escape from the constraints on personal freedom imposed by Western bourgeois culture is so frequently construed through a particularly colonial framework because different peoples and landscapes are able to function as a backdrop to a Western, aristocratic adventure story (and hence the gesture of escape remains totally inside Western culture, a variation or repetition of a Western model).

Certainly part of becoming cosmopolitan for an American such as Bowles or the characters in the novel is learning to take on European sophistications and appropriate European fantasies and obsessions. The desert nomad is an enduring feature of the Western canon of exotica, and a great deal of European literature exists on the romance of the camel nomad (most notably T. E. Lawrence's *Seven Pillars of Wisdom,* which articulates the trope of the corruption of town versus the purity and nobility of the desert). The French presence in Algeria gave rise and referred to a longstanding Orientalist literature, which further refers to the aristocratic Crusader tradition of the chansons de geste and various other heroic tales of knights going off to fight the infidel.

Sexual Ambivalences

The exotic is often marked through sexuality or, rather, is made to represent a certain kind of sexual encounter to the extent that stories of Europeans going to foreign countries and having sex with attractive natives have become a constant and persistent cliché of film and literature.[22] Difference is immediately made to collapse into sexuality but to exceed it as well insofar as such encounters become a convenient signpost that the European has indeed experienced difference (and lived to tell the tale). Colonial stories generally trace the (supposed) ability of the colonized woman to provide a properly exotic experience for the European man, yet become somewhat more ambivalent and complicated when it is a white woman who experiences sexual adventure in the colony. Whereas the native woman tends to be presented as unthreatening (although treacherous), the native man is characterized as extremely dangerous to white women. In *The Sheltering Sky* Kit's sexual encounters are explicitly linked to rape, death, and madness.

Port's encounter with a Saharan woman, Marhnia, in the early part of the story quickly reproduces the figure of the Ouled Naïl dancer-prostitute in French literature and pornography, the Moorish woman unveiled and available to the colonist in *Algerie Française*.[23] This first engagement with a Saharan nomad is sexual, made available to Port through a relatively uncomplicated cash transaction. Betrayal is nevertheless built into the encounter. With Marhnia, he pays, she submits, but in this apparent submission lurks dissimulation: She attempts to steal his wallet. Port's ambivalence about Marhnia surfaces in his suspicion and his desire, and the question of trust is raised during an intimate moment of the encounter: "They lay on the couch together. She was very beautiful, very docile, very understanding, and still he did not trust her."[24]

Marhnia's "treachery" is ineffectual, and Port remains in control of the situation, easily foiling her attempt to steal his wallet and leaving the scene of the encounter unscathed. The liaison between Kit and Belqassim is much more violent and ambivalent, and Kit loses all control over the events taking place, literally held down by Belqassim. Here is her experience of their first sexual contact: "There was an animal-like quality in the firmness with which he held her, affectionate, sensual, wholly irrational—gentle but of a determination that only death could gainsay."[25]

Describing colonized people as animals who lack the ability to reason is a long-standing tradition in colonial texts, but the ambivalence of this characterization is evoked in the preceding passage: Kit immediately falls in love with Belqassim. The association between sex with Belqassim and death comes up again after he has taken her to his house in the Sahara and confined her, first on the roof, then in his bedroom:

> Now that he owned her completely, there was a new savageness, a kind of angry abandon in his manner. The bed was a wild sea, she lay at the mercy of its violence and chaos as the heavy waves toppled upon her from above. Why, at the height of the storm, did two drowning hands press themselves tighter and tighter about her throat? Tighter, until even the huge grey music of the sea was covered by a greater, darker noise—the roar of nothingness the spirit hears as it approaches the abyss and leans over.[26]

Irrationality, savagery, violence, chaos, and death—the native man brings these to the white woman, yet Kit's sexuality is her enemy as well, something equally alien and destructive, that enables her to seek oblivion in deathlike experiences with deadly, alien men. The colonized male, then, is presented as doubly treacherous: He demands submission from the white woman and at the same time calls forth the madness and savagery within her.

Bertolucci's film differs from the book precisely around the issue of sexual contact between colonists and natives, and this shift is symptomatic of a certain ambivalence and unease with such encounters in colonial tales. In the book Marhnia's passivity with respect to Port is emphasized; after the wallet incident, he shoves her, and she cries out, alerting the men in nearby tents. In Bertolucci's film Marhnia's gesture is deliberate, and she follows Port to the door of the tent and ululates loudly to call the men to assist her (Bertolucci obviously finds the Arab ululation threatening, as he uses this woman's cry throughout the film to mark moments of danger for the protagonists).[27]

In Bowles's version of the story he focuses on, and reiterates, the extremely equivocal nature of the contact between the white woman and the man of color in colonial situations. Belqassim and his friend in effect rape Kit soon after she joins the caravan; despite the violence of the encounter, Belqassim is tender and amorous but always dangerous. Bertolucci emphasizes the affectionate, seductive qualities of Belqassim, and it is not clear if he and Kit have sex during the journey in the desert. Bertolucci's charming Belqassim treats Kit as a lady, ordering a palanquin to be constructed to protect her white skin from the sun. Thus, in Bertolucci's film the native woman becomes more dangerous and threatening and the native man less so, more an object of pleasure for the female colonist. Ambivalence about such encounters in colonial texts remains forty years after the novel was written, but the anxiety seems to have shifted to the woman of color (here we recall films such as *Full Metal Jacket* [1987], where it is the Vietnamese woman who is the enemy).

Land and Madness

Bowles spoke of *The Sheltering Sky* in a recent interview: "The book is about the desert, not about people. The desert does away with people. It swats them like we swat flies. It's hard to get through the desert and come out on the other side alive."[28] (See Figure 5.3.) This remark is somewhat disingenuous, given that people have been living in the desert for a long time and have been able to coexist with the terrain. Clearly for Bowles, "people" here mean Europeans. The story traces the personal disintegra-

FIGURE 5.3 Kit Morseby (Debra Winger) in The Sheltering Sky. *(Copyright ©*

tion of Port and Kit and the disastrous consequences of their encounters with North African peoples. Although the vastness and (presumed) indifference of the Sahara Desert come up again and again in the text, indigenous desert peoples are made to represent or collapse into the desert landscape and to stand for an indifferent and treacherous natural world. Bowles's view of the Sahara landscape as hostile and destructive to human life seems indicative of the peculiarly Western notion of land and space as abstract, yet dangerous categories.

Bowles suggests that the land is harsh and indifferent and that the characters, especially Kit, are unprepared to encounter this emptiness. Baudelaire suggests that the Sahara itself is able to produce certain effects, including madness, in the visitor. But perhaps it is the very notion that the land is hostile that precludes visitors having a sense of place in the desert, existing with it and not resisting it as an enemy. The European's unease with wild, uncultivated landscape has a history, and there is a sense of inevitability to this unease, which serves to underline the separation from the land at the heart of Kit and Port's disaster.

People live on this supposedly uninhabitable desert land, but their presence tends to be occluded in the colonial text. In a peculiar double move the inhabitants are both abstracted from the land and wholly identified with it. Bowles produces an equivalence between the harsh, indifferent landscape and the Arab, the colonized native. In a key scene in the novel Port and Kit, staying in a town on the border of the Sahara, bicycle into the desert at sunset. To them, the landscape appears to go on and on, broken by jagged outcrops of rock. Port speaks of the sky that shelters and protects them from darkness, the void, and his words function as a premonition that something is very wrong. They encounter two Arabs, one praying and totally oblivious to their presence and the other, who looks at them indifferently, shaving his pubic hair with a knife. The Arabs are silent and disclose nothing to the visitors and hence function as a spectacle for Kit and Port that is at once impure and quotidian. Their activities—prayer (Baudelaire's fanaticism) and a particular kind of bodily hygiene—have for the European a degraded quality and consequently occur indoors and in private. Here they occur outdoors and on the land. These everyday activities take place in counterpoint to Kit and Port's profound talk of infinity and alienation, and in the narrative the Arabs seem to merely subsist on the land, unable to appreciate its intensities. Another disjunction is produced, here between the sublime and the everyday, which elides the way that the banal, everyday activities of the two Arabs suggest a different, perhaps less alienated relation to the land than that maintained by the visitors. And we recall here that it is Port, who assures himself that he is stronger than the land, who does not survive.

The Sheltering Sky has a didactic function, regardless of whether Bowles intends it. Certainly the story presents the view that the land is somehow alienated from the people who live on it. Because the relations of the protagonists with Algerians are structured around incidents of betrayal and suspicion, the story suggests that it is impossible and indeed undesirable to relinquish colonial authority and, furthermore, that it is impossible for the Westerner to respect or comprehend cultural differences. Indeed, Bowles links contact with African people to insanity; of course Kit is going to go crazy, the result of an alien landscape, masquerading as a boy, and sleeping with dark-skinned men, or perhaps it was her madness that impelled her to do these things in the first place.

In colonial tales such as *The Sheltering Sky* the authors seem to recognize at some level that power makes people weak and stupid. The colonist is stupid precisely because he or she has learned to rely on the external structures of colonial authority and on the benefits the colonial system provides to the colonizers.[29] The colonist has limited experience in dealing with difference and ambivalence in a way that challenges her privilege and hence finds it extremely difficult to survive without the colonial authority that defines and orders her relations with colonized peoples. The colonist becomes severely disoriented without that structure (unless she is able to recognize her own relation to colonialism and can begin to relinquish her authority and privilege) because she is taught to think that if she gives up authority, she will and must be subject to someone else's power. This is, as we know, a central feature of Western, hierarchical culture: We learn that somebody has to be in charge while at the same time learning to elide the ways in which actual political power (such as colonialism) structures relations among people. It is authority or rather the attempt to hang onto it that makes the colonist sick, but in books such as *The Sheltering Sky* any attempt to confront or relinquish this authority either never comes up, is doomed, or results in disaster.

Near the end of the story, after Kit runs away from Belqassim, she meets Amar, a black man who attempts to help her when she is confronted by an angry crowd. At this stage of the adventure the repetition of the alien face produces only exhaustion. As they walk through the streets of the African town, "outside the sun seemed more dazzling than before. The mud walls and the shining black faces went past. There was no end to the world's intense monotony."[30] This exhaustion indicates a shift in Kit's experience of difference: She is no longer standing above the people she encounters and enjoying the spectacle of difference, as Port sought to do when he walked the streets of Oran. Yet Kit is still alienated from the people she walks among, and difference still remains a repetition, marked through the morphological quality of skin color. Difference has become a kind of sameness akin to the gray monotony of Western culture that initially provoked her visit to the Algerian desert. Kit remains a colonist, but one who through her actions has lost status. The narrative reveals an important point here: The colonist must affirm and maintain her position and privilege or lose status and be subject to colonial authority as a native or, worse, a traitor. Because Kit is dressed as an Arab woman, she is initially treated as such and barred from entering a café that does not allow native women inside; she is called "*saloperie*" (filth). When the café owner discovers she is European, confusion ensues for a moment, but Kit is quickly referred to as a "*sale putain*" (dirty whore) and a "creature." And, of course, despite Kit's ambivalent position, the native remains treacherous in the story: After making love to her and promising to "save" her, Amar steals her money and traveling case.

Bowles is right in underlining the risks of sexual tourism in the colony but for the wrong reasons. If the quest for difference as articulated by Kit and Port necessarily results in betrayal, it is not because this is the nature of indigenous people or of the landscape: Betrayal is built into the quest itself and is in fact an autobetrayal that has to do with the way desire is dreamed by the colonialist subject. This is what creates the catastrophes in the desert. We could say that Kit gave up authority (or it was taken from her by circumstances), in a manner of speaking, but in a way that is identical to madness. Is this the only way relinquishing colonial authority can be thought of in a colonial tale? All we (and the we constructed by the text is Western and probably white) learn from the story is that women of color are treacherous but ultimately harmless, whereas men of color are extremely destructive and to be avoided.

Escape and Authority

> "Europe has destroyed the whole world," said Port. "Should I be thankful to it and sorry for it? I hope the whole place gets wiped off the map."[31]

The desire to escape the repressiveness and negative intensity of Western culture is not, if I am to be honest, a wholly unreasonable or unattractive idea. But this desire for escape so often is consistent with a colonialist ethos and consequently so often returns as a reiteration of Western authority. The problem lies in how lines of escape, or a notion of an outside, come to be constructed as conventionally as they are, and why the sense of an outside to Western culture is so often articulated within an aristocratic, colonialist ethos (which in this instance means travel at will with many changes of clothing, which implies money, leisure, and porters). In one sense the characters in *The Sheltering Sky* are successful in their quest for nomadic adventure in that they do manage to travel great distances and, in Kit's case, migrate across the Sahara with nomadic people. But the real question becomes, Where will resistance to the effects of Western culture occur, and how is a colonized outside constructed as the place where a person may find difference and intense experience?

As much as the Algerian Sahara exists as a site of desire, it does not float in space and time. When both Baudelaire and Bowles were writing, the Sahara was colonized land. Because the desert was colonized territory, Europeans could live out fantasies not possible at home and subscribe to a peculiar notion of rebarbarization in which the colonists would become more enracinated in the desert landscape, and more native, than the Algerians.[32] The Algerian desert was *available* to the colonist, whether French or American, and the experience that this landscape was able to provide existed as a commodity in the colonized market. Is a forgetting of such historical events as colonial wars possible in a market economy where land and people are subject to exchange as commodities? Is this attempt to forget or to escape Western culture the source of the sickness to which Port and Kit succumb in the desert? It seems clear that whatever drove them out of the West, going elsewhere as a colonist will only make matters worse.

In colonial tales such as *The Sheltering Sky* the characters seem to (or always/already) think of escape or an outside in the most literal way, which means that their escape or sense of what it could mean will always remain within a gesture of appropriation; they locate their own difference or refusal of bourgeois culture in both the ancien régime and the putative absolute difference of Arab and Tuareg people. The conventionality of the gesture means that the colonist will escape by physically going outside of European or U.S. cities and by utilizing the trappings of difference as an intriguing backdrop to the adventure. The ability to experience different customs (and especially different bodies) means that the colonist is able to select the traits of difference that interest her, decide what difference is, and capture and accumulate some of that difference as a way of breaking through the alienation she feels in Paris or New York. The colonist remains in control.

There need be no actual engagement with difference or with different people save in their capacity as servants, prostitutes, or opaque backdrops to this experience. In *The Sheltering Sky* difference and authenticity are represented by North African Arabs and Saharan nomadic peoples but could just as easily be represented by something else given that the story does not engage with Arab and Saharan people. For Western aesthetes such as the characters in the story, all cultural difference is the same and provides the same order of experience: There are Western subjects, and there are all those others who provide color and intensity for the amusement of the former (we note that, by the end of the story, Kit discovers that all men are able to please her).

Because nomadic peoples occupy a particular place in Western colonial fantasies of exoticism and cultural difference, the nomad functions as a metaphor for radical exteriority, for the possibility of pure flows of movement and escape. In a certain type of colonial literature this metaphor is linked to the Westerner's desire to become a nomad, to wander across the desert and somehow locate authentic experience in precisely that movement and in the encounter with different peoples and cultures. But if Deleuze and Guattari are right in suggesting that nomads inhabit space rather than move through it,[33] then the colonialist dream of escaping Western culture through nomadic wanderings and incursions into nomadic territory raises questions about the relation among movement, appropriation, and colonial authority.

Bowles's desert adventure is constructed through an allegory of loss, which both draws on and affirms a tradition of European writing and, by implication, the structures of colonial authority on which these writings were and continue to be based. For Bowles, the redemption of the Western project is no longer possible, but the way in which he (rightly) rejects this project renders resistance and healing impossible as well. There is no way out, only disastrous attempts at escape. It is perhaps surprising, given the recent popularity of his work, how very Western Bowles's notion of land is. The landscape is at once inert and malevolent, much as the colonized people are opaque and dangerous. Bowles maintains a series of binary categories, which underpin Kit and Port's experience of the desert (wild/tame, dangerous/safe, Native/European), similar to the equally dualistic disjunctions articulated by Baudelaire and Bataille. Any possibility of undermining these categories is rendered hopeless in *The Sheltering Sky,* and the precise nature of the relation between people and land, colonizer and colonized is not called into question.

Part of the problem lies in thinking of our culture and their culture and imagining each as cohesive, discrete entities. To think of ourselves as escaping or rejecting Western culture is at some level to affirm our culture's view of itself as monolithic and universal and to risk reproducing the rhetoric of mastery that characterizes colonial discourse. There are many margins and roads inside, margins at the heart of this culture, in capital cities and in the wild places, many ways of escaping the culture's purview without slipping into what we like to think of as absolute difference. And to escape from the inside can be much more subversive than riding a camel across the desert. At the basis of the impasse is the notion of radical difference—a colonial notion that remains pervasive—and an alienated relation to the land. I question the extent to which abstract difference exists at all, as opposed to the many local differences of culture, territory, and tradition.

6

The Smoking Mirror

I began *Cannibal Culture* with the story of the two Aztec god-brothers, Tezcatlipoca and Quetzalcoátl, as a way of exemplifying a problem of representation and power. The Aztecs recognized that vision is linked to an imperial moment and that the act of gazing into a mirror lies at the root of the triumph of human sacrifice and militarism. It is perhaps not surprising that the Aztec stories are enlivened by many instances of conflict and warfare. A certain truth can be located in discord. One of the most notable accounts also involves strife between two siblings, this time Huitzilopochtli, or Hummingbird on the Left, and his sister Coyolxauhqui, or Copper Bells on Her Cheeks. Huitzilopochtli was the tutelar god of the Aztec nation (and incidentally was also the blue Tezcatlipoca of the south) who guided the migrating Aztecs toward their destiny from inside a bundle carried by the procession of wayfarers. The Méxica sought advice from the spirit contained in this bundle, consulting it as they made their way to the swamp that would become imperial Tenochtitlán. In the story of Huitzilopochtli's birth Coyolxauhqui leads an army against her mother Coatlicue, who has incurred dishonor by miraculously becoming pregnant with Huitzilopochtli. The texts describe Coyolxauhqui and her army preparing for war, carefully dressing and fastening regalia onto their bodies before Coyolxauhqui leads them toward her mother. They come on, relentlessly, toward Serpent Mountain, where Coatlicue waits apprehensively. But at the moment the army arrives on Serpent Mountain, Huitzilopochtli springs fully armed from his mother's womb, strikes Coyolxauhqui with a serpent-shaped stick, and instantly decapitates her. As the headless Coyolxauhqui rolls down Serpent Mountain, her body falls into pieces. Huitzilopochtli then pursues her army without pity. The text says:

> And when Huitzilopochtli had killed them,
> when he had expressed his anger, he took from them their finery,
> their adornments,
> their destiny, put them on, appropriated them,
> incorporated them into his destiny, made of them his own insignia.[1]

On the way to empire the Méxica learned that appropriation was an instrument of conquest, a way of subsuming subject peoples into an Aztec future and transforming them into a chapter in an Aztec story. Capturing regalia—and displaying this testimony of victory for all to see—has always been part of conquest and its aftermath, which is when the real process of conquest takes place as the initial victory repeats itself again and again. The confiscation of another people's cultural artifacts is a way of marking and remarking the defeat of the enemy and is always closely linked to the repetition of the moment of conquest, a repetition that can occur in how the world comes to be represented aesthetically.

Huitzilopochtli's victory over the army of his sister was reenacted repeatedly on top of the sacrificial pyramid, with the moment at which he struck the mortal blow echoed again and again on the bodies of the prisoners of war, bodies that continually rolled down the steps of the pyramid before being dismembered and distributed to the priests. Coyolxauhqui is incapacitated, and her anger against her mother is rendered impotent. Huitzilopochtli demonstrates that it is the brother who will decide the good and that his victory over his sister and her allies must be absolute. Thus, the formation of the Aztec state—as represented by Huitzilopochtli's triumph at Serpent Mountain—is reiterated again and again in the sacrifices.

What do the Aztec stories have to do with contemporary problems of representation and the arts, exoticism, appropriation, and other issues of cultural difference? These tales of discord reveal the link between vision and empire and teach us that the vast range of aesthetic practices undertaken and valorized in a conquest culture are able simultaneously to inform and veil other, more explicitly violent practices. Certainly the extent to which violence is a central organizing principle of our own society has been concealed in part by the way aesthetics are able to function as an alibi. We ought not forget that the Aztec priests maintained a special temple in Tenochtitlán that contained representations of all the gods of subject people, something like an ethnographic museum. Part of the aestheticization of conquest involves the way history itself is understood and aestheticized: Like all imperial peoples, the Aztecs rewrote the history books of the people they conquered as a way of manipulating the past and the pasts of their subjects. What is illuminating is the way the Méxica explicitly tied acts of appropriation and overcoding to an imperial moment.

Imperial victories do exact a price from the conquerors. In the 1991 film *Retorno a Aztlán* Mexican director Juan Mora Catlett suggests that it was the Méxica's transformation into an imperial society (with priests, hierarchies, writing systems, and other paraphernalia hauled along in the wake of the state machine) that made it impossible for them to find their way back to the place they came from. When the Aztecs became an expansionistic state, they forgot their origins; they forgot Coatlicue, who was also their mother the earth (strangely, this earth deity is the same Coatlicue defended by Huitzilopochtli). Huitzilopochtli promised his people, "The four corners of the world shall ye conquer, win, and subject to yourselves. . . . It shall cause you sweat, work and pure blood."[2] But he lied or, rather, neglected to tell the whole story. Huitzilopochtli promised victory in battle and the conquest of vast amounts of territory, but (as always) this promise was really about the seduction of being in charge, of deciding the good. The Aztecs—by which I mean the people of the court and the city who lived off the fruits of the empire—learned the truth behind the lie when the story turned and the Spaniards arrived with their own certainties and pitilessness.[3]

What is the price of empire? We can try to answer this question in a roundabout way by looking at other motives that complicate the problem of appropriation. Capturing culture, which in effect means usurping a cultural tradition not one's own, can also reflect an attempt to fill the void created when a society follows the path of empire and cannibalism. To embark on a project of conquest, a society needs to organize itself to carry out this project. This means no deviance from the constant preparation for war and no questioning of the agenda of conquest and cultural superiority. It is no accident that the wars against witches and heretics occurred during the early colonial period, when Europe was transforming into a conquest culture. It is also no accident that the more recent imperial societies have been characterized by rigid hierarchical distinctions between categories of people. Militarism requires a hard heart, and if people have not transformed themselves into machines, they do tend to recognize that something is wrong with the society in which they live. Seizing the sacred objects of conquered people can become a way of feeding the endless emptiness and hunger produced within conquest cultures. Although appropriation does not work, it does constitute an attempt to escape from the box in which victory has placed the conquerors. Power does corrupt, and it has bad effects on everyone.

The we that is constructed within and through Western culture is an imperial people. Those of us who live in North American and European cities are taught that we alone know the good, an education that has nothing to do with anything we might think about the matter (this can be true even if we are disenfranchised within this empire because everyone is subject to the same images, something that can create all kinds of difficulties with internalized racism). Because the West has behaved as an empire for so long, those of us who live under its purview are profoundly alienated from what we used to call the natural world (I realize that the notion of the natural is a construction as well, but I am using it to refer to something actually in the world—in other words, the land that sustains life and without which everyone dies). This alienation means that we are no longer able to communicate with the spirit world—which is to say, we are alienated from a ceremonial system and practice that provide meaning to existence, that begin to untangle the dilemma of temporality, and that can help prevent the proliferation of cannibal disease. (Christianity has provided sustenance to many but cannot really be called an earth religion, as orthodox practice has always feared the spirit world.) This alienation has occurred in the name of science and rationality, but a paradox remains: Many people in the West still need the oak groves and spirits killed off by science and orthodox Christianity, which means they turn to other traditions, sometimes to confiscate their paraphernalia of the sacred in the hope of finding sustenance. Again, although this desire for meaning is not a bad thing, it has been twisted together with power relations of the most unsavory kind.

New Zealand Maori director Barry Barclay's film *Te Rua* (1991) gives more depth to the configurations of appropriation and colonialism by pointing to some of the effects of colonialism on the people doing the appropriating. The film tells the story of a Maori community's attempts to retrieve three sacred carvings from an ethnographic museum in Berlin. The community needs the carvings to heal itself and live as a people again. Certain spirits inhabit the carvings, and the carvings embody these spirits. Although the carvings are beautiful and possess an aesthetic sensibility, they are not precisely art (in the sense of being created to look at); rather, they are aesthetics and spirituality brought together within a specific community for specific spiritual reasons. The film is clear in its association of objects and power, here spiritual power, and although the narrative is not primarily concerned with the spiritual impoverishment of Western culture, it is able to offer insights about the motives of collectors that are germane to this issue. The European museum director who finally comes to support the return of the carvings initially appears as a desiccated cannibal-man who can survive only by feeding on the presence of spiritual objects in the museum he administrates, objects he imagines he in some way owns. (I have tried to show how the museum is a special home of the *wétiko*.) The spirits that live in the objects seem to sustain him, but they are spirits he has stolen, and at some level he recognizes this theft. This museum director is only one individual, but it is possible to claim that precisely the same desire for ownership of the spirits occurs on a larger scale when spiritual objects are collected and displayed in national museums or in the living rooms of individuals who can afford them.

Most museums and galleries understand ceremonial objects in terms of their aesthetic or scientific value, which is to say, according to a contemporary Western belief system. But *Te Rua* suggests that the spiritual and ceremonial qualities of these objects are at some level recognized and understood within Western culture and that this desire for proximity to the spirit world secretly animates the project to acquire and display the objects in the first place. The collector of reproduction Ghost Dance paraphernalia (see Figure 6.1) feeds off the mystical beliefs of the Ghost Dancers as much as

FIGURE 6.1 Ghost Dance collection from Prairie Edge arts and crafts gallery

off the beauty of the objects—and both attributes continue to be confused with the pleasures of ownership. Conquering a people means usurping their power, as Huitzilopochtli seized the finery and destiny of his enemies. Keeping in mind this spiritual dimension of colonialism, we can begin to understand why the Canadian government banned the potlatch for so many years and confiscated the dance regalia of the winter ceremonies: These measures were designed to break "the spirit" of the people and to acquire their power, that which made them strong in the face of colonial encroachment. (The white government understood things far too literally, however. Given the choice between going to jail and surrendering dance masks, most people gave up the masks. As the grandson of someone charged with potlatching in the 1920s explained to me, the matter was quite simple: The community could always make more masks, but it could not make more elders.) Appropriation becomes a question of the colonial powers acquiring spiritual objects such as masks and renaming them art in an attempt both to legitimize their capture and display and to incorporate them into a Western narrative. People in colonizing nations could simultaneously derive strength from this alien sacred and render it harmless. (In a rather different sense than art collectors and ethnographers, Christian missionaries also sought to capture an alien sacred as a way of eradicating it and replacing it with their own version of the spirit world.)

In the early colonial period notions of Christian religious orthodoxy sought to silence the spirits, with this task later delegated to science. It is not simply a question of science now commandeering the function of the sacred in Western culture but of the extent to which scientific discourses have made it possible to elide the absence of a sacred, ceremonial arena in Western culture (a lack that many people nevertheless try to fill up with television preachers and odd cults). Michel de Certeau points out that as the locus of beliefs shifted from paganism to Christianity to the modern nation-state, there were a progressive devaluation and exhaustion of these beliefs. He writes, "What was not transportable, or not yet transported, into the new areas of progress appeared as 'superstition,' what could be used by the reigning order was accorded the status of a conviction."[4] So often talk about the sacred or spirit world embarrasses Western intellectuals; in the name of various kinds of progress the spirits are made to stand for romanticism and reaction. In the dominant streams of Western thought smart always equals rational.

Even at the heart of Western culture there have always been some signs of unease with the imperial capture of the spirit world, even if this disquiet has been construed ambivalently. Legends of hideous curses have followed the removal of sacred objects from tombs and temples to museums in the West, for instance, as in Wilkie Collins's nineteenth-century novel *The Moonstone* and in the rumors of madness and possession that filtered back to Europe from the colonies. Perhaps the most famous example is the curse of the tomb of King Tutankhamen that followed the opening of the Egyptian tomb in 1926 and that gained credence after people involved in the opening of the tomb began to meet with bizarre fates. We can see the rumors of the cursed tomb as an implicit recognition that science's arrogance had limits and that the warnings carved into the tomb's entrance did, in fact, express another reality. But this recognition was, not surprisingly, subject to rapid commodification, and it helped sell a fascination with Tutinspired fashion in the 1920s and later in the 1970s when the grave goods went on tour in North America. The tendency to play with the idea of a deadly curse against which modern science is powerless is a way of discharging the anxiety generated by the confiscation of sacred objects.

Te Rua makes the point that if we (Maori, Pakeha, German) are to undo the social and political apparatuses that enabled sacred objects to be abstracted from their ceremonial settings, simply announcing our identities or producing increasingly rigid binary categories of us and them will not be enough. Such categories tend to reproduce the simplistic views of the colonial era, and identity politics is especially limited when it designates bloodline as the primary criterion of inclusion or classifies huge groups of people as corrupt or wicked. People occupy vastly different positions within systems of authority, but everyone experiences points of complicity and compromise with these systems. There is no absolutely pure space, but there are communities with shared histories, and everyone is better off when people treat each other with respect. At the end of *Te Rua* one of the elders recites the genealogies to show that everyone in the community is related to the Maori man who originally helped the German collector seize the carvings.

When it comes to the acquisition of ceremonial art as a type of spiritual misuse, could feeding off the power of other cultures be dangerous to the people or society that does so? Colonial victories last only so long, and capital follows the money, having no loyalty to a particular place or people. The West increasingly seems to have had its time, as is apparent from recent examples ranging from balance-of-payment difficulties, to infant mortality rates in the United States, to the condition of once-imperial Britain, whose government now imports the toxic waste of other countries to generate revenue. Internal violence continues virtually unchecked, neofascist organizations are on the rise, and Western governments are unable to prevent their activities (even if these governments want to do so). The colonial ideal of European superiority remains just under the surface of Western culture, informing so much high and low aesthetic endeavors, but the ideal is little more than nostalgia.

The bad effects of imperial thinking on the colonizers were occasionally recognized in the colonial period in a way that can continue to provide lessons. The projection of an idealized Western universal knowledge can fall back and recoil onto the well-meaning individual: People in the colonizing countries may have an imaginary relation to the real, but the real has an unsettling tendency to speak back. This is very apparent in the colonial world of E. M. Forster's *A Passage to India,* where the young Englishwoman's expectations of what will happen to her if she is alone with an Indian man structures her perceptions of what actually does happen. Adela is not a bad person, but her understanding of events has, in all the ways that matter, been decided in advance and has nothing to do with anything Aziz does or does not do. Rather, Adela drives herself mad, and everything takes place inside her own head. Her profound self-absorption, which she is able to take for granted because of her position as an Englishwoman traveling through the British raj, means that she is unable to conceive of any agency on Aziz's part. To say this is not to claim that this process is simple, and Forster was well attuned to the complexities of ethnicity and gender in a colonial setting. But at base it is British colonialism in India that makes the Englishwoman sick and that causes the effects of her sickness to ripple outward across the British and Indian communities.

Adela's fate is an example of autoconsumption, of the way cultural cannibalism directed outward—her assumption that she knows, that she is in charge by virtue of her identity as an Englishwoman, that India is an experience to be consumed—turns on itself because it cannot survive an encounter with real people, places, or events. This cannibalism is based on a set of assumptions that conceals the true nature of the British project in India, which is to consume bodies and images as much as wealth, always leaving the Westerner hungry for more. The colonist can never uncover the heart of the colonized, the holy grail of the truth of difference, that moment when the colonist can be absolutely certain that s/he is in charge. I think Forster is telling us that Westerners have two choices: Either relinquish preconceived ideas about difference (along with authority), or go crazy. I have spoken of the universalization of Western values and ontological systems and wish to stress again that it can occur only if people believe they know everything about whatever they are making judgments about. The myth of universal knowledge tells them that when they see something, they possess a template that will explain what it all means. And this is how authority manifests itself.

Westerners whose great exotic adventures go sour can and will blame the Vietnamese, the Arabs, or even the landscape for the problems they encounter, but it is their expectations that do them in. The problem is, again, deciding in advance what things will be like, imposing an imperial operation on the world. This is what brings disaster down on people like Kit and Port, Adela, Rene Gallimard, and indeed anyone who thinks he understands the other and runs smack up against the substantive reality of actual people and places, usually with devastating results for everybody. Their conceit tells them that they are in charge, but the reality they must face is always shifting: Sometimes difference is so much more different than they could ever imagine, and other times it is not that different at all. But anticipation always constructs a blind spot, even in those who consider themselves especially knowledgeable. It is perhaps unsurprising that North American anthropologists working in Peru were unable to predict the rise of the Sendero Luminoso movement because they assumed that the indigenous people of the Andes were concerned with the past rather than with the future or with the injustices that white people worried about (the Andean people were, after all, Indians).[5] The models of culture that these specialists had studied in graduate school had assured them of these facts, and they were predisposed to believe in these models because they thought they were in a position to know the real: They imagined that their training gave them access to universal knowledge. In a similar vein, even the well-funded CIA was unable to gauge the extent of anti-Shah sentiment in Iran just before the revolution. Power does make us stupid, or as Nietzsche said in *Twilight of the Idols,* macht truly verdumpts.[6]

The State, Again

Am I falling into imperial thinking by appropriating the Aztec empire as an analogy for the most violent and rapacious qualities of Western culture? I think the answer to this question partially depends on the use to which examples from another culture are put. I also think empires are fair game, regardless of when and where they occur. The Aztec state can illuminate the nature of power by provoking a moment of shock in Westerners ("Oh no, we can't possibly be like *that!*" has been the cry ever since Cortés saw his first sacrificial pyramid) and by vividly demonstrating what an empire actually does, despite all the gilding of fine art, culture, fancy talk, and diplomatic maneuvers.

There is another reason to approach the problem of imperial representation through the analogy of Aztec society. After all is said and done, I accept a materialist analysis of culture. To suggest that certain aesthetic forms are more likely to be taken up and valorized in certain societies is not to maintain a rigid determinism but rather grounds and permits a recognition of cultural topographies and of the tendency of traits to cluster in patterns. Imperial cultures share certain basic characteristics, regardless of whether the society is located in Rome, China, or Great Britain and aside from quibbles over differences (such as the Asiatic mode of production and other theoretical esoterica). In the first volume of *Anti-Oedipus* Deleuze and Guattari explain how despotic representation works by coding cultural matter through the body of the despot, who can be Pharaoh, Jehovah, or any figure that functions as the sole quasi cause; the "fictitious voice from on high" gives the orders and obliterates other ways of doing things.[7] It is not simply that the portrait will always be of Caesar but that all other portraits will be imagined to exist in reference to Caesar. Unfortunately it is not always easy to tell which characteristics will be significant to the problem of an imperial aesthetic, particularly in regard to the complex and manifold issues of representation. It is a fact that imperial societies create monumental architecture, but the nuances of opera plots or clothing styles are more difficult to interpret and link to a system of imperial representation.

When we are able to look at our own society as a cluster of traits like any other, we can begin to undo the transparency and the naturalization of the cannibal regimes. The dominant stream of Western culture is imperial and has been for some time, but today the imperial mode has shifted and crossed an entirely new threshold. The effects of this shift are as frightening as they are unpredictable. Violence is both nearer and more distant than in any previous empire, nearer because we see both fictional and real acts of violence every day on endless television programs and farther away because the people making decisions that cause mass death and upheaval are bureaucrats rather than sacrificial priests. The relation between cause and effect is attenuated, and Hannah Arendt's "banality of evil" is apparent in the bureaucratic fondness for euphemisms that obscure the nature of the activities they describe: There is something monstrous about the terms *friendly fire* and *collateral damage,* as there is in the more insidious *development.* Violence is sublimated, and other voices are rendered inaudible. The elders remind us that every time we flick on a switch, something dies, but this is a message many people seem unable to hear.

The obvious problem with cultural generalizations and analogies is that these can end up obscuring the specificity of both cultural and aesthetic forms. For instance, the Aztec elites maintained a sacrificial system for reasons that had to do with the organization of political and economic authority in the valley of Mexico and with regional historical events, such as the great famine of 1450–1454, which led to a sharp increase in sacrifices. Sacrificial violence has a history and involves a precise empire building that occurs slowly, step by step, with each decision implying similar decisions in the future. The lightning-swift appearance of the state that Nietzsche speaks of is only part of the story. (Again, people do not start out ripping other people's hearts out.) Similarly, rather than identifying monocausal reasons for social and cultural phenomena, we are wiser to map out the multiple configurations of aesthetics and power that make these goings-on possible.

I believe that it is possible to generalize about culture without falling into the trap of deciding in advance what cultural phenomena mean—which is to say, I think there are certain trajectories of cause and effect that account for the cultural disposition of contemporary society. It should be clear by now that my agenda involves bringing the Aztecs into the genealogy of empire so that when we try to grasp the nature of power we think of Tenochtitlán as much as imperial Rome or Washington. The exclusion of Mexico has made it difficult to look at what civilization truly involves, what power actually looks like, and what we are up against in any project to shift the status quo. The Méxica can be a mirror in which the face of power, our own as much as theirs, begins to emerge from the mist. They moved quickly and were brought down equally quickly: by themselves, not by Cortés, but by the tens of thousands of subject peoples who saw the chance to finally overthrow their masters. The face in the mirror can come as no real surprise: The West still longs to be imperial, a desire manifested in its thinking, if not in overt political control over territory. (We all know about covert means to establish and maintain power and about proxy wars: The lesson of Vietnam is that it is cheaper to let others do the actual fighting unless there are clear propaganda advantages, as was true for the Falklands/Malvinas War, the Gulf War, and the invasions of Grenada and Panama.)

Ideas that continue to circulate in the constructions of culture and history are repeated on television and in mainstream cinema and confuse our understanding of the culture in which we live. People continue to assert that Adolf Hitler was a madman, as if that explains anything; they say that all the violent events in the world today are either totally incomprehensible or have something to do with human nature. After a certain point it becomes very difficult to locate the moment when events could have turned out differently (the former Yugoslavia comes to mind), but this does not mean that extreme events are impenetrable. I reject the idea that violence, whether individual or societal, is random and inexplicable, a fiction that seems dependent on the view that Western culture possesses greater virtues and values than other societies and is not an imperial society in which violence is immanent and valorized for its own sake.

Nietzsche explains in some detail how power stupefies and ultimately renders those who think they are in charge both stupid and melancholy. Power is self-referential, as Fanon points out, and is fundamentally a system of display in which the colonizer does not have to take into account the concerns of the people being sacrificed and displayed. So much of the supposed interest in difference ends up being self-referential—it is so boring, this us us us, even when it is run through cultural difference—but this self-referentiality is important to keep in mind when we think through problems of colonialist representation. Remember Quetzalcoátl's terror when he examined his face in the mirror that his evil brother spitefully offered to him. This story tells us that there is something about vision, about the representation of the self to the self, that can make us sick (contra the construction of the self as a transparent, universal entity) and that we try to escape by representing the other. We can never quite see ourselves except by accident. We cannot see the other, we cannot see the self, the image in the mirror is constantly shifting, but it continues to make us nervous.

Signs and Omens

Motecuzoma and the people of Tenochtitlán were given omens that warned them of the destruction of their world. There are signs in the air today that the world many in the West have taken for granted is also breaking down.

Gradual breakdown and rapid collapse are two different things: I certainly do not think that the edifice of Western capitalism is going to collapse in the immediate future (capitalism has proved infinitely adaptable, it seems), but the old configurations of power at the very heart of the empire are shifting in the New World Order.

The old empire was a regime of intense and manifest cruelty. The Caribbean sugar plantations and the slums in London and Manchester needed and fed off each other, and both affected the course of the wars against indigenous people in the Americas. Then for a time, perhaps after World War I or even more briefly after World War II, it seemed that the world might get better, that people might come to their senses, that the shackles of the past might indeed be thrown off, if only people would clap their hands and say, "I believe." The violence and carnage of the two world wars did not in fact end up shocking people and their governments out of their romance with power. Even when "the people" saw that new versions of fascism were alive and well, they decided not to rise up after all (much to the surprise of many on the Left, who believed that to demonstrate the existence of evil would be enough). Unfortunately things have become profoundly worse, especially as the land has increasingly and possibly irrevocably become damaged. When the frogs recently stopped singing in many parts of the world, some of the old people in Native communities matter-of-factly interpreted this as a sign that the earth can no longer cleanse itself. We approach a time of great change.

Life is becoming harder in North America, the old golden mountain, the land of plenty of our dreams. This, too, is occurring at the level of basic sustenance of life. The alienation and commodification of culture have affected how people experience their lives, and conditions of extreme stress will certainly not improve matters, despite all the fine talk about people pulling together in hard times. *Wétiko* psychosis flourishes in a climate of isolation, when people are unable or unwilling to help one another, when they cannot imagine anything outside of the box in which they find themselves all alone. This means that deep in the heart of Western culture there are strange and unpredictable consequences of the ideologies of individualism. Or to put the matter slightly differently, colonialism has made Western culture sick and has duplicated all the violence and desperation and turned them inward (as it has always done). This has happened despite the attempts to feed off difference, despite the search for excitement in exotic locales, and despite all the lovely commodities. These are not enough to fill the hole.

It seems increasingly difficult to survive both economically and psychically with the minimum wage service jobs that seem the fate of so many, but people seem unable to imagine mutual aid as a way out of their desperation. They have become even more individualized than I ever thought possible, even in my most cynical and pessimistic moments. On a recent visit to the United States nearly everyone I spoke to said they would be able to manage in the New World Order only if they were completely independent, never forced to rely on others. This, they think, will keep them safe from paranoia, anger, and confusion. Television has definitely done its job, and people are much more apt to say that everyone should take care of themselves and quit their whining and expectations rather than suggest that people should find ways to help one another. People who lived through the Great Depression say that the level of individualism is why things are worse now. So many people in North American cities look pinched and ill and seem extremely disoriented by the situations in which they find themselves. They are puzzled because life did not turn out as they were led to expect. Poor children are shot in New Orleans. White, middle-class teenagers sit blankly on the sidewalk in Victoria, B.C., blinking up at passersby in the watery sunlight as if they have just survived a disaster, which in a sense they have.

Tension is in the air on the streets of American cities. Anything can happen, which does not mean that violence is actually as random as people imagine. The term *random violence* occludes the extent to which such phenomena are a natural consequence of the way society has been arranged. People are trained to be aggressive, but often this training backfires, and the violence spins out further and further until someone opens fire in a mall for apparently no reason. But these events are not particularly mysterious or unpredictable. Think of the way marines were trained in Stanley Kubrick's film *Full Metal Jacket* (bear in mind the one who went crazy). (Canada is just a few years behind in the violence department, so Canadians ought not imagine themselves too superior to Americans.) This propensity to feed off and aestheticize violence travels and intensifies everywhere and makes anything else seem impossible. In *Tristes Tropiques* a pessimistic Claude Lévi-Strauss wrote in 1955, "The atmosphere thickens, everywhere."[8]

There are (moneyed) North Americans who seem quite happy to continue deluding themselves that everything is just fine or that the situation on the street is manageable, at least in terms of the potential effects on them. Increasingly people who can afford to are choosing to live behind walls: What works in Bogotá can also work in the gated communities of California, a state of affairs that reveals the fear behind the confident words.

Most people are not evil; they just want to pass their time as happily as possible, with a certain amount of space in which they can live their lives. Very few people start out wanting to unload an M-16 into a crowded store, but financial pressure, lack of choices, individualism, and aestheticized violence make an extremely dangerous cocktail. There are not a lot of choices: You can transform yourself into a highly productive, highly competitive professional, if you can get a job and do not go crazy from overwork in the process (*Vogue* magazine informs us that successful women average about five hours of sleep a night, a truly depressing thought.) Or you can end up in a low-paying service industry job, if you can survive on the wages, also with no time to think or to imagine a way to make an alternative possible. Or you can bail out, as many young people seem to be doing, and create another version of self-sufficiency on the land.[9] But space is a luxury, and bailing out has its consequences.

In these times we must ask what function violence serves in contemporary culture because it would probably not exist without a good reason. And making television producers and advertisers money does not really explain anything. Richard Townsend writes that Méxica human sacrifice was "greatly emphasized as a general policy aimed at inuring the population to violence and bloodshed as a way of life."[10] If people become used to violence as a way of life, they will accept all kinds of cruelty, and they will accept a government that solves problems by force rather than negotiation. To constantly kick ass, and to want to do so, will seem normal. It is curious that the incessant representation of rage and terror is accompanied by therapeutic discourses that seek to individualize the problem and cure the effects on the individual or the nuclear family. One debate concerns whether there is indeed increasing violence in families, with some claiming that it is just being talked about more. I suspect that with the fetishization of violence in culture more and more people will act this violence out and will do so in the most convenient setting, which is to say, in their own homes.

It is also curious that people periodically appear on television to deplore the rising tide of violence in society. But it is unusual to hear people talk about how violence is produced and rewarded in our culture, which is true both in real life and on television. Violence has become normalized, which bears on the necessity for people to exhibit "attitude" (another term for aggression) and the truly unpleasant spectacle of George Bush telling people to read his lips à la Dirty Harry.

I am very uneasy about the way the current romance with violence links up to people's inability to locate a center to the culture in which they live. By center I do not mean a fixed conceptual template that insists on imposing order on unstable cultural, aesthetic, or ceremonial material; nor do I mean a cabal of high art experts who deem themselves best qualified to judge what the culture actually is (in other words, who succeeds and who fails). I am not using the term *center* as an alibi for a scale of values that dictates and oppresses because everything is decided from above. I am thinking of how many earth-based societies maintain an idea of the cultural center as the heart of the social body, a heart that everyone can recognize and to which people feel connected. This existence of a shared, mutually understood center might irritate from time to time, but it remains a source from which people can draw strength and experience belonging and responsibility for one another. What has made this idea of a cultural heart seem an impossible—and in many respects unappealing—fantasy in the West? Since the earliest days of European colonial expansion, there has been a constant effort to construct cultural identity through reference to those other, supposedly inferior cultures over which the West has triumphed. At the same time, there has been a tendency to locate authenticity and meaning outside the West in the commodified and easily digested versions of difference that have so fascinated colonists old and new. There is far more interest in the other than in how dominant Western values have systematically sought to destroy margins and alternatives in the West and have attempted to subdue everyone else. This will to cannibalize difference ends up revealing more about the West than it does about the cultures that have been subject to appropriation. Just past the bluster, everywhere we look there are emptiness, elision, blind spots, and, finally, weakness.

If the effort to transform difference into deadened and deadening commodities (which can be offered up for consumption to a market well prepared in advance) is an indication of the West's weakness, how do we account for the equally constant trumpeting of Western superiority? How do we account for the elision of the fascination with violence and hierarchy that is the true source of this weakness and for the damage this does to people inside and outside of dominant society and to the earth itself? The process of commodification feeds back and forth; the economic system is arranged to keep people consuming, so new aesthetic and cultural territory must continually be "discovered" and colonized. The fruits of these conquests must be displayed in a way that is attractive to buyers. At the same time, precisely because no cultural heart exists in the most dominant stream of Western society, people continue to cannibalize other cultures and fictionalized versions of their own past in order to survive. In this way appropriation serves both economic and spiritual needs, the latter of which are occluded and denied.

But there seems to be a paradox with this formulation: On the one hand, the West appears as a hungry predator; on the other, it appears as something horribly confused and ill. The two actually do go hand in hand. The *wétiko* is one way to describe this conjunction. I also imagine contemporary culture as a large, dangerous, wild animal—say, a nine-foot-tall silvertip grizzly bear—that has been confined to a cage. This animal has been wounded but not yet mortally. Bears can be dangerous at the best of times (not because they are evil, I hasten to add, but because it is their way), and everybody knows that wild animals are at their most dangerous when they have been hurt. Western culture may be breaking down, but it is still capable of inflicting a great deal of damage on the world. The critical mass of histories, languages, and aesthetic and intellectual traditions that make up

Western culture is sick *and* predatory, and the safest thing to do is to leave it alone. Do not attempt to engage the beast; go find something else to do. To paraphrase the oft-quoted words of Deleuze, the only sensible course of action is to run away, but while running make sure to pick up a stick.

Refusing the Cannibal

Can we turn away from the cannibal path? Have things gone too far to do so? Before I can answer these questions, others need to be addressed. What is at stake in clinging so persistently to the view that the European conquest of the world was a nearly effortless endeavor, one that quickly and permanently succeeded in annihilating Native cultures, with the exception of those that could be commodified? This fiction continues to close off possibilities in the present. Part of the problem has to do with how history is imagined. We read statements of this sort again and again: "In this unequal struggle Spain triumphed rapidly over the indigenous peoples. The Aztec and Inca empires succumbed in holy terror before the power of Spanish harquebuses, cannons, horses, bloodthirsty dogs, and weapons of iron and invincible armor. A mere handful of men conquered a continent with millions of inhabitants. ... This entire indigenous civilization was defeated by the Spanish."[11]

In this extremely peremptory account of the European invasions, everything seems to have already been decided. Interestingly, the author of this quotation, Enrique Dussel, has been involved for many years in the struggle against oppression in Latin America. To question this passage is not to doubt the sincerity of the author's intentions in this regard, although sincerity clearly has its own blind spots. Yet there is something about the tone of the passage that makes me extremely uneasy, a sense of inevitability that appears as a form of pacification in itself. This kind of history induces paralysis and makes another version of the story seem impossible. Dussel deplores the violence involved in the process of colonization, yet at the same time insists that there was in fact a rapid and absolute indigenous defeat. Is this not another form of conquest, one that makes his ethical stance on colonial violence seem somewhat equivocal? (His tone reminds me of the sixteenth-century friars who believed the conquest to have been necessary but condemned the violence of the conquistadors.)

Certainly the fall of Tenochtitlán (to name only one example) seems to provoke in many writers a desire to articulate European strength and efficiency again and again and to characterize the Aztecs in terms of weakness and exhaustion (for Christian writers such as Dussel, this can also refer to a certain idealization of the oppressed and weak in Christian theology). The Aztecs lost the war against the Spaniards in 1521, which led to a transformation of many features of the old pre-European Mexican society. But many peoples have been conquered, with varying degrees of brutality; the same tone of finality and termination does not appear in discussions of, for instance, the relatively rapid and efficient German invasions of the Low Countries and northern France in the twentieth century. Passages like Dussel's reinforce the belief that Europeans alone are the agents of history, which denies any possibility of agency to those who refuse to assimilate into dominant Western culture or who prefer a more distanced relation to the centers of power. Certeau articulates something that anyone close to contemporary indigenous struggles will immediately recognize as true: Conquest is never absolute, and the "weak" have many ways to trick the "strong."[12] Nothing is ever decided once and for all.

What is at stake in the occlusion of indigenous resistance and the survival of precolonial cultural and linguistic traditions?[13] Perhaps in Dussel's text we can discern a reason for this elision of indigenous action and resistance. In his description of the Aztec and Inca empires, Dussel writes, "Their pantheons had not as yet been codified nor adequately organized, their theogonies and beliefs were still heterogeneous, and their philosophical reflection had hardly begun."[14]

The use of "yet," "not ... adequately," "still," and "hardly begun" reinforces a long-standing and persistent conceptual hierarchy in which non-Western societies are made to express the failures and omissions that Western culture has been able to overcome. This kind of thinking runs deep, and it is here that we can see why Aztecs, Native people, Asian women, and so many others had to disappear from the story or, rather, be made to disappear from any role but a passive one, the role of supposedly inferior but possibly interesting object of consumption. The assertion that the world, because of its supposedly backward nature and general unruliness, deserved to be conquered is no longer articulated explicitly but remains disguised in contemporary writings. And this approach to the world continues to be affirmed, although now for reasons that have more to do with the universalization of notions of science and history rather than with theology. Evolutionist notions of history and culture are extremely persistent; even well-meaning people such as Dussel and white environmentalists believe that they know what is good for the land and hence refuse to trust the indigenous people who have lived on this land for millennia.[15] The difference expressed by other cultures must be presented as both absolute and obsolete, and the reiteration of this difference becomes a way to affirm the Western dream of global history, which can be made to appear seamless, authoritative, and capable of subsuming all other histories.

What is at stake in clinging to the notion that everything has been decided, that the earth is, in fact, a dead thing? Such ideas are debilitating, which perhaps is the point, and produce nothing but stasis and despair.

(Remember Motecuzoma's experience of profound dread and paralysis when he observed the Spaniards in his mirror.) If the possibilities for change are not all over, if a few tricks still remain up the sleeves of those who have no wish to be masters, and if culture is more resilient and layered than advertisers would have us believe, then where to now? How do we locate margins right here now? How do we tame the cannibal monster?

In Chapter 1 I approvingly quoted Leslie Marmon Silko on the moment of recognition between the Spaniards and Aztecs and how the blood worshippers of Mexico called their equivalents from across the ocean. In Chapter 2 I criticized Georges Bataille for suggesting that at some level the Aztecs longed for and affirmed the Spanish conquest and that it was an intensification of their own sacrificial moment. My approach to these writers is not as contradictory as it might seem at first glance. What Silko and Bataille are saying is in some respects not all that different, but there are very different implications in the way each writer has formulated the problems of conquest, defeat, and survival. Bataille sees the Aztecs as wholly different from Europeans and indeed as an opposite that is "morally at our antipode."[16] Bataille maintains the Aztecs as an object to delight and horrify, whereas Silko is interested in the lessons they continue to offer about the ruses of power. Bataille has his own theoretical agendas and accordingly reads Aztec society as completely concerned with the sovereign expenditure of blood. Silko refuses to mystify either the Aztecs or the Spaniards and sees the Aztecs as a society like any other, although one that followed a particular path in which energy was derived from the violence the state produced and aestheticized. The imperial exemplar is available to all peoples to choose or reject and was taken up in Europe, eventually dominating Western thinking.

The difference between Bataille and Silko suggests another way to look at the problem of culture and representation. Rather than objectifying difference and turning it into something to entertain, we can see difference as a mirror that allows us to recognize the extent to which the society we live in has come to feed off violence and alienation from the land. We can choose—and reject—certain paths. Those of us who come from the imperial, Western tradition need to decolonize our eye and carefully examine the cultural and aesthetic phenomena we have been taught to find interesting. We might then cease imagining empire as fascinating and as somehow higher on the great chain of being than earth-based societies. If there is such a thing as a cannibal path, then surely it is possible to walk away.

Cannibal stories are a way of seeing the imperial exemplar for what it is. The beautiful dead Asian women, the Native clan key chains, the vast numbers of museums and galleries stuffed with booty, are all food for the monster, which continues to grow and grow and becomes hungrier with each meal. Because the cannibal flourishes in a climate of frozen isolation, confronting the monster in ourselves and in our culture begins to break down the experience of separation; we can belong to the world again. The heart of ice softens, and imagining other people and cultures as deadened objects becomes less appealing, if we can bear to look in the mirror. Perhaps the cannibal monster will continue to bite from time to time, but this is better than its consuming everything in sight. We will never entirely get rid of it.

Notes

Chapter 1

1. According to current terminology, the name *Méxica* is considered more correct than *Aztec,* which properly refers to the three cities making up the Triple Alliance confederacy.

2. See, for instance, Pierre Clastres, *Society Against the State* (Oxford: Basil Blackwell, 1977); and Pierre Clastres, *The Archaeology of Violence* (New York: Semiotext[e], 1994).

3. *Annals of Cuahtitlan,* quoted in Laurette Sejourne, *Burning Water* (London: Thames and Hudson, 1978), p. 57.

4. *Florentine Codex, Rhetoric, and Moral Philosophy,* vol. 4 (Santa Fe: School of American Research Monograph, 1969), p. 41.

5. Claude Lévi-Strauss, *Tristes Tropiques,* trans. John Russell (New York: Atheneum, 1967), p. 388. For a discussion of Aztec sacrifice, see Inga Clendinnen, *The Aztecs* (Cambridge: Cambridge University Press, 1991). The point is that human sacrifice is so often framed as an enigma. That said, there are careful studies of the institution, such as Christian Duverger, *La fleur létale: Économie du sacrifice azteque* (Paris: Seuil, 1979); and Elizabeth H. Boone, ed., *Ritual Human Sacrifice in Mesoamerica* (Washington, D.C.: Dumbarton Oaks, 1984).

6. Leslie Marmon Silko, *Almanac of the Dead* (New York: Simon and Schuster, 1991), p. 570.

7. See Francois Hartog, *The Mirror of Herodotus: The Representation of the Other in the Writing of History* (Berkeley and Los Angeles: University of California Press, 1988).

8. Paul Chaat Smith, "Home of the Brave," *C Magazine* 42 (Summer 1994): 30–42.

9. Bruce Johansen, and Robert Maestas, *Wasi'chu: The Continuing Indian Wars* (New York: Monthly Review Press, 1979). John Redhouse explains in the introduction, "The Lakota used a metaphor to describe the [European] newcomers. It was *Wasi'chu,* which means takes the fat, or greedy person. Within the modern Indian movement, *Wasi'chu* has come to mean those corporations and individuals, with their governmental accomplices, which continue to covet Indian lives, land, and resources for private profit. *Wasi'chu* does not describe a race; it describes a state of mind" (p. 11).

10. See Miguel Leon-Portilla, *The Broken Spears: The Aztec Account of the Conquest of Mexico* (Boston: Beacon Press, 1962).

11. Jack Forbes, *Columbus and Other Cannibals* (New York: Autonomedia, 1992). Forbes explains, "*Wétiko* is a Cree term (*windigo* in Ojibway, *wintiko* in Powhatan) which refers to a cannibal or, more specifically, to an evil person or spirit

who terrorizes other creatures by means of terrible evil acts, including cannibalism. *Wetikowatisewin,* an abstract noun, refers to 'diabolical wickedness or cannibalism'" (p. 33).

12. Friedrich Nietzsche, *Thus Spoke Zarathustra,* trans. R. J. Hollingdale (Harmondsworth: Penguin Books, 1969), p. 75.

13. Michael Taussig, *The Nervous System* (New York: Routledge, 1992), p. 27.

14. See Dean MacCannell, *Empty Meeting Grounds: The Tourist Papers* (London: Routledge, 1992), pp. 17–73.

15. I wish to thank Wedlidi Speck for helping me out with this concept.

16. Forbes, *Columbus and Other Cannibals,* p. 46.

17. Théophile Gautier, quoted in Joanna Richardson, *Théophile Gautier: His Life and Times* (New York: Coward and McCann, 1959), p. 76.

18. See Gilles Deleuze and Felix Guattari, *Anti-Oedipus: Capitalism and Schizophrenia,* trans. Robert Hurley, Mark Seem, and Helen R. Lane (New York: Viking Press, 1977), esp. ch. 3, on the function of the despot in representation.

19. Susan Sontag, "Introduction," in *Antonin Artaud: Selected Writings* (Berkeley and Los Angeles: University of California Press, 1988), p. xl.

20. John Lloyd Stephens, *Incidents of Travel in Central America, Chiapas, and Yucatan* (New York: Harper and Brothers, 1841), vol. 1, p. 115, quoted in Curtis M. Hindslay, "In Search of the New World Classical," in *Collecting the Pre-Columbian Past,* ed. Elizabeth Hill Boone (Washington, D.C.: Dumbarton Oaks, 1993), pp. 105–122, 111.

21. Stephen E. Weil, *Rethinking the Museum* (Washington, D.C.: Smithsonian Institution Press, 1990). This essay, "Who Owns the Nataraja?", was also published in *ARTnews* 88(5) (May 1989):188.

22. For an excellent critique of the (disingenuous) notion of postcolonialism, see Anne McClintock, "The Angel of Progress: Pitfalls of the Term 'Post-Colonialism,'" *Social Text* 31–32 (1992):84–98.

23. Iain Chambers, *Migrancy, Culture, Identity* (London: Routledge, 1994), p. 76.

Chapter 2

1. David Henry Hwang, *M. Butterfly* (New York: Plume, 1988), p. 17.

2. See Doreen K. Kondo, "*M. Butterfly:* Orientalism, Gender, and a Critique of Essentialist Identity," *Cultural Critique* 16 (Fall 1990):5–30.

3. See Lucy Lippard, *Mixed Blessings: New Art in a Multicultural America* (New York: Pantheon Books, 1990), for a discussion of how contemporary artists have approached questions of syncretism and power.

4. Many PBS shows have taken this tack. For instance, the *Tribal Eye* series of the 1970s sought to address non-Western aesthetics, but some episodes reinforced Western prejudices about the inherent violence or sublimity of traditional peoples. With educational programs the Western viewer can still find foreign cultures titillating and exotic, but s/he gets to feel good about it, even edified, as the images appear in the name of science. *National Geographic* magazine is another example of how educational material can fail to come to terms with problems of colonialist representation and, indeed, in some instances affirm it.

5. For a discussion of this concept, see Sally Price, *Primitive Art in Civilized Places* (Chicago: University of Chicago Press, 1989), pp. 37–55.

6. See Dean MacCannell, *Empty Meeting Grounds: the Tourist Papers* (London: Routledge, 1992), pp. 17–73.

7. The standoff took place during the summer and autumn of 1990 and involved a Mohawk community near Montreal setting up a blockade to prevent the expansion of a municipal golf course onto sacred land. The conflict escalated after provincial police stormed the barricade, leaving an officer dead, and ultimately involved the Canadian Army. To date, the land rights issue that was the source of the standoff has not been resolved. "Change" appeared in titles and in the body of articles in the Canadian weekly *Maclean's* as an agent in its own right: in "Creating a New Way of Life: Changes Threaten Cree Traditions" and "Northern Agony: Change Leaves Canada's Arctic Grappling with an Alarming Array of Tragic Social Ills," the titles orient the reader toward a specific set of conclusions. This trope was also articulated by Supreme Court Justice of British Columbia Allan McEachern's decision to reject Gitksan-Wet'suwet'en land claims, in which he remarked, "The difficulties in adapting to changing circumstances, not limited land use, is the principal cause of Indian misfortune" (*Financial Post,* March 14, 1992, p. 1). Thus, when the media began to report on the Oka standoff, the Mohawk community was already framed as a community existing in an unhealthy or feeble state, unable to adapt to inevitable change (here symbolized by a golf course).

8. See Malek Alloula, *The Colonial Harem,* trans. Myrna Godzich and Wlad Godzich (Minneapolis: University of Minnesota Press, 1986).

9. See Hwang, *M. Butterfly,* p. 45.

10. Libretto, *Madama Butterfly* (New York: London Records, 1974), p. 12. See Catherine Clement, *Opera, or the Undoing of Woman,* trans. Betsy Wing (Minneapolis: University of Minnesota Press, 1988).

11. Eugenio Donato, "The Museum's Furnace: Notes Toward a Contextual Reading of *Bouvard and Pécuchet,*" in *Textual Strategies,* ed. Josue V. Harari (Ithaca: Cornell University Press, 1979), p. 225.

12. This function seems even clearer when the cost of the opening night party is considered: $750,000 in what must have been an orgy of self-congratulation in recession-hit and increasingly multicultural Toronto. We can also ask how *Miss Saigon* fits into the revisionist right-wing histories of the Vietnam War, in which the only consideration is whether "we" lacked the will to win.

13. See Jeffrey Richards, *Visions of Yesterday* (London: Routledge and Kegan Paul, 1973), esp. ch. 12.

14. See Marjorie Garber, *Vested Interests: Cross-Dressing and Cultural Anxiety* (New York: Harper, 1992).

15. Franz Fanon, *The Wretched of the Earth* (New York: Grove Press, 1963), p. 53.

16. Quoted in Shonagh Adelman, "Maryse Holder Liked to Fuck," *Fuse Magazine* (September 1988):36.

17. See Gawitrha', *Dwanoha: One Earth, One Mind, One Path* (Brantford, Ont.: Pine Tree, 1992), for a view of the failure of Western political systems from the perspective of Iroquois Great Law of Peace.

18. My grasp of this issue has benefited from discussions with Dot Tuer, who has noted the extent to which Latin America continues to be a site of contestation for Western capital. She locates an example of this in the failure of Western architectural styles of the 1950s and 1960s in Latin America.

19. See Stephen Spender, "Introduction," in Malcolm Lowry, *Under the Volcano* (New York: Plume, 1971), pp. xi–xxx.

20. An exception is the novel *Aztec,* which seemed to be around for a while and is now available in a Spanish-language version in nearly every bookstore in Mexico City.

21. Richard Rodriguez, *An Argument with My Mexican Father* (New York: Penguin, 1992), p. 2.

22. For an excellent discussion of surrealism and cultural difference, see Peter Woolen, *Raiding the Icebox: Reflections on Twentieth-Century Culture* (Bloomington: Indiana University Press, 1993), ch. 3; and James Clifford, *The Predicament of Culture: Twentieth-Century Ethnography, Literature, and Art* (Cambridge, Mass.: Harvard University Press, 1988), pp. 117–151.

23. Here we can see how the codes of exoticism are able to migrate across time and space.

24. Georges Bataille, "Extinct America," *October* 36 (Spring 1986):4.

25. More recently Cambodia/Kampuchea has filled this function.

26. Bataille, "Extinct America," p. 3.

27. See Georges Bataille, *Visions of Excess,* trans. Alan Stoekl (Minneapolis: University of Minnesota Press, 1985), pp. 116–129.

28. Bataille, "Extinct America," p. 7.

29. Bataille, *Visions of Excess,* p. 10.

30. Bataille, "Extinct America," p. 7.

31. Ibid., p. 9.

32. Ibid.

33. According to one reading of the Spanish invasion of Tenochtitlán, this interpretation might even be true: If the Aztecs had not been so willing to conquer and oppress their neighbors, these tens of thousands of Mexicans from surrounding nations might not have been so willing to ally themselves with Cortés in his war to bring down the Aztec empire. But I do not think this is what Bataille means.

34. Bataille, "Extinct America," p. 9.

35. This use of a constructed version of difference to illuminate Western concerns is certainly not uncommon. In a similar vein Sally Price notes the "implicit asymmetry" in the appropriation of primitive art by Europeans in that "their" art will be used to illuminate "our" concerns. See Sally Price, *Primitive Art in Civilized Places* (Chicago: University of Chicago Press, 1989), p. 34.

36. Sergei M. Eisenstein, *Immoral Memories,* trans. H. Marshall (Boston: Houghton Mifflin, 1983), p. 182.

37. Ibid., p. 181.

38. Inga Karetnokova, *Mexico According to Eisenstein* (Albuquerque: University of New Mexico Press, 1991), p. 55.

39. See, for instance, Ward Churchill, ed. *Marxism and Native Americans* (Boston: South End Press, 1982). Of course, what is and is not possible for intellectuals have changed since the 1930s: An urban intellectual such as Frida Kahlo could

wear the indigenous dress of Tehuana women as a way of marking her political and aesthetic sensibility. This would be unthinkable today, in North America at least, and it scarcely bears imagining what the response would be to a mostly white woman in Toronto wearing traditional porcupine quill regalia and a deerskin dress as a way of marking her identification with First Nations people in Canada.

40. Eisenstein, *Immoral Memories*, pp. 181–182.

41. Karetnokova, *Mexico According to Eisenstein*, p. 69.

42. Ibid., p. 53.

43. Antonin Artaud, *Selected Writings*, ed. Susan Sontag (Berkeley and Los Angeles: University of California Press, 1976), p. 353.

44. J.M.G. Le Clézio, *The Mexican Dream: Or, the Interrupted Thought of Amerindian Civilizations*, trans. Teresa Lavender Fagan (Chicago: University of Chicago Press, 1993), pp. 161–172.

45. See Ronald Hayman, *Artaud and After* (Oxford: Oxford University Press, 1977), p. 108.

46. Artaud, *Selected Writings*, p. 537.

47. Hayman, *Artaud and After*, p. 106.

Chapter 3

1. With respect to terminology, some people object to the term *Native Canadians* because they are not actually Canadian in the sense of being a member of the Canadian nation, as opposed to, for instance, the Mohawk nation. The term *First Nations* can be a bit unwieldy in everyday usage, so I generally use the more common description *Native* (not *Indian* for the obvious reason that India is located on another continent). Also, there seems to be some confusion on the part of some non-Natives over the term *traditional*, which, as it has been explained to me, is a relatively fluid concept. Some people can consider themselves traditional and live in the city; others would find that impossible. Traditional usually refers to a system of values that stresses doing things in a good way and recognizes many of the negative effects of contemporary, Western-based society. Traditional can also refer to matters of style, including aesthetic, decorative, and discursive.

2. The issue of tourism can become quite complex. Some communities in British Columbia, such as Tofino near Clayoquot Sound, promote tourism as an alternative to slash-and-burn resource extraction, specifically clear-cutting. Some Native communities in British Columbia have developed heritage centers to draw tourist dollars and at the same time educate visitors, such as the new heritage complex in the Cowichan nation on Vancouver Island. I think the question of how exploitative the tourist industry is really depends on who is organizing the tourism and for whose benefit tourism is being promoted.

3. Marcia Crosby, "Construction of the Imaginary Indian," in *Vancouver Anthology: The Institutional Politics of Art*, ed. Stan Douglas (Vancouver: Talonbooks, 1991), pp. 267–294; Joane Cardinal-Shubert, "In the Red," *Fuse Magazine* (Fall 1989):20. See also Rosemary Coombe, "The Properties of Culture and the Politics of Possessing Identity: Native Claims in the Cultural Appropriation Controversy," *Canadian Journal of Law and Jurisprudence* 6 (1993):249–285.

4. Crosby, "Construction of the Imaginary Indian," p. 274.

5. Marie-Ange Brayer, "Lothar Baumgarten," *Forum International* 19 (October-November 1993):105. I am indebted to Christine Davis for drawing my attention to this article.

6. The Western notion of time was a site of contestation even in the West, with Gnostic and Stoic conceptions of temporality challenging the Greek and Christian views. See Giorgio Agamben, *Infancy and History: Essays on the Destruction of Experience,* trans. Liz Heron (London: Verso, 1993), pp. 100–101.

7. For a discussion of this point, see Paul Chaat Smith, "Home of the Brave," *C Magazine* 42 (Summer 1994):30–42.

8. Crosby, "Construction of the Imaginary Indian," p. 279. This is not an isolated incident; recall James Clifford's report of the Mashpee trial in Massachusetts in which similar concepts were deployed. Like the Gitksan-Wet'suwet'en, the Mashpee nation lost in the white courtroom. See James Clifford, *The Predicament of Culture* (Cambridge, Mass.: Harvard University Press, 1988), 277–348.

9. See Christopher B. Steiner, *African Art in Transit* (Cambridge: Cambridge University Press, 1994), esp. ch. 5.

10. For a discussion of some of the issues surrounding tourism, see Haunani-Kay Trask, "Lovely Hula Lands: Corporate Tourism and the Prostitution of Hawaiian Culture," *Border/Lines* 23 (Winter 1991-1992):22–34.

11. In the thousands of medicine shields and pipes that appear on the New Age market, and in all the images of eagles, we never actually see genuine eagle feathers for sale because their sale is prohibited by the U.S. and Canadian governments. Not surprisingly, of course, the manufacturers of these items are prepared to obey federal law—which is to say, white law—at the same time they are prepared to willfully break traditional, customary Native laws that concern similar issues. The refusal to respect Native conventions occurs in the name of being able to do what they want—in other words, in the name of personal freedom—although it really does seem to come down to a question of power and the potential consequences of ignoring law.

12. "Resolution of the 5th Annual Meeting of the Traditional Elder's Circle," quoted in Ward Churchill, *Fantasies of the Master Race* (Monroe, Maine: Common Courage Press, 1992), p. 223–224. For a discussion of appropriation in the men's movement, see Ward Churchill, *Indians Are Us?* (Toronto: Between the Lines, 1994), pp. 207–272.

13. Leslie Marmon Silko, *Almanac of the Dead* (New York: Simon and Schuster, 1991), p. 719.

14. See Deborah Doxtator, *Fluffs and Feathers: An Exhibit on the Symbols of Indianness* (Brantford, Ont.: Woodland Cultural Centre, 1992), p. 34.

15. Think of the continuing popularity of the Curtis photographs of Chief Joseph and other defeated Native leaders. For discussions of images of Native people in photographs, see Lucy Lippard, ed., *Partial Recall* (New York: New Press, 1992).

16. Trudell has made this important point in the public talks he occasionally gives. These ideas are also expressed in his poetry and music. See the recording *Tribal Voice* (produced and released by John Trudell, 1979), in which he reads his poetry accompanied by traditional Native music.

17. Franz Fanon, *The Wretched of the Earth* (New York: Grove Press, 1963), p. 53.

18. Sometimes appropriation can come down to something very simple, like economics. I recall an older Native friend telling me that it sometimes hurts Native peo-

ple to see wealthy white people wearing the beautiful Native jewelry they cannot afford.

19. Wendy Rose, "The Great Pretenders: Further Thoughts on Whiteshamanism," in *The State of Native America,* ed. M. Annette Jaimes (Boston: South End Press, 1992), p. 416.

20. See Akwesasne Notes, *Basic Call to Consciousness* (Summertown, Tenn.: Book Publishing, 1978).

21. Lovat Dickson, *Wilderness Man: The Strange Story of Grey Owl* (Toronto: Macmillan, 1973), p. 255.

Chapter 4

1. Sally Price, *Primitive Art in Civilized Places* (Chicago: University of Chicago Press, 1989); Ivan Karp and Steven D. Lavine, ed., *Exhibiting Cultures: The Poetics and Politics of Museum Display* (Washington, D.C.: Smithsonian Institution Press, 1991); Peter Vergo, ed., *The New Museology* (London: Reaktion Books, 1989); Michael Ames, *Cannibal Tours and Glass Boxes: The Anthropology of Museums* (Vancouver: University of British Columbia Press, 1992).

2. Durandus (no date), quoted in David Murray, *Museums: Their History and Their Uses,* vol. 1 (Glasgow: Maclehose Press, 1904), p. 8 n.

3. Sidney Galler, John Oliver, Harriet Roberts, Herbert Friedmann, and David Squires, "Museums Today," *Science* 161 (1968):550.

4. Edward Said, *Orientalism* (London: Routledge and Kegan Paul, 1978), p. 42.

5. See Mary Beard, "Souvenirs of Culture: Deciphering (in) the Museum," *Art History* 15(4) (December 1992):505–532.

6. I use the word *preferred* deliberately because I think writing is a choice, something I address in greater detail in Chapter 5.

7. See Gilles Deleuze and Felix Guattari, *Anti-Oedipus: Capitalism and Schizophrenia* (New York: Viking Press, 1977), ch. 3, for a discussion of the despotic function of writing.

8. Peter Corley-Smith, *The Ring of Time: The Story of the British Columbia Provincial Museum* (Victoria: British Columbia Provincial Museum, 1985), p. 27.

9. For a contemporary example of this refusal to recognize Aztec writing as writing, see Tzetvan Todorov, *The Conquest of America* (New York: Harper and Row, 1985). For a critique of Todorov's formulation of symbolic competence, see Deborah Root, "The Imperial Signifier: Todorov and the Conquest of Mexico," *Cultural Critique* 9 (Spring 1988):197–219.

10. See, for instance, Johannes Fabian, *Time and the Other* (New York: Columbia University Press, 1983).

11. See, for instance, Ray A. Young Bear, "Journal of a Mesquakie Poet," in *Without Discovery,* ed. Ray Gonzalez (Seattle: Broken Moon Press, 1992), pp. 145–152. See also Deborah Doxtator, *Fluffs and Feathers* (Brantford, Ont.: Woodland Cultural Centre, 1992).

12. See Robert E. Bieder, "The Collecting of Bones for Anthropological Narratives," *American Indian Culture and Research Journal* 16(2) (1992):21–35; Larry J. Zimmerman, "Archaeology, Reburial, and the Tactics of a Discipline's Self-Delusion," *American Indian Culture and Research Journal* 16(2) (1992):37–56;

and Douglas Cole, *Captured Heritage: The Scramble for Northwest Coast Artifacts* (Seattle: University of Washington Press, 1985).

13. For a discussion of the Ishi phenomenon, see Gerald Vizenor, "Ishi Bares His Chest: Tribal Simulations and Survivance," in *Partial Recall,* ed. Lucy Lippard (New York: New Press, 1992), pp. 64–71.

14. See Sander Gilman, "Black Bodies, White Bodies: Toward an Iconography of Female Sexuality in Late-Nineteenth-Century Art, Medicine, and Literature," *Critical Inquiry* 12(1) (Autumn 1985):204–242.

15. Roger F.H. Summers, *The History of the South African Museum* (Capetown: Balkema Books, 1975), pp. 104–105.

16. David Carrasco, *Quetzalcoátl and the Irony of Empire* (Chicago: University of Chicago Press, 1982).

17. Quoted in J. M. Cohen, "Introduction," in *The Conquest of New Spain,* by Bernal Diaz del Castillo (Harmondsworth: Penguin, 1963), p. 9. See also Benjamin Keen, *The Aztec Image in Western Thought* (New Brunswick: Rutgers University Press, 1971), p. 60.

18. Art also enters popular culture in somewhat less dignified forms. Think of how an entire generation was introduced to high culture—opera, especially Richard Wagner—by Bugs Bunny cartoons.

19. For an extremely astute description of Amazonian tourism, see Pierre Clastres, *The Archaeology of Violence* (New York: Semiotext[e], 1994).

20. John Berger's remarks on the link between oil painting and fashion advertisements are truer than we think. See John Berger, *Ways of Seeing* (Harmondsworth: Penguin, 1972). The relation among high art, cultural appropriation, and fashion has a history. For instance, in the 1960s Courreges manufactured dresses based on the paintings of Piet Mondrian. Over the years haute couture styles have meandered through culture after culture, some very explicitly. For instance, Isaac Mizrahi's showed what he called totem pole dresses (based on Northwest Coast designs, but here in sequins) in 1991, and Norma Kamali produced beaded vests the same season, both of which claimed to celebrate and affirm the Native cultures that were the sources of the designs. Again, what is appropriated are stylistic fragments that have come to stand for the culture as a whole. Thus, this type of appropriation works as the taking up of partial aesthetic codes and recoding these through the nonexotic, much as we see with European high art. But the same problem remains as for exoticism in general: How is it decided which fragments are exotic or attractive?

21. Pierre Bourdieu, *Distinction: A Social Critique of the Judgement of Taste,* trans. Richard Nice (Cambridge, Mass.: Harvard University Press, 1984). For a comprehensive discussion of sociological theories of art, see Vera Zolberg, *Constructing a Sociology of the Arts* (Cambridge: Cambridge University Press, 1990).

22. See Gilles Deleuze and Felix Guattari, *A Thousand Plateaus,* trans. Brian Massumi (Minneapolis: University of Minnesota Press, 1987), p. 178, for a discussion of exclusion as a process of marking deviations.

23. Theodor W. Adorno, *Prisms* (Cambridge, Mass.: MIT Press, 1981), p. 173.

24. Museum cities, such as Florence, also have a moribund quality: They know they are beautiful, and certainly they aggrandize their beauty, but this beauty can-

not move. It certainly is their fortune. (Rome is more interesting than Florence precisely because it is messy.)

25. At the art college where I currently teach, an institution reputed to be progressive, there is only one course that explicitly addresses non-Western art (itself an odd concept, as it suggests the lumping together of an entire world). Along with world aesthetics, this course is also supposed to cover the canon of Western art, all in thirteen weeks. The students clamor for more noncanonical material, but in these days of cutbacks many of the faculty are resistant to new approaches.

26. Octavio Paz, *Essays on Mexican Art* (New York: Harcourt Brace, 1993), p. 292. My discussion of the commodification of criticality has benefited from discussion with contemporary artist Christine Davis.

27. Note John Berger's discussion of Hans Holbein the Younger's *The Ambassadors* (1533) and his work on display in *Ways of Seeing* (Harmondsworth: Penguin, 1972). A great deal of credit is due to Berger's seminal work, which demonstrated that a political analysis of the art object involves more than the social background or intention of the artist. Rather, political analysis can show what the painting actually does to construct meaning and underline relations of power. Many of the meanings are unpleasant and subvert the ideal of the nobility of high art, but paintings picture—and conceal—reality in a range of ways.

28. Jimmie Durham, *A Certain Lack of Coherence: Writings on Art and Cultural Politics* (London: Kala Press, 1993), p. 111.

29. See Bourdieu, *Distinction;* and Pierre Bourdieu, *In Other Words: Essays Towards a Reflexive Sociology,* trans. Matthew Adamson (Cambridge: Polity Press, 1990).

30. bell hooks, "Altars of Sacrifice: Re-membering Basquiat," *Art in America* (June 1993):71.

31. Cited in Eilean Hooper-Greenhill, *Museums and the Shaping of Knowledge* (London: Routledge, 1992), p. 2.

32. Walter Benjamin, *Illuminations* (New York: Schocken Books, 1969), pp. 217–252. See also Susan Buck-Morss, "Aesthetics and Anaesthetics: Walter Benjamin's Artwork Essay Reconsidered," *October* 62 (Fall 1992):3–42.

Chapter 5

1. Linda Hogan, "Journeys and Other Stories," in *Without Discovery,* ed. Ray Gonzalez (Seattle: Broken Moon Press, 1992), p. 224.

2. Jack Forbes, *Columbus and Other Cannibals* (New York: Autonomedia, 1992), p. 46.

3. My use of the term *Araby* is an attempt to circumvent the problem of expressions such as *Middle East, Near East,* or *Orient,* all of which are relational to Europe. One drawback to Araby is that it technically excludes Turks and Persians, who are not Arab, but I think the word's archaic quality reminds us of the historical status of this part of the world as an adversary and the extent to which Crusader polemics continue to obtain.

4. Pierre Clastres, "On Ethnocide," *Art and Text* 28 (March-May 1988):50–58.

5. This naturalization is nothing new if we think about how the classical Greek slave system has been naturalized to the extent that in the vast majority of under-

graduate history textbooks, it is not seen as particularly relevant to discussions of the Greeks' artistic or philosophical tradition.

6. This dream has become increasingly questionable, even in popular culture. The science fiction movies of the 1950s and 1960s have given way to extraordinarily popular book/film combinations such as *Jurassic Park* (1993), which explicitly questions the conceits of science. A mathematician, however, is the character who best understands why science cannot live up to its own claims. Thus, in *Jurassic Park techne* is redeemed, along with the Anglo-Saxon family.

7. See Edward Said, *Orientalism* (Harmondsworth: Penguin, 1978); Norman Daniel, *Europe, Islam, and Empire* (Edinburgh: Edinburgh University Press, 1964); Annelies Moors and Steven Wachlin, "Postcards of Palestine," *Critique of Anthropology* 7(2) (Autumn 1987):61–77; Meyda Yegenoglu, "Veiled Fantasies: Cultural and Sexual Difference in the Discourse of Orientalism," *Cultural Studies* (forthcoming 1995); and Mahmut Mutman, "Pictures from Afar: Shooting the Middle East," *Inscriptions* 6 (1992):1–44.

8. Quoted in Dorothea M. Gallup, *The French Image of Algeria: Its Origin, Its Place in Colonial Ideology, Its Effect on Algerian Acculturation* (Ann Arbor: University Microfilms, 1973), p. 186.

9. Quoted in Mohammed Bennoune, "The Origin of the Algerian Proletariat," *Dialectical Anthropology* 1(3) (1976):221.

10. Linda Nochlin, *The Politics of Vision: Essays on Nineteenth-Century Art and Culture* (New York: Harper and Row, 1989).

11. See John Berger, *Ways of Seeing* (Harmondsworth: Penguin, 1972), ch. 3.

12. Charles Baudelaire, *Art in Paris, 1845–1862: Salons and Other Exhibitions* (London: Phaidon, 1970), p. 184.

13. Brown University, *All the Banners Wave: Art and War in the Romantic Era 1792–1851* (Providence, R.I.: Department of Art, Brown University, 1982), p. 80.

14. See Michel Sandoz, *Theodore Chasseriau, 1819–1856* (Paris: Art et Metiers Graphiques, 1974), p. 317.

15. Paul Bowles, *The Sheltering Sky* (New York: Vintage International 1990), p. 8.

16. Ibid., p. 191.

17. Bernardo Bertolucci's film version of the story reflects a revival of interest in Bowles's work. The film was not a commercial success. It was miscast, and I quickly tired of John Malkovich's studied ennui and Debra Winger's vapidity; the characters appeared merely petulant rather than riddled with Western angst (although perhaps the two come to the same thing in the end). Also, at some level we cannot help but read this film through *Lawrence of Arabia* (1962) and similar movies, so that for all its ponderousness Bertolucci's version seems almost a parody of the desert adventure story.

18. For a historical discussion of this issue, see Norman Daniel, *Islam, Europe, and Empire* (Edinburgh: Edinburgh University Press, 1966). Daniel comments on the European view of the Orient in the colonial period, "This imperial attitude meant thinking of a people as different and inferior: agreeable or disagreeable, but always different" (p. 154).

19. Bowles, *The Sheltering Sky,* p. 14. See also Yegenoglu, "Veiled Fantasies," which addresses the representation of the veiled face in Western writing.

20. For a discussion of the notion of the *pharmakon,* see Jacques Derrida, "Plato's Pharmacy," pp. 61–172. *Desseminations,* trans. Barbara Johnson (Chicago: University of Chicago Press, 1981).

21. Bowles, *The Sheltering Sky,* p. 6.

22. We can see how this type of exoticism continues to function in capitalism, for instance, in airline and other tourist advertisements.

23. We note that for the film version of the story Bertolucci selected an actress with enormous breasts to play Marhnia. We are reminded of Malek Alloula's analysis of the European's obsession with the "Moorish bosom" in French colonial postcards from Algeria. See Malek Alloula, *The Colonial Harem,* trans. Myrna Godzich and Wlad Godzich (Minneapolis: University of Minnesota Press, 1986).

24. Bowles, *The Sheltering Sky,* p. 33.

25. Ibid., p. 285.

26. Ibid., p. 304.

27. This use of ululation may be a filmmaker's quotation of *Women of Algiers.*

28. Bryan Appleyard, "Desert Song: Sand and Some Really Major Stars," *Mirabella* (October 1989), pp. 71–77.

29. We are reminded here of bell hooks's discussion of marginality and resistance and her observation that in white supremist societies black people must comprehend both the margin and center, whereas whites often comprehend only the center. See bell hooks, "Choosing the Margin," *Yearning: Race, Gender, and Cultural Politics* (Toronto: Between the Lines Press, 1990).

30. Bowles, *The Sheltering Sky,* p. 318.

31. Ibid., p 93.

32. For a discussion of the notion of colonial rebarbarization, see Dorothea M. Gallup, *The French Image of Algeria.*

33. Gilles Deleuze and Felix Guattari, *A Thousand Plateaus,* trans. Brian Massumi (Minneapolis: University of Minnesota Press, 1987), pp. 318–382.

Chapter 6

1. Eduardo Matos Moctezuma, "The Templo Mayor of Tenochtitlán: History and Interpretation," in *The Great Temple of Tenochtitlán: Center and Periphery in the Aztec World,* ed. Johanna Broda, David Carrasco, and Eduardo Matos Moctezuma (Berkeley and Los Angeles: University of California Press, 1987), p. 54.

2. Quoted in Laurette Sejourne, *Burning Water* (London: Thames and Hudson, 1957), p. 20.

3. I am certainly not suggesting that earth-based, egalitarian societies had an easier time during the European invasions. I am trying to suggest that imperial peoples are unable to imagine the turn, the lament of defeat, because their distance from the earth blinds them.

4. Michel de Certeau, *The Practice of Everyday Life,* trans. Steve Rendall (Berkeley and Los Angeles: University of California Press, 1984), pp. 178–179.

5. See Orin Starn, "Missing the Revolution: Anthropologists and the War in Peru," in *Rereading Cultural Anthropology,* ed. George Marcus (Durham, N.C.: Duke University Press, 1992), pp. 152–180.

6. Friedrich Nietzsche, *Twilight of the Idols,* and *The Anti-Christ,* trans. R. J. Hollingdale (Harmondsworth: Penguin, 1968), p. 60.

7. Gilles Deleuze and Felix Guattari, *Anti-Oedipus: Capitalism and Schizophrenia* (New York: Viking Press, 1977), p. 209.

8. Claude Lévi-Strauss, *Tristes Tropiques,* trans. John Russell (New York: Atheneum, 1976), p. 37.

9. Governments such as Great Britain's seem to find dropout culture highly threatening if the new laws designed to restrict the movements of the youths known as travelers are any indication.

10. Richard Townsend, *State and Cosmos in the Art of Tenochtitlán* (Washington, D.C.: Dumbarton Oaks, 1979), p. 31.

11. Enrique Dussel, *History and Theology of Liberation* (Maryknoll, N.Y.: Orbis Books, 1976), p. 126.

12. Certeau, *The Practice of Everyday Life.* In one impressive sentence he writes, "The spectacular victory of Spanish colonization over the indigenous Indian cultures was diverted from its intended aims by the use made of it: even when they were subjected, even when they accepted their subjection, the Indians often used the laws, practices and representations that were imposed on them by force or by fascination to ends other than those of their conquerors; they made something else out of them; they subverted them from within—not by rejecting them or transforming them (though that occurred as well), but by many different ways of using them in the service of rules, customs or convictions foreign to the colonization which they could not escape" (pp. 31–32).

13. In this vein I question why, for so many European writers on the invasion of Mexico, the tens of thousands of Tlaxcalan and Cempoalan soldiers who fought alongside Cortés against the Aztecs are absent or elided in their texts, as are the months of street fighting in Tenochtitlán, the rebellions, the lies to the authorities, and the secret resistance to Spanish rule.

14. Dussel, *History and Theology of Liberation,* p. 127.

15. This has been an issue in Canada, where environmental groups have a tendency to support the creation of national parks rather than Native land rights on those same lands.

16. Georges Bataille, *La part maudite* (Paris: Editions de Minuit, 1967), p. 84.

Bibliography

Adelman, Shonagh. "Maryse Holder Liked to Fuck." *Fuse Magazine* (September 1988):35–37.

Adorno, Theodor W. *Prisms*. Cambridge, Mass.: MIT Press, 1981.

Agamben, Giorgio. *Infancy and History: Essays on the Destruction of Experience*. Trans. Liz Heron. London: Verso, 1993.

Akwesasne Notes. *Basic Call to Consciousness*. Summertown, Tenn.: Book Publishing, 1978.

Alloula, Malek. *The Colonial Harem*. Trans. Myrna Godzich and Wlad Godzich. Minneapolis: University of Minnesota Press, 1986.

Ames, Michael. *Cannibal Tours and Glass Boxes: The Anthropology of Museums*. Vancouver: University of British Columbia Press, 1992.

Artaud, Antonin. *Collected Works*. Vol. 4. London: Calder and Boyars, 1974.

______. *Selected Writings*. Edit. Susan Sontag. Berkeley and Los Angeles: University of California Press, 1976.

Bataille, Georges. "Extinct America." *October* 36 (Spring 1986):3–9.

______. *La part maudite*. Paris: Editions de Minuit, 1967.

______. *Visions of Excess*. Trans. Alan Stoekl. Minneapolis: University of Minnesota Press, 1985.

Baudelaire, Charles. *Art in Paris, 1845–1862: Salons and Other Exhibitions*. London: Phaidon, 1970.

Beard, Mary. "Souvenirs of Culture: Deciphering (in) the Museum." *Art History* 15(4) (December 1992):505–532.

Benjamin, Walter. *Illuminations*. New York: Schocken Books, 1969.

Berger, John. *Ways of Seeing*. Harmondsworth: Penguin, 1972.

Bieder, Robert E. "The Collecting of Bones for Anthropological Narratives." *American Indian Culture and Research Journal* 16(2) (1992):21–35.

Boone, Elizabeth Hill, ed. *Collecting the Pre-Columbian Past*. Washington, D.C.: Dumbarton Oaks, 1993.

______. *Ritual Human Sacrifice in Mesoamerica*. Washington, D.C.: Dumbarton Oaks, 1984.

Bourdieu, Pierre. *Distinction: A Social Critique of the Judgement of Taste*. Trans. Richard Nice. Cambridge, Mass.: Harvard University Press, 1984.

______. *In Other Words: Essays Towards a Reflexive Sociology*. Trans. Matthew Adamson. Cambridge: Polity Press, 1990.

Bowles, Paul. *The Sheltering Sky*. New York: Vintage International, 1990.

Brayer, Marie-Ange. "Lothar Baumgarten." *Forum International* 19 (October-November 1993):103–112.

Broda, Johanna, David Carrasco, and Eduardo Matos Moctezuma, eds. *The Great Temple of Tenochtitlán: Center and Periphery in the Aztec World.* Berkeley and Los Angeles: University of California Press, 1987.

Brown University. *All the Banners Wave: Art and War in the Romantic Era, 1792–1851.* Providence, R.I.: Department of Art, Brown University, 1982.

Buck-Morss, Susan. "Aesthetics and Anaesthetics: Walter Benjamin's Artwork Essay Reconsidered." *October* 62 (Fall 1992):3–42.

Cardinal-Schubert, Joane. "In the Red." *Fuse Magazine* (Fall 1989):20–28.

Carrasco, David. *Quetzalcoátl and the Irony of Empire.* Chicago: University of Chicago Press, 1982.

Castillo, Bernal. *The Conquest of New Spain.* Harmondsworth: Penguin, 1963.

Certeau, Michel de. *The Practice of Everyday Life.* Berkeley and Los Angeles: University of California Press, 1984.

Chambers, Iain. *Migrancy, Culture, Identity.* London: Routledge, 1994.

Churchill, Ward. *Fantasies of the Master Race.* Monroe, Maine: Common Courage Press, 1992.

———. *Indians Are Us?* Toronto: Between the Lines, 1994.

———. ed. *Marxism and Native Americans.* Boston: South End Press, 1982.

Clastres, Pierre. *The Archaeology of Violence.* New York: Semiotext(e), 1994.

———. "On Ethnocide." *Art and Text* 28 (March-May 1988):50–58.

———. *Society Against the State.* Oxford: Basil Blackwell, 1977.

Clement, Catherine. *Opera, or the Undoing of Woman.* Trans. Betsy Wing. Minneapolis: University of Minnesota Press, 1988.

Clendinnen, Inga. *The Aztecs.* Cambridge: Cambridge University Press, 1991.

Clifford, James. *The Predicament of Culture: Twentieth-Century Ethnography, Literature, and Art.* Cambridge, Mass.: Harvard University Press, 1988.

Cohen, J. M. "Introduction." In *The Conquest of New Spain,* by Bernal Díaz del Castillo. Harmondsworth: Penguin, 1963.

Cole, Douglas. *Captured Heritage: The Scramble for Northwest Coast Artifacts.* Seattle: University of Washington Press, 1985.

Coombe, Rosemary. "The Properties of Culture and the Politics of Possessing Identity: Native Claims in the Cultural Appropriation Controversy." *Canadian Journal of Law and Jurisprudence* 6 (1993):249–285.

Corley-Smith, Peter. *The Ring of Time: The Story of the British Columbia Provincial Museum.* Victoria: British Columbia Provincial Museum, 1985.

Crosby, Marcia. "Construction of the Imaginary Indian." In *Vancouver Anthology: The Institutional Politics of Art,* ed. Stan Douglas. Vancouver: Talonbooks, 1991.

Daniel, Norman. *Islam, Europe, and Empire.* Edinburgh: Edinburgh University Press, 1966.

Deleuze, Gilles, and Felix Guattari. *Anti-Oedipus: Capitalism and Schizophrenia.* Trans. Robert Hurley, Mark Seem, and Helen R. Lane. New York: Viking Press, 1977.

———. *A Thousand Plateaus.* Trans. Brian Massumi. Minneapolis: University of Minnesota Press, 1987.

Derrida, Jacques. *Dessemінations.* Trans. Barbara Johnson. Chicago: University of Chicago Press, 1981.

______. *Of Grammatology.* Trans. Gayatri Spivak. Baltimore: Johns Hopkins University Press, 1976.

Dickson, Lovat. *Wilderness Man: The Strange Story of Grey Owl.* Toronto: Macmillan, 1973.

Donato, Eugenio. "The Museum's Furnace: Notes Toward a Contextual Reading of *Bouvard and Pécuchet.*" In *Textual Strategies,* ed. Josue V. Harari. Ithaca: Cornell University Press, 1979.

Doxtator, Deborah. *Fluffs and Feathers: An Exhibit on the Symbols of Indianness.* Brantford, Ont.: Woodland Cultural Centre, 1992.

Durham, Jimmie. *A Certain Lack of Coherence: Writings on Art and Cultural Politics.* London: Kala Press, 1993.

Dussel, Enrique. *History and Theology of Liberation.* Maryknoll, N.Y.: Orbis Books, 1976.

Duverger, Christian. *La fleur létale: Économie du sacrifice azteque.* Paris: Seuil, 1979.

Eisenstein, Sergei M. *Immoral Memories.* Trans. Herbert Marshall. Boston: Houghton Mifflin, 1983.

Fabian, Johannes. *Time and the Other.* New York: Columbia University Press, 1983.

Fanon, Franz. *The Wretched of the Earth.* New York: Grove Press, 1963.

Forbes, Jack. *Columbus and Other Cannibals: The Wétiko Disease of Exploitation, Imperialism, and Terrorism.* New York: Autonomedia, 1992.

Gallup, Dorothea M. *The French Image of Algeria: Its Origin, Its Place in Colonial Ideology, Its Effect on Algerian Acculturation.* Ann Arbor: University Microfilms, 1973.

Garber, Marjorie. *Vested Interests: Cross-Dressing and Cultural Anxiety.* New York: Harper, 1992.

Gawitrha'. *Dwanoha: One Earth, One Mind, One Path.* Brantford, Ont.: Pine Tree, 1992.

Gilman, Sander. "Black Bodies, White Bodies: Toward an Iconography of Female Sexuality in Late-Nineteenth-Century Art, Medicine, and Literature." *Critical Inquiry* 12(1) (Autumn 1985):204–242.

Gonzalez, Ray, ed. *Without Discovery: A Native Response to Columbus.* Seattle: Broken Moon Press, 1992.

Harari, Josue V., ed. *Textual Strategies.* Ithaca: Cornell University Press, 1979.

Hartog, Francois. *The Mirror of Herodotus: The Representation of the Other in the Writing of History.* Berkeley and Los Angeles: University of California Press, 1988.

Hayman, Ronald. *Artaud and After.* Oxford: Oxford University Press, 1977.

Hogan, Linda. "Journeys and Other Stories." In *Without Discovery: A Native Response to Columbus,* ed. Ray Gonzalez. Seattle: Broken Moon Press, 1992.

hooks, bell. "Altars of Sacrifice: Re-membering Basquiat." *Art in America* (June 1993):69–75.

______. *Yearning: Race, Gender, and Cultural Politics.* Toronto, Between the Lines Press, 1990.

Hooper-Greenhill, Eileen. *Museums and the Shaping of Knowledge.* London: Routledge, 1992.

Hwang, David Henry. *M. Butterfly.* New York: Plume, 1988.

Jaimes, M. Annette, ed. *The State of Native America: Genocide, Colonization, and Resistance.* Boston: South End Press, 1992.

Johansen, Bruce, and Robert Maestas. *Wasi'chu: The Continuing Indian Wars.* New York: Monthly Review Press, 1979.

Karetnokova, Inga. *Mexico According to Eisenstein.* Albuquerque: University of New Mexico Press, 1991.

Karp, Ivan, and Steven D. Lavine, ed. *Exhibiting Cultures: The Poetics and Politics of Museum Display.* Washington, D.C.: Smithsonian Institution Press, 1991.

Keen, Benjamin. *The Aztec Image in Western Thought.* New Brunswick: Rutgers University Press, 1971.

Kondo, Doreen K. "*M. Butterfly:* Orientalism, Gender, and a Critique of Essentialist Identity." *Cultural Critique* 16 (Fall 1990):5–30.

Le Clézio, J.M.G. *The Mexican Dream: Or, the Interrupted Thought of Amerindian Civilizations.* Trans. Teresa Lavender Fagan. Chicago: University of Chicago Press, 1993.

Leon-Portilla, Miguel. *The Broken Spears: The Aztec Account of the Conquest of Mexico.* Boston: Beacon Press, 1962.

Lévi-Strauss, Claude. *Tristes Tropiques.* Trans. John Russell. New York: Atheneum, 1967.

Lippard, Lucy. *Mixed Blessings: New Art in a Multicultural America.* New York: Pantheon Books, 1990.

Lowry, Malcolm. *Under the Volcano.* New York: Plume, 1971.

MacCannell, Dean. *Empty Meeting Grounds: The Tourist Papers.* London: Routledge, 1992.

Marcus, George, ed. *Rereading Cultural Anthropology.* Durham, N.C.: Duke University Press, 1992.

McClintock, Anne. "The Angel of Progress: Pitfalls of the Term 'Post-Colonialism.'" *Social Text* 31–32 (1992):84–98.

Michaels, Eric. *Bad Aboriginal Art.* Minneapolis: University of Minnesota Press, 1994.

Moors, Annelies, and Steven Wachlin. "Postcards of Palestine." *Critique of Anthropology* 7(2) (Autumn 1987):61–77.

Murray, David. *Museums: Their History and Their Uses.* Vol. 1. Glasgow: Maclehose Press, 1904.

Mutman, Mahmut. "Pictures from Afar: Shooting the Middle East." *Inscriptions* 6 (1992):1–44.

Nietzsche, Friedrich. *Thus Spoke Zarathustra.* Trans. R. J. Hollingdale. Harmondsworth: Penguin, 1969.

———. *Twilight of the Idols* and *The Anti-Christ.* Trans. R. J. Hollingdale. Harmondsworth: Penguin, 1968.

Nochlin, Linda. *The Politics of Vision: Essays on Nineteenth-Century Art and Culture.* New York: Harper and Row, 1989.

Paz, Octavio. *Essays on Mexican Art.* New York: Harcourt Brace, 1993.

Price, Sally. *Primitive Art in Civilized Places.* Chicago: University of Chicago Press, 1989.

Richards, Jeffrey. *Visions of Yesterday.* London: Routledge and Kegan Paul, 1973.
Richardson, Joanna. *Théophile Gautier: His Life and Times.* New York: Coward and McCann, 1959.
Rodriguez, Richard. *An Argument with My Mexican Father.* New York: Penguin, 1992.
Root, Deborah. "The Imperial Signifier: Todorov and the Conquest of Mexico." *Cultural Critique* 9 (Spring 1988):197–219.
Sahagun, Bernardino de. *Florentine Codex, Rhetoric, and Moral Philosophy.* Vol. 4. Santa Fe: School of American Research Monograph, 1969.
Said, Edward. *Orientalism.* Harmondsworth: Penguin, 1978.
Sandoz, Michel. *Theodore Chasseriau, 1819–1856.* Paris: Art et Metiers Graphiques, 1974.
Sejourne, Laurette. *Burning Water: Thought and Religion in Ancient Mexico.* London: Thames and Hudson, 1957.
Silko, Leslie Marmon. *Almanac of the Dead.* New York: Simon and Schuster, 1991.
Smith, Paul Chaat. "Home of the Brave." *C Magazine* 42 (Summer 1994):30–42.
Sontag, Susan, ed. *Antonin Artaud: Selected Writings.* Berkeley and Los Angeles: University of California Press, 1988.
Spurr, David. *The Rhetoric of Empire: Colonial Discourse in Journalism, Travel Writing, and Imperial Administration.* Durham, N.C.: Duke University Press, 1993.
Starn, Orin. "Missing the Revolution: Anthropologists and the War in Peru." In *Rereading Cultural Anthropology,* ed. George Marcus. Durham, N.C.: Duke University Press, 1992.
Steiner, Christopher B. *African Art in Transit.* Cambridge: Cambridge University Press, 1994.
Stephens, John Lloyd. *Incidents of Travel in Central America, Chiapas, and Yucatan.* New York: Harper and Brothers, 1841.
Summers, Roger F.H. *The History of the South African Museum.* Capetown: Balkema Books, 1975.
Taussig, Michael. *The Nervous System.* New York: Routledge, 1992.
Todorov, Tzetvan. *The Conquest of America.* New York: Harper and Row, 1985.
Townsend, Richard. *State and Cosmos in the Art of Tenochtitlán.* Washington, D.C.: Dumbarton Oaks, 1979.
Trask, Haunani-Kay. "Lovely Hula Lands: Corporate Tourism and the Prostitution of Hawaiian Culture." *Border/Lines* 23 (Winter 1991–1992):22–34.
Vergo, Peter, ed. *The New Museology.* London: Reaktion Books, 1989.
Vizenor, Gerald. "Ishi Bares His Chest: Tribal Simulations and Survivance." In *Partial Recall,* ed. Lucy Lippard. New York: New Press, 1992.
Weil, Stephen E. *Rethinking the Museum.* Washington, D.C.: Smithsonian Institution Press, 1990.
Werckmeister, O. K. *Citadel Culture.* Chicago: University of Chicago Press, 1991.
Woolen, Peter. *Raiding the Icebox: Reflections on Twentieth Century Culture.* Bloomington: Indiana University Press, 1993.
Yegenoglu, Meyda. "Veiled Fantasies: Cultural and Sexual Difference in the Discourse of Orientalism." *Cultural Studies* (forthcoming 1995).

Young Bear, Ray A. "Journal of a Mesquakie Poet." In *Without Discovery: A Native Response to Columbus,* ed. Ray Gonzalez. Seattle: Broken Moon Press, 1992.

Zimmerman, Larry J. "Archaeology, Reburial, and the Tactics of a Discipline's Self-Delusion." *American Indian Culture and Research Journal* 16(2) (1992):37–56.

Zolberg, Vera. *Constructing a Sociology of the Arts.* Cambridge: Cambridge University Press, 1990.

About the Book and Author

In Arizona, a white family buys a Navajo-style blanket to be used on the guest-room bed. Across the country in New York, opera patrons weep to the death scene of *Madame Butterfly*. These seemingly unrelated events intertwine in *Cannibal Culture* as Deborah Root examines the ways Western art and Western commerce co-opt, pigeonhole, and commodify so-called "native experiences." From nineteenth-century paintings of Arab marauders to our current fascination with New Age shamanism, Root explores and explodes the consumption of the Other as a source of violence, passion, and spirituality.

Through advertising images and books and films like *The Sheltering Sky*, *Cannibal Culture* deconstructs our passion for tourism and the concept of "going native," while providing a withering indictment of a culture in which every cultural artifact and ideology is up for grabs—a cannibal culture. This fascinating book raises important and uncomfortable questions about how we travel, what we buy, and how we determine cultural merit. Travel—be it to another country, to a museum, or to a supermarket—will never be the same again.

Deborah Root teaches art history at the Ontario College of Art and postcolonial theory in the Faculty of Architecture and Landscape Architecture at the University of Toronto.

Index

Adorno, Theodor, 137
Advertisements
  and class markers, 130
  in constructing desire, 121, 122, 122(fig.), 123–124, 125(fig.), 127–130
  and corporate sponsorship of art, 147–148
  and cultural appropriation, 69(fig.), 74, 74(fig.), 89(fig.), 90–92, 91(fig.), 96, 96(fig.)
  exoticism in, 38, 39(fig.), 40, 46, 133–136, 134(fig.), 135(fig.), 217(n22)
  tourism, 68, 70, 71(fig.), 82, 83(fig.)
  and women, 132, 133–136
Aestheticization
  and appropriation of art, 18–25
  and commodification/consumption of art, 17–18, 121, 124–126
  in concealing violence, 188
  of cultural difference, 30–31, 33, 50, 162, 163–171. *See also* Exoticism
  museums and, 111–114
  of violence, 13–15
  See also Art
Aesthetic taste
  and the aristocrat, 46
  and criticality, 144
  and landscapes, 159–160
  link with class, 130–132
Africa, 36, 81, 133
AIDS, 36
Alaska Airlines, 68, 69(fig.)
Algeria
  French colonization/invasion of, 19–20, 47–48, 162–163
  French representation of, 40, 163–171
Alienation
  authentic experience in curing, 175, 176, 182
  and contemporary Western culture, 15–16, 189–190, 198–199
  post–World War II, 172, 173
  and Western attitude toward land, 151, 153, 158, 159
Alloula, Malek, 38–40
Almanac of the Dead, The (Silko), 8, 98
al-Qadr, Abd, 162
Altered States (Russell), 64
Althusser, Louis, 3, 79, 107, 154, 161
Ambivalence
  and commodification of difference, 69
  and exoticism, 44–51
  and experiencing difference, 175, 178–179
  in representations of Mexico, 56, 57–58
  toward otherness and nature, 160–161, 162, 165, 166–167, 171
Ames, Michael, 109
Anabaptists, 156
Anti-Oedipus (Deleuze and Guattari), 84–85, 195
Apollinaire, Guillaume, 56
Appropriation
  aesthetic, 19–21, 33–34, 127, 212–213(n18)
  and authenticity, 80–82, 103–106
  of exoticized fragments, 42–43, 214(n20)
  in lessening danger of otherness, 160

New Age movement and spiritual, 87–98, 101, 106
politics of, 210–211(n39)
recoding/deterritorializing meaning through, 82–87
and resistance in 1960s, 98–101
role in conquest cultures of, 188, 189–193
and Western cannibalism, xi–xii, 201
and Western power/entitlement, 68–73, 76–78, 101–102, 212(n11)
See also Commodification; Museums
Arab Horsemen Taking Away Their Dead After Battle (Chasseriau), 169–171, 170(fig.)
Araby
definition, 215(n3)
Western representation of, 157, 161, 162–172
Western tropes of, 36, 37, 38, 40
Archaeology, 51–52
romance and, 123–127
Archaeology (magazine), 123, 124
Aristocrats
and experiencing difference, 177
Mayans as, 52
as romanticized collector, 45–46, 121, 124, 147
and vampirism, 13
Arizona, 86–87
Art
as alibi for appropriation, 18–25
as ceremony, 149
commodification of, 67–68, 73, 121, 124–126, 139–142
corporate financing of, 147–148
and criticality, 142–145, 215(n27)
landscape painting, 159–160, 165–167
and museums, 111–114, 136–139
Orientalist painting, 163–165
paganism in, 157
pre-Columbian Mexican, 52, 56–57
surrealist, 55–56
Artaud, Antonin, 55, 56–57, 63–66
Asia, 37, 38, 40
Assimilation policy, 33
Astorga, Nora, 49
Aswan, Egypt, 82–84
Australia, 153
Authenticity
and appropriation of identity, 103, 105
and art, 144–145, 146
in commodification, 69–70, 78–81, 90, 92, 93
exoticism in locating, 31, 34
and experiencing difference, 175, 176
as located in otherness, 201
as located in the past, 115–116
and museum objects, 110, 111, 114, 118–120
Authority, 175–176, 177, 181–182. *See also* Power
Aztec, 210(n20)
Aztecs, 207(n1)
museums and, 113
representations of violence and power, xiv, 1–3, 4–8, 16, 187–189, 202–203, 204
Spanish conquest of, 119–120, 210(n33), 218(n13)
use as analogy, 195, 196–197
Western representations of, 36, 49, 51, 52, 53, 56

Baartman, Saydie, 118
Barclay, Barry, 190
Basquiat, Jean-Michel, 145–147
Bataille, Georges, 55–60, 204
Battle of Aboukir (Gros), 166, 168–169, 168(fig.)
Baudelaire, Charles, 166–167, 172, 180
Baumgarten, Lothar, 75
Beauty, 3, 17, 57–58. *See also* Aestheticization
Belaney, Archie (Grey Owl), 103–106, 104(fig.)
Benjamin, Walter, 76, 149
Benjamin-Constant, Jean-Joseph, 165
Berger, John, 164–165, 215(n27)
Beuys, Joseph, 142
Black Robe (film), 36

Blue Lagoon (film), 40
Bohemianism, 142
Bonaparte Visits the Pesthouse at Jaffa (Gros), 167
Bouchard, Paul-Leon, 165
Bourdieu, Pierre, 130, 131, 144
Bowles, Paul, 171–184
Bram Stoker's Dracula (film), 13, 14(fig.)
Braque, Georges, 55
Brayer, Marie-Ange, 75
Breton, André, 64
British Columbia
  commodification of Native culture, 67–68
  land disputes in, 79, 152–153
  museum of, 112–113, 115–116
  tourism in, 211(n2)
British Museum, 111–112, 113, 120, 127, 132

Caligula (PBS), 41
Canada
  colonization of, 152
  land/treaty disputes in, 105, 152–153, 218(n15)
  and Native ceremonies, 191–192
  See also British Columbia
Cannibalism/cannibalization
  of cultural difference, xiii–xiv
  effect of cultural, 194
  and exotification, 30
  as a mirror, 204–205
  and museum display of human remains, 117
  in representations of indigenous people, 36, 37
  and Western alienation, 198, 201
  and Western consumption psychosis, 9–18
Cardinal-Shubert, Joane, 70
Carey, Ken, 93
Carrasco, David, 119
Carry On Up the Khyber (film), 46
Cartier, Jacques, 152
Casmir perfume, 38, 39(fig.)
Catharism, 157
Catlett, Juan Mora, 188
Celebrities, 17–18
Ceremonial items, 191(fig.)
  appropriation and ownership of, 22–24, 68, 107, 190–193
  and authenticity issues, 80–81
Ceremony
  appropriation of, 95
  art as, 149
  in controlling evil, 16
  power inherent in, 191–192
Certeau, Michel de, 192, 203, 218(n12)
Chambers, Iain, 25
Champoillon, 111–112
Chanel perfume, 129
Change, inevitability of, 38, 209(n7)
Chasseriau, Theodore, 169–171, 170(fig.)
Cherokee sex workshop, 88–90, 94
Chiapas, 63
China, tropes of, 37, 46
Chinese Bungalow, The (film), 44
Christianity
  attitude toward land, 151–153, 155–158, 162–163
  on excessive consumption, 12
  legitimacy in, 94
  object display and, 110
  savagery and nature in, 99
  suppression of spirits by, 192
  victimization in, 100
  and Western alienation, 190
Churchill, Ward, 94
CIA, 195
Class
  aesthetic taste and fluidity of, 130–132
  and exoticism, 35–36
Clastres, Pierre, 157
Coatlicue, 187, 188–189
Collins, Wilkie, 192
Colonialism
  and aesthetic appropriation/entitlement, 19–25, 72–73, 102, 107–108. *See also* Appropriation
  art/literature in representations of difference, 163–185
  in contemporary society, x–xi

effect on conquerors, 193–195
in ethnographic discourse, 112
and exotification, 30, 32–34, 40–41, 47–49. *See also* Exoticism
museum treatment of, 109, 115–116
in New Age movement, 93–94
object commodification and romance of, 121–127, 132–136. *See also* Commodification
and victimization, 100
and Western attitudes toward land, 152–153, 157, 159, 160–163
See also Western culture
Columbus and Other Cannibals (Forbes), 10–11
Commodification
of aesthetic forms, 24–25, 139–141
of authenticity, 78–81
and constructing desire, 121–130, 132–136
of criticality, 143–149
of cultural difference, ix, x–xii, 33, 201
entitlement/power in, 72–74, 76–78
of experience, 176, 183
of land, 158
and recoding/deterritorializing meaning, 75–76, 82–87
and sacred objects, 80–81, 192–193
salvage paradigm in, 74–75
of spirituality, 88–97, 106
and tourist industry, 67–70
See also Consumption
Conquest
as absolute, 202–203, 218(n12)
of Aztecs, 119–120, 210(n33), 218(n13)
and corporate values, 148
descriptions of, 119–120
and display of human remains, 116
French invasion of Algeria, 19–20, 162–163
Orientalist painting and display of, 164–165
role of appropriation in, 188–189, 191–192
spiritual appropriation and, 96–97
See also Colonialism; Power
Conquest of New Spain, The (Díaz del Castillo), 119–120
Consumption
and authenticity, 69–70
and ceremonial items, 80–81, 192–193
and class markers, 130–132
constructing desire for, 120–127
and exotification, 30, 33. *See also* Exoticism
link with violence and power, xii–xiv, 58
museums and, 108
role of alienation in, 15–16
and vampire stories, 12–15
Western display of, 16–18
in Western value system, 9–11, 12
and women, 132–133
See also Commodification
Contradictions, 57–58, 61, 65. *See also* Ambivalence
Control, 50–51, 53. *See also* Authority; Power
Corporations. *See* Multinationals
Cosby (television), 131
Counterculture, 98–101
Country Life, 103
Coyolxauhqui (Copper Bells on Her Cheeks), 187, 188
Cree, 153, 207–208(n11)
Criticality, commodification of, 140–145, 146–147
Cronenberg, David, 27
Crosby, Marcia, 70, 74–75, 79
Crusades, 157, 162–163
Crying Game, The (film), 45
Cultural difference, x
and aesthetic appropriation/ entitlement, 19–25, 33, 68–70. *See also* Appropriation
cannibalization of, xiii–xiv, 201. *See also* Cannibalism/cannibalization
colonial expectations of, 194–195
commodification of, ix, x–xii, 33, 121–127. *See also* Commodification

and exoticism, 30–31, 41–66. *See also* Exoticism
experiencing radical, 174–185
as a mirror, 204–205, 210(n35)
and representations of otherness, 160–161, 162, 163–171
tropes of, 34–41
Cultural exchange, 77–78
Cultural integrity, *versus* authenticity, 80
Cultural superiority
in contemporary society, 69, 171, 193, 203
and display of art, 73, 108, 136–137
as integral to conquest culture, 163, 165, 189
as Western characteristic, 154

Dance, 82, 84–85
David (Michelangelo), 120, 120(fig.), 127
Death
Aztecs and, 50, 59
and commodification of criticality, 147
juxtaposition with beauty, 57–58
and museum high art, 137–139
museums and displaying, 108–109, 116–118
of the other in self-identity, 170–171
See also Violence
Death of Sardanapalus (Delacroix), 164
Decamps, Alexandre, 165
Dee, John, 6
Degas, Edgar, 127
Delacroix, Eugène, 47–48, 164
Deleuze, Gilles, xii, 84–85, 97, 158, 184, 195
Deliverance (film), 160
Deskaheh, 105
Deterritorialization, of meaning
and appropriation/commodification, 84–87, 97
and introduction of science, 158
Dialectical materialism, 61
Díaz del Castillo, Bernal, 119–120
Dinesen, Isak, 133
Displacement
of cannibalism, 15, 16
recoding of meaning and population, 84
sexual, 118
and tropes of difference, 41
Display
of consumption, 16–18
and exoticism, 46
and museums, 107–120
role in conquest, 101–102, 164–165, 188, 197
of sacrifice, 29
Documents (journal), 56
Donato, Eugenio, 42–43
Doxtator, Deborah, 100
Duras, Marguerite, 47
Durham, Jimmie, 143
Durkheim, Émile, 56
Dussel, Enrique, 202, 203
Dyak bis-poles, 112

Egypt, 82–84
Eisenstein, Sergei, 55, 60–63
Engels, Friedrich, 33
Entitlement, 21–25, 72–73, 93–94. *See also* Appropriation
Environmental problems, 155, 198
Eroticism
and celebrities, 17
and vampirism, 13
as Western trope, 38–41, 44–46, 62
See also Sexuality
Escape, 183–185
"Essai sur le don" (Mauss), 34
Ethnographic museums, 108, 109, 111, 114–116, 136
Ethnology, 43, 55–56, 119
orality and, 112–113
Evil, 16
Exhibiting Cultures, 109
Exoticism
ambivalence and self-referentiality of, 45–49
versus appropriation, 78
cultural fragmentation in, 41–43, 214(n20)

high art and legitimacy of, 130
history of, 32–34
and representations of Mexico, 49–66
and tropes of difference, 34–41
Western fascination with, 27–31, 210(n23)
women as consumer targets for, 132–136
Experience
authentic, 175, 176, 183–185
unconscious, 54, 63–65, 66, 146
"Extinct America" (Bataille), 57

Fanaticism, 36, 40
Fanon, Franz, 45, 102, 197
Fantasies
exoticism and power, 32, 40–41
Mexico and unconscious experience, 63–64, 66
Fashion industry, 129
Fear/terror
and alienation from land, 158, 160
and contemporary society, 199
state use of, 12
Feather People (The Americas) (Baumgarten), 75
Femmes d'alger (Delacroix), 47–48
Film
cultural appropriation through, 92, 99–100, 101
on effects of appropriation, 190, 193
exoticism in, 33, 44, 45, 46, 47
and fear of nature, 160
and imperial states, 188
Mexican representations in, 53, 55, 60, 61
representations of Western tropes in, 36, 37, 40
science and, 216(n6)
social class and aesthetic taste in, 131
vampire, 13, 14(fig.)
violence in, 199
women in, 49, 179
Flaubert, Gustave, 42–43
Forbes, Jack, xii, 10–11, 155
Forster, E. M., 193–194
Foucault, Michel, xii
Fragmentation
commodification and cultural, 76, 78, 93, 122–123
and exotification, 31, 42–43, 60
France
colonization of Canada, 152
intellectuals/artists on cultural difference, 55–60, 63–66
invasion of Algeria, 162–163
Orientalism and Algerian colonization, 19–20, 47–48, 163–171
Freedom, personal, 90, 94
French impressionism, 140
Fromentin, Eugene, 166, 167
Full Metal Jacket (film), 179, 199
Fusco, Coco, ix

Gauguin, Paul, 62
Gautier, Théophile, 19–20, 22, 24, 142
Gender, 35–36. *See also* Women
Germany, 116
Ghost Dance, 190–191, 191(fig.)
Gilgamesh sculptures, 112
Girodet, 168
Golub, Leon, 145
Gómez-Peña, Guillermo, ix, xi
Great Britain, 218(n9)
Greeks, 215–216(n5)
Gros, Antoine-Jean, 166, 167–169, 168(fig.)
Guatemalan Peten region, 51
Guattari, Felix, xii, 84–85, 97, 158, 184, 195

Haida, 67
Hawaiian Shaman Training, 96, 96(fig.)
Hayman, Ronald, 66
Heart of Darkness—Apocalypse Now, 174
Hegel, Georg, 55
Hendrix, Jimi, 53
Hierarchy
and Aztecs, 5, 7

in Christianity, 157
as integral to conquest culture, 189
as Western organizing principle, 154, 155, 156
as Western trope of Araby, 169
Hindu temple sculptures, 113
History
aestheticization of, 188
conquest as absolute in representing, 202–203
details in constructing, 118–120
exoticism and interpreting, 55, 59–60
paintings, 167–171
of Vietnam War, 209(n12)
Hogan, Linda, 151
Holland, 116
Holy Inquisition, 157
hooks, bell, 146, 217(n29)
Hooper-Greenhill, Eilean, 147–148
Hugo, Victor, 170
Huitzilopochtli (Hummingbird on the Left), 5–6, 187, 189
Human nature, 36
Human remains, 116–118
Human sacrifice, 207(n5)
Aztecs and, xiv, 2–3, 58, 188, 196
links with consumption, 9
and repression in Christianity, 156
Hwang, David Henry, 27–29, 41–42, 43
Hydro Quebec, 153

Identity
and appropriation, 102–106
commodification and cultural, 86
fixed ethnic and gender, 29, 31
politics of otherness, 193
rediscovering cultural, 200–201
representations of difference in self-, 162, 163, 171, 176
Imaginaries
exotic, 51–53. *See also* Exoticism
of Mexican difference, 53–66
Incidents of Travel in Central America, Chiapas, and Yucatan (Stephens), 22
Independent (London newspaper), 147–148
India, 23, 37, 113, 193–194
"Indian Culture" (Artaud), 65
Indigenous Art Inc., 124
Individualism
in contemporary society, 198–199
and object display, 131
as Western value, 97, 99, 158
Ingres, Jean, 165
Insanity
in representations of difference, 166–167
and spiritual curses, 192–193
through experiencing difference, 173–176, 181
Intellectuals
and appropriating cultural difference, 210–211(n39)
and representations of Mexico, 53–66
Iran, 195
Iroquois, 36, 105
Irrationality, 169, 178–179. *See also* Fanaticism
Ishi: The Last of His Tribe (PBS), 117
Islam
European representation of, 157, 161, 162–172
Western tropes of, 36, 37, 38, 40
Isolation. *See* Alienation
Italian Renaissance, 140

Japan, 37
Java Head (film), 37
Jewelry, 126
Jews, 157
Jurassic Park (film), 216(n6)

Kachinas, 86–87
Kahlo, Frida, 53, 60
Kahnawake, x
Kamali, Norma, 214(n20)
Kandinsky, Wassily, 131
King, Serge, 96, 96(fig.)
Knowledge
commodification of, 123–124

universal, 194–195
Kojève, Alexandre, 55
Koons, Jeff, 141
Kroeber, Alfred, 117
Kubrick, Stanley, 199
Kwagiutl, 67

La bataille perdu (Hugo), 170
Lacan, Jacques, 161
La Grande Odalisque (Ingres), 165
Lakota, 10, 207(n9)
l'Amérique disparue (Bataille), 56
Land
and Orientalist painting, 165–171
Western attitude toward, 151–153, 154–160, 163, 180–181, 184–185
Land/treaty disputes, 209(n7)
appropriation and salvage paradigm in, 105
authenticity issues in, 79, 212(n8)
racism in, 67
and Western views on land, 152–153, 218(n15)
La part maudite (Bataille), 56
Las Casas, Bartolomé de, 37
Last of the Mohicans (film), 36
Lawlessness, 52–53
Lawrence, T. E., 177
League of Nations, 105
Le Clézio, J.M.G., 64
Left (political), 61–62, 158, 198
Legends of the Hidden Temple, 126
Legitimacy
and high art, 130
universalizing and issues of, 94
See also Authenticity
"Les Arts anciens de l'Amérique" (art exhibit), 56–57
Les Muets de Serail (Bouchard), 165
Lettres persanes (Montesquieu), 32
Lévi-Strauss, Claude, 8, 199
Literacy, 112, 113, 114, 213(n6)
Literature
romantic, 52
The Sheltering Sky (Bowles), 171–184
Western women in, 49
Little Big Man (film), 99
Louis, Saint, 162
Lowry, Malcolm, 50, 53, 66
Luddite movement, 158

M. Butterfly (Hwang), 27–29, 31, 41–42, 43, 45
MacCannell, Dean, 37
Maclean, 209(n7)
Madame Butterfly (Puccini), 27, 28(Fig. 2.1), 31, 42
Madonna, 53
Magical thought. *See* Fantasies
Maori, 190
Marginality, 217(n29)
Markham, Beryl, 133
Marx, Karl, 33
Mashpee nation, 212(n8)
Matisse, Henri, 137
Mauss, Marcel, 32, 34, 55, 56
Mayans, 51–52, 73
McEachern, Allan, 209(n7)
McLaren, Malcolm, 27
Meaning, deterritorializing/recoding, 84–87
Melanesia, 36, 37
Mendieta, Ana, 149
Metraux, Alfred, 56
Metropolitan Museum of Art, 126, 127, 128(fig.), 129, 129(fig.), 132
Méxica, 207(n1). *See also* Aztecs
Mexico
exoticism and representation of, 49–66
land disputes in, 153
museums and art of, 113
Western tropes of, 36
See also Aztecs
Mexico City, ix–x, 64
Michelangelo, 120, 120(fig.), 127, 128(fig.), 136
Midnight Express (film), 36
Mission, The (film), 37
Miss Saigon, 27, 28(Fig. 2.2), 43–44, 209(n12)
Mizrahi, Isaac, 214(n20)
Mohawks, x, 38, 153, 209(n7)

Montesquieu, 32
Moonstone, The (Collins), 192
Moonstruck (film), 131
Moore, Henry, 137
Motecuzoma, 1, 6, 197, 204
Multinationals, 43, 145
Musee de l'Homme (Paris), 112, 118
Museo Preistorico ed Etnografico, 107
Museum cities, 214–215(n24)
Museums
  display and, 107–120, 190
  and entitlement, 23–24
  marketing by, 123–127, 129–130, 131, 132
  and Western high art, 136–139
Museums and the Shaping of Knowledge (Hooper-Greenhill), 147–148
"Museum's Furnace, The" (Donato), 42–43

Napoleon, 111–112, 167, 169
National Gallery (London), 138
National Geographic, 41, 208(n4)
Native Carrying Some Guns, Bibles, Amorites on Safari (Basquiat), 146
Natives
  authenticity and marketing items of, 79, 80
  commodifying culture of, 67–68, 70–78, 82, 86–87
  commodifying spirituality of, 88–97, 101
  counterculture appropriation of, 98–101
  definition of, 211(n1)
  Western tropes of, 36, 37, 38
Navajos, 77–78
New Age movement, 63, 87–98, 101, 106
New Guinea, 37
New Mexico, 82, 83(fig.)
New Necklace, The (Paxton), 35–36, 35(fig.)
New World Order, 198
Nietzsche, Friedrich, xii, 11, 100, 195, 197
Night of the Iguana, The (film), 53, 66
Nochlin, Linda, 164
Nomadism, 184
Nostradamus, 6
Nuu'chah'nulth, 67

Objectification. *See* Commodification
Oka standoff, x, 38, 153, 209(n7)
Ontology, Western, 154–161
  appropriation and effect on, 75–76
  and spiritual appropriation, 95
  universalization of, 194
  See also Western culture
Orality, 112. *See also* Literacy
Orientalism, 161–165, 216(n18)
  in literature, 171–173
Orientalism (Said), 33, 112
Otherness
  and displacement of cannibalism, 15, 16
  in exoticization, 54–55
  and identity politics, 193
  locating authenticity in, 201
  and museum displays, 109
  representation of, xi, 160–161
  See also Cultural difference
Ottoman Turks, 168

Paganism, 156–157
Painting
  exoticism in, 35–36, 47–48
  history, 167–171
  landscape, 159–160, 165–167
  Orientalist, 161, 163–165
Paradox. *See* Contradictions
Pasha, Mustapha, 168
Passage to India, A (Forster), 193–194
Passivity trope, 37–38
Paxton, William McGregor, 35–36, 35(fig.)
Paz, Octavio, 140–141
PBS. *See* Public Broadcasting Service
Performance art, ix, 149
Physical anthropology, 117–118
Picasso, Pablo, 55
Pietà (Michelangelo), 127, 128(fig.)
Poema de Mío Cid, 120

Politics
appropriation and, 105–106
authenticity issues in, 79–80
and criticality in art, 140–145, 215(n27)
identity, 193
Polynesia, 38, 40
Popular culture
appropriation through, 99–101
and commodification of fine art, 121, 214(n18)
and Mexican exoticism, 53
representations in, 197
social class and aesthetic taste in, 131
See also Film; Literature
Portuguese, 152
Power
and aesthetic appropriation/ entitlement, 18–19, 21–25, 68–73, 76–78, 191–192
and authority in the colonial system, 154–155, 181–182
colonialism and fantasies of, 32, 40–41
and consumption as a value, 9, 13–15, 17–18
and contemporary society, x–xiv, 198
cultural representations of, x–xiv, 1–6
effect on conquest culture of, 189, 194–195, 196–197
and exotification of cultural fragments, 31
and scientism, 158
of tradition, 101
violence implicit in, 6–8
See also Colonialism; Control
Prescott, William, 60, 119
Price, Sally, 36, 109, 210(n35)
"Price and Meaning" (Paz), 140–141
Primitive Art in Civilized Places (Price), 109
Primitivism
ambivalence in, 36–37, 41
and innocence, 167
intellectuals/artists and, 54, 55–56, 62–63
and nostalgia, 32, 33–34
Proper names, commodification of, 127–130
Public Broadcasting Service (PBS), 41, 117, 208(n4)
Puccini, Giacomo, 27, 42
Punishment of the Hooks, The (Decamps), 165

Quetzalcoátl-Topilzín, 1–2, 4–5, 6, 197
¡Que Viva Mexico! (film), 55, 60, 61

Racism
and artistic criticality, 145–146, 147
in British Columbia, 67
fear and greed in, 160
fixed identities and, 29, 31
objectifying difference to justify, 46
Rains Came, The (film), 44
Rajneesh, Baghwan, 88
Ralph Lauren's Safari perfume, 133, 134(fig.)
Rationality
versus Arab irrationality, 169
and Christianity, 157–159
and denying the sacred, 192
role in Western alienation, 190
and Western worldview, 152
See also Science
Recoding, of meaning
and appropriation/commodification, 84–87, 97, 214(n20)
and introduction of science, 158
Redemption, 54, 66
Religion
and art, 136, 138, 141, 148
and Western tropes of difference, 37
See also Ceremony; Spirituality
Renoir, Pierre-Auguste, 127
Repression, Christianity and, 156, 157. *See also* Colonialism
Retorno a Aztlán (film), 188
Return of the Bird Tribes, The (Carey), 93
Revolt in Cairo (Girodet), 168
Revolution, 64
Rijksmuseum voor Volkendunde, 115
Rivera, Diego, 60, 129–130, 129(fig.)

Rodriguez, Richard, 53
Romanticism
of colonialism and object commodification, 121–127
and Mexican exoticism, 51–53
See also Exoticism
Rose, Wendy, 94, 102–103
Roseanne (television), 131
Rosetta Stone, 111–112
Royal British Columbia Museum, 112–113, 115–116
Royal Ontario Museum, 123
Russell, Ken, 64

Sacrifice, 29. *See also* Human sacrifice
Sade, Marquis de, 57–58
Sahagun, Bernardino de, 60
Sahara Desert, 171–173, 179–180, 183
Said, Edward, 33, 112, 161
Salammbô (Flaubert), 43
Salvage paradigm, 74–75, 99–101, 103
and museums, 109
Saskatchewan, 70, 71(fig.)
Savagery
in Christianity, 99
gentle primitive *versus* violent, 36–37, 41
in Western representations of Araby, 169
Schliemann, Heinrich, 127
Schnabel, Julian, 145
Science
and Christianity, 157–159
in denying the sacred, 192–193
exoticism and archaeology, 51
and museums, 116–118
role in Western alienation, 190
and Western cultural superiority, 22, 34, 208(n4)
in Western ontology, 154, 155, 216(n6)
Sendero Luminoso movement, 194–195
Sepúlveda, Juan Ginés de, 37
Serrano, Andres, 97
Seven Pillars of Wisdom (Lawrence), 177
Sexuality
ambivalence toward exotic, 177–179
Cherokee sex workshop, 88–90, 94
displacement of, 118
in Western representations of Araby, 164, 169, 217(n23)
See also Eroticism
Shamanism, 66, 94–96, 96(fig.)
Shaman's Drum (magazine), 92
Sharif's Justice, The (Benjamin-Constant), 165
Sheltering Sky, The (Bowles), 171–184
Sheltering Sky, The (film), 44, 173, 174, 176, 179, 180(fig.), 216(n17), 217(n23)
Silko, Leslie Marmon, xii, 8, 98, 204
Sistine Chapel, 136
Smith, Paul Chaat, 9
Smithsonian Institution, 120, 132
Soldier Blue (film), 99
Sontag, Susan, 21
South Africa, 118
Spanish, 8–9
Spirituality
appropriation of, 63, 190–193
commodification of, 70, 86–97, 106
and representations of Mexico, 64
and Western dislocation/alienation, 97–101
Star Trek (television), 99
State, the imperial
as cannibal, 2–3, 4
characteristics of, 5, 6–8, 195–197, 217(n3)
use of violence and fear/terror, 11–12
Steiner, Christopher, 81
Stephens, John Lloyd, 22
Sublimity trope, 37, 41
Sufism, 37
Sumer, 155
Surrealism, 49–50, 53–57, 58
Survival International, 74, 74(fig.)

Tarahumara, 64–65
Taussig, Michael, 11–12
Taxidermy, 108–109, 114–115
Tehuantepec, 61, 62

Television
cultural appropriation through, 92, 99, 101
and isolation in contemporary society, 199
PBS, 41, 117, 208(n4)
social class and aesthetic taste in, 131
Temporality
appropriation and approaches to, 75–76
and corporate messages, 148
museums and effect on, 113–114, 115–116
timelessness as Western trope, 37–38, 62, 164
Western contestations over, 212(n6)
Tenochtitlán, 1, 2, 4, 5, 49, 57, 197
Terra nullius, 152
Te Rua (film), 190, 193
Tezcatlipoca (Smoking Mirror), 1–3, 2(fig.), 4–7, 9, 187
Theater, 27–29, 31, 43–44
Thelma and Louise (film), 53
Timelessness trope, 37–38, 62, 164. *See also* Temporality
Toltecs, 1–2, 4
Toronto, Canada, ix, xii
Tourism
and commodification of Native cultures, 67–70, 71(fig.), 81, 82–84, 83(fig.), 85, 86
exploitative nature of, 211(n2)
and museums, 116
and romance of discovery, 123–124
Townsend, Richard, 200
Traditional, definition of, 211(n1)
Traditional Elders' Circle, 94–95
Tribal Eye (PBS), 208(n4)
Tribù perfume, 133, 135(fig.)
Tristes Tropiques (Lévi-Strauss), 199
Tropen Museum, 116
Tropes
ambivalence about, 46–47
of difference, 34–41, 42, 62
madness and exoticism, 173
Mexican contradictions, 58, 61
Trudell, John, 101, 212(n16)
Tuer, Dot, 210(n18)
Tula, 4–5, 102
Tutankhamen, King, 192–193

Unconscious experience
and art, 146
and Mexican exoticism, 54, 63–65, 66
Under the Volcano (Lowry), 50, 53, 66
United States, 33, 162
University of British Columbia, Museum of Anthropology, 109

"Valéry Proust Museum" (Adorno), 137
Valuation
aesthetic, 21, 120–130, 139–142. *See also* Commodification
of hierarchical systems, 155
Value(s)
and commodification of art, 121, 126
consumption as Western, 9–11, 17–18
corporate, 147–148
individualism as Western, 97, 99
universalization of Western, 94, 194
See also Ontology, Western
Vampires, 12–15
Vatican Museum, 136
Victimization, 99–101
Violence
aestheticization of, 188
and Aztec representation of power, 2–3, 4–6
and contemporary society, 196, 197, 199, 200
as implicit in power, 6–7, 155
and Western consumption, 8–16, 58
Western denial of, xii, 7–8
in Western representations of difference, 36, 38, 164, 169, 178–179
See also Power